Arabi-Malayalam: Linguistic Cultural Traditions of Mappila Muslims of Kerala

Arabi-Malayalam: Linguistic Cultural Traditions of Mappila Muslims of Kerala

M.H. Ilias
Shamshad Hussain

GYAN

Published by

Indira Gandhi National Centre for the Arts, New Delhi

Gyan Publishing House
5, Ansari Road
Daryaganj, New Delhi-110002
Phone: 011-47034999, 9811692060
E-mail: books@gyanbooks.com

Distribution Network
gyanbooks.com
India, USA, Canada, UK, Australia, France

ISBN: 978-93-6280-059-6 (PB)

First Published, 2024

Printed at: Gyan Press, Delhi.

Arabic Malayalam: Linguistic Cultural Traditions of Mappila Muslims of Kerala
Author: M. H. Illias, Shamshad Hussain

Contents

Preface

Arabi-Malayalam: Linguistic-Cultural Traditions of Mappila Muslims of Kerala is the outcome of a research project which was carried out under the programme, *Confluence of Traditions and Composite Cultures* of the Janapada Sampada Division of Indira Gandhi National Centre for the Arts (IGNCA). One of the major concerns of this programme is to study the processes that characterize creative transcendence of diverse religious identities and cultural symbioses through interactions in the realm of arts. Setting composite cultures as the major area of enquiry, this programme keeps keen interest in exploring the multi-layered nature of Indian cultural heritage created through intricate patterns and webs of interconnectedness.

Mappila community of Kerala embodies a cultural hybridity as their identity offers an interesting mix of regional and Arab. Although their faith remains largely Islamic, Mappila Muslims are the inheritors of mainly two different traditions; Islam and Kerala. Though tracing their inheritance to the Arabs, who came to the region and married local women, Kerala Muslims have imbibed native culture, customs and manners, making certain variations to the newly accepted religious faith. This cultural blend, according to the authors, has been the hallmark of art and literature of the community.

The evolution of Arabi-Malayalam language, the chief medium for the creative expressions of the community, also represents some cosmopolitan moments which can be comprehended only by understanding the movements of peoples and exchange of cultures, ideas and materials spanning across a wider region. The overwhelming presence of Arabi-Malayalam caused not only the poor growth of Urdu but also resulted in the lesser influence of the Indo-Persian brand of Islam in Kerala. Mappila community's isolation from the rest of India is more significant as they have by-passed not just the political sway and tradition of it, but the cultural heritage and theological affinity as well.

What this work does is a reconceptualization of history of the community and its linguistic and cultural orientations which are otherwise understood as a practice or a set of practices pertaining only to given set of actors within specific territorial unit. The significance of this work lies in such a reconceptualization, describing the particular cosmopolitan moments that the history of the community stands for, which, of course, has not been written about adequately by local or international scholarship. Along with this work, Janapada Sampada Division has also carried out an audio-visual documentation of Arabic-Malayalam language and various art forms, cultural performances, rituals and liturgical practices of Mappila community which are the theatres of literary expression for this language.

Acknowledgements

This work is the outcome of a documentation project entitled *Arabi-Malayalam: Linguistic Cultural Traditions of Mappila Muslims of Kerala* conducted as part of the programme on "Confluence of Traditions and Composite Cultures" of the Janapada Sampada Division of Indira Gandhi National Centre for the Arts (IGNCA), New Delhi. The strong faith and appreciation of the multi-cultural fabric of Kerala that we shared have been the driving force behind this endeavour right from its inception. First of all, we wish to record our profound sense of gratitude toward Dr. Sachchidanand Joshi, Member Secretary, IGNCA whose encouragement and support were invaluable in working through this project and finally turning the monograph into publication. We would also like to express our gratitude to Professor Molly Kaushal, Head of the Department, Janapada Sampada Division for her consistent support at various stages of this project and for her critical comments which helped in the revision of the work. The Co-ordinator of this project, Dr Sreekala Sivasankaran, Associate Professor, Janapada Sampada Division who has supported this project throughout deserves special thanks.

Significant administrative and institutional supports have come from Jamia Millia Islamia (JMI). Prof. Talat Ahmad, Vice Chancellor and Prof. Shahid Ashraf, Pro.Vice Chancellor JMI have extended generous support to us in every phase of the project. Prof.Zikrur Rahman, Prof. Javed Ahamad Khan and Mr Ayatullah of JMI and Prof. Sushama L. of Sree Sankaracharya University of Sanskrit, Thirur Centre deserve special thanks for their assistance of various sorts. We are also grateful to Professor A.K. Ramakrishnan (Centre for West Asian Studies, JNU) and Professor Basheer Ahmad (Centre for Arabic and African Studies, JNU) for making valuable comments on previous drafts of the text. In transliterating the Arabic and Arabi-Malayalam terms, we have benefitted a lot from the advice of Professor K.M. Shareef (Department of English, University of Calicut), Vinod Kumar (Department of Sanskrit, University of Kerala) and Anees Alangadan (Department of Arabic, Farook College). Our warm thanks go to Smitha and Elizabeth Philip for copyediting the manuscript. We would like to underline our special thanks to Saleel, Anees, Jaleel and Sajid for typing and designing the manuscript.

We have incurred innumerable debts in conceptualising and materialising this work. We are deeply grateful to the research and documentation team consisting Mohamed Ashraf, Aniyan Chitrasala and Shamej Sreedhar. In Kerala, where we conducted field work, we have debts that we can never repay to the people we worked with, the singers and performers of art forms and keepers of traditions whose generosity and insights animated this project throughout. We thank Sunil, and Jerrin for their willingness to help this project with their photographs.

Abdulla Thanima, P.P. Fathima, Shabrez Anwar, Shamiya Anwar, M.N. Karassery, P. Pavithran, Hussain Randathani, Ummar Tharamel, T.K. Hamza, A.P. Ahmed, Samad Pookkad, BF Abdul Rahiman,

Pareed Gurukkal, Nallalam Kabeer, Abu Vellayil, Ramla Beegum and Backer Thamarayoor helped us by giving interviews and providing valuable information for improving the manuscript. Sayyid Salih Shihab, Yousafali Pandikkad, Iqbal Koppilan, Abdul Sathar, Gafoor Edathola and Mehaboob helped locate some of the rare works published in Arabi-Malayalam. We are thankful for their generosity. The staff at several libraries including Farook College, PSMO College, Darul Huda Islamic University and Moinkutty Vaidyar Smarakam provided indispensable information. We thank them for their great help. At a more personal level, we are indebted to a number of friends and colleagues Hudaifa, Ophira, Fazaruddin, Mathew, Sreerekha, Yousafali, Amindas, Salam, Mohammed Syed, Noushad, Zainul Abid, Limseer, Sadik, Sakeer, Rafeek, Nahas, Basheer, Aftab, Rafiulla, Nazmi, Vakil, Hafis, Mujeeb Rahman Kinalur, Feroz, Anoop, Baburaj and Gopikrishnan and we thank all who encouraged the project from the start and supported it in every way they could. Also to be mentioned here is our families, thanks a lot for their love, care and concern throughout this project.

M.H. Ilias

Shamshad Hussain

1
Introduction

> I was literate and well-read in Arabi-Malayalam, a locally devised language of Mappila Muslims of Kerala and the chief medium of instruction at madrassa in Malabar[1]...[M]ost ironically, when 'modern' education got the prominence and people turned to it, I became 'illiterate'. As a part of their effort to make Kerala a state with hundred percent literacy in the early 90s, volunteers of Sakshratha Mission, the state agency assigned with the purpose, identified me 'illiterate' and offered 'remedial' classes. I sadly remember the painful experience, struggling to write corresponding Malayalam letters for the Arabi-Malayalam alphabets which were sentimentally attached to me. The state sponsored *Total Literacy Campaign*[2] has done cruelties of similar sort to many in the Malabar region.[3]

The poignant story of Kunji Beevathumma as shared with the authors demonstrates well, how the painful transition from Arabi-Malayalam to Malayalam took place during the early 1990s for many who were literate in the former in Malabar. Historically, Muslim women whose education was confined to Arabi-Malayalam were the major victims of this stereotyping; they were portrayed 'marginalized' in most of the modern-secular narratives depicting them as illiterate and uneducated.

Arabi-Malayalam language was otherwise an immensely rich language with a number of scientific, philosophical, and literary works and a large number of Mappilas were highly literate in this tradition in spite of the fact that they were considered illiterate by 'modern' standards. Mappilas lived in an environment where Arabi-Malayalam texts were read and learnt by-heart and histories were told publicly through the genres of songs, ballads and other modes of narration. The public recital of texts or poems meant that its message reached many listeners simultaneously. The realm of literacy in the

---

[1] Malabar, northern part of Kerala comprising seven districts, was once under British East India Company-controlled Madras State.

[2] This was a campaign spearheaded by the Government of Kerala with an objective to eradicate illiteracy for the whole of the state. Kerala was finally declared a 'totally literate state' on the 8th April 1991.

[3] As narrated to the authors.

context of Mappila Muslims contained a vast domain, encompassing many linguistic forms, various genres and literary fusions.

Under the colonial rules (both Portuguese and the British), the practice of sending children to the 'secular' schools, established mainly by the colonial administration and Christian missionaries, was restricted because of the strong anti-colonial position. The knowledge was imparted either through the traditional *madrassa* system or indoctrination of a collective sort carried out through *v'alu* or midnight preaching. "Popular *fatwas* were issued then by the *ulema* to discourage 'secular' education among the Mappilas", writes Ummar Moulawi, a renowned scholar of Islamic theology and the leader of Salafi movement in Kerala, in his autobiography.[4]

> I have not been sent to the school despite the fact that my parents were literate in Malayalam language...that practice (sending children to the 'secular' school) was quite alien to the Mappila community of that time. Ulemas in the locality were against it and they inculcated the worthlessness of 'modern' education in midnight preaching. A recurring prayer on such occasions was: "the Lord, king of *khojas* save us from the damages that those who speak refined Malayalam make...and from those who use English, the language of infidels and the language of hell, as well.[5]

Moulawi's words underline the importance given to Arabi-Malayalam in the education of Mappila Muslims of Kerala. Though Malayalam remained as the mother tongue of many in the community, the first language learned in a systematic way in the Mappila life was Arabi-Malayalam. People used to switch over conveniently to other languages including Malayalam as the situation demanded. The *dars* attached to mosques happened to be the place where Mappilas learned Malayalam language in a systematic way. Moulawi narrates his experience of learning Malayalam as follows:

> Because of the abstinence from 'modern' knowledge imparted in Malayalam and English, there was a widely-held tendency to portray the members of Mappila community as illiterates...I learned to write and read Malayalam with the help of a teacher who volunteered to teach me the language while reading the Quran at a *dars*...Arabi-Malayalam letters were to be written first. Corresponding alphabets in Malayalam would be written below. Malayalam letters were mastered one by one and eventually turned to writing small and big sentences.[6]

There is of course a lot to infer from taking up these experiences seriously; especially in socio-cultural terms, experiences of this sort often deal with routine and institutionalized aspects of social settings and representations. Intercultural personal experiences in particular, as short narrative texts, provide channels for knowing best the ethnocentric and hierarchical settings in each society. These experiences also touch significantly upon the new sense of 'modern' emerged in the state of Kerala, which, to some considerable extent was premised so much on the conception of 'secular.'

---

[4] Umar Moulawi, *Ormakaḷude Thīrath,* (Cochin: Da'wa Books, 2009), p. 24.

[5] Ibid.

[6] Moulawi, *Ormakaḷude Thīrath*, p.38

Interestingly, to this new sense of 'modern-secular', because of its innate religious orientation, Arabi-Malayalam language became a significant 'other' that could conveniently be neglected.

Within the realm of 'secular' literature also there was a pronounced skepticism towards Arabi-Malayalam literary works which have often been seen as associated with the less prestigious genre, of 'vernacular' community literature. Most of the standard texts of Kerala's literary history in both Malayalam and English did not recognize or mention the term Arabi-Malayalam as the authors often tried to put it in the basket of 'Muslim' or 'Mappila' literature.[7] Similarly, citing the overwhelming production of liturgical texts and prayer books in Arabi-Malayalam, the 'secular' historians of literature always showed a keen interest in belittling it yet another religious language in addition to Arabic.[8] For some[9], the major issue was linguistic fusions and foreign words from Arabic and Persian genres that placed Arabi-Malayalam outside the master narrative of Malayalam literature, though the adoption of loaned words is a common feature of every South Indian language including Malayalam in which one can find numerous words borrowed from languages such as Sanskrit, Hebrew and Portuguese.[10] Nevertheless, the adoption of plots related to Arab culture and narrative strategies close to Arab and Persian tradition has historically made Arabi-Malayalam stories and verses more popular cutting across the community lines in Kerala. The 'standard' literary journals did not review them and literary theorists kept them at arm's length. It was difficult for them to be presented in 'serious' literary conferences and festivals.

Within the area of Kerala literature also, one can detect certain hesitancy towards conducting research into the alternative literary spaces that Arabi-Malayalam created.[11] It is noteworthy that in most of the writing of literary history of Kerala, the analysis of Arabi-Malayalam literature seldom appeared and if at all, only as a passing genre that essentially identified with the writing of the Mappila community. Despite its considerable body of literature and literary credentials, mainstream history of literature in Kerala does not consider Arabi-Malayalam tradition as a part of its inheritance.[12] It may be striking in this context that the conventions of literature in Kerala are mixed up with the identity of Malayalam in its variety works, and yet Arabi-Malayalam does not come under its preview. Krishna Chaitanya, for example, presents the efforts of traditional Muslims in Arabi-Malayalam language as "almost completely isolated."[13] Scholars who have written the literary history of Kerala considered that only with the modern education and the resultant switch over of the community to Malayalam language, Muslims did enter into the field of serious literary writing.[14] Chaitanya's comment on Arabi-Malayalam literary tradition is reflective of that:

---

[7] Balakrishnan Vallikkunnu, *Mappila Sahityavum, Navodhanavum*, (Kozhicode: Yuvata Books,2008)

[8] P.Mohamed Kuttasesry, Adunika Arabi Sāhityavum Malayalatile Asparśyatayum, Chandrika Weekly (Republic Day Special Issue, 1972).

[9] Krishna Chaithanya, *A History of Malayalam Literature*, (Hyderabad: Orient Longman, 1971)

[10] Malayalam has a set of words taken from Portuguese language. *Kasēra* for chair, *mēsa* for table and *kakkūs* for toilet are the most popular ones among them.

[11] K. Aboobacker, *Malayāḷatile Eṣal Vazhi* (Calicut : Islamic Publishing House, 2014), pp.7-12.

[12] Udaya Kumar, "Shaping a Literary Space: Early Literary Histories in Malayalam and Normative Uses of the Past", in Hans Harder (ed.) *Literature and nationalist Ideology,* (New Delhi: Social Science Press, 2010), p. 32.

[13] Chaithanya, *A History of Malayalam Literature*, p. 196.

[14] Ibid.

> The traditional Muslim literary effort has remained almost completely isolated till very recent time. It is only recently that the Muslim community has taken into modern education...[T]he script (Arabi-Malayalam) made the situation verse... [T]oday an attempt is being made to rewrite and publish many of the works in Malayalam script.[15]

In more ways than one, such remarks are symptomatic of the ways in which the contribution of Kerala Muslims figures in popular discourses. This ignorance has been reflected in many other works on the literary history of Kerala which either neglected the entire corpus of literary writing produced in Arabi-Malayalam or addressed only certain bits of it. M. Leelavathy's *Malayāḷa Kavita Sāhitya Caṛitram*, a comprehensive work dealing with the history of poetry in Kerala, for instance, contains only a passing reference to Arabi-Malayalam poetry. Paying little attention to poetry in Arabi-Malayalam (known popularly as Mappila songs), Leelavathy engages in broad-brush painting and puts all the works belonging to this genre under the common basket of ballads.[16] The renowned poet and a scholar of Malayalam language Ulloor S. Parameswara Aiyyar also has made an attempt in writing a literary history of Kerala confining himself to the works in Malayalam language. The neglect of Arabi-Malayalam is more evident as his voluminous work *Kerala Sāhitya Caṛitram*, which is otherwise considered to be the most authoritative one of its kind in the history of literature in Kerala, has only half a page description of Arabi-Malayalam literature.[17] It excludes not only seminal writing, but also popular authors in this language like Moyinkutty Vaidyar.

With the presence of foreign vocabularies and aesthetics, some of the writers of literary history presented Arabi-Malayalam as something totally foreign to the literary sensibilities in Kerala.[18] This issue requires further discussion which we have done in the portions to follow. Many such elaborations of the "us" and "them" in literature in Kerala served to reinforce the conceptual split between the secular/Malayalam on the one hand, and the communal/Arabi-Malayalam on the other. Occasionally, this was presented as a division between 'native' and 'foreign' though the latter was evolved fully banking on local artistic resources and aesthetic senses. This easy construction of Malayalam as the real native and the others-especially Arabi-Malayalam as foreign, is unhelpful to any cohesive understanding of the diversity that literature in Kerala stands for.

Beyond National/Secular Boundaries

There is also tendency towards considering Arabi-Malayalam literature as a divergence from 'national' norm. This is, of course, true. Because of its multi-regional, cross-cultural origin (a detailed account of the genesis of this language has been given in the following chapter), Arabi-Malayalam seldom bears the characteristic of one place. It is less tied to national boundaries or defined linguistically and geographically within the socio-cultural milieu of a particular region. As the history of its origin entails a complex interaction of histories of different regions, peoples and times merged together in the cultural backdrop of maritime trade, the enquiry into the marginalization of Arabi-Malayalam requires a bit of telescoping.

---

[15] Ibid., 196-197.

[16] M.Leelavathi, *Malayāḷa Kavitasāhityacaritram*, (Thrissur: Kerala Sahitya Academy, 2011).,p.32.

[17] Ulloor S Parameswara Iyer, *Keraḷa Sāhityacaritram*, vol. 1, (Trivandrum: University of Kerala, 1955), p.269.

[18] Iyer, *Keraḷa Sāhitya Caritram* & K.M.George, *A Survey of Malayalam Literature*, (Bombay: Asia Publishing House, 1968).

The history of evolution of Arabi-Malayalam language and literature represent some cosmopolitan[19] moments which have not been written about adequately by colonial or local scholarship. So, any discussion on it, first and foremost, should involve a re-conceptualization of the literary history of this language one which is presently understood as a practice or a set of practices of past pertaining only to given set of actors within a specific territorial unit, namely Kerala. This is basically a problem involved in the writing of Kerala Muslim history- presenting the past of the region something confined to the history of land-based societies. Paying little attention to history of maritime trade and trade or faith-based diasporas, most current categories of analysis are developed by archaic scholarship to understand the Kerala Muslim history without perspectives from the sea.[20] A study of Arabi-Malayalam thus opens up the possibility for a greater interest in the strained relationship between national and cosmopolitan.

No study of history of Arabi-Malayalam language could be completed without such a thoughtful consideration of the movements of peoples, cultures and goods across the Indian Ocean region. This was the site where many cultures flourished and sustained. Cultures that often seem so widely divergent were in fact in constant contact and exchange with each other in the synthesis of this language. A new thinking about Arabi-Malayalam language and literature from various submerged strands of history and different vantage points is therefore essential.[21] There is the need of a larger rethinking or inevitability of a new historical approach in which the unit of study should be the Indian Ocean region in its entirety.

Retelling history of Mappilas along *thalassological* lines, of course, has its own significance as the community held a pivotal position in medieval and early modern history of the Indian Ocean region. Quite naturally, the orientation of literary works in their language was outward, more specifically, toward the Indian Ocean. The development of literature in Arabi-Malayalam reflects trade and faith-induced cosmopolitanism with its effects spread across far-flung regions like Southern Yemen, East Africa and South East Asia. The limitation that characterizes current discussion about the genealogy of Arabi-Malayalam language and literature is its tendency to reduce the scope of it to the specific situation prevailed in Kerala. An attempt to reposition the history of this language in the framework of cosmopolitanism, therefore, speaks of broader inter-regional interconnectedness in which people, goods and ideas were in constant motion without a hegemonic cultural or political centre.

Many early works in Arabi-Malayalam literature had been profoundly influenced by the influx of some Arabic poems and other literary forms within Southern Arabia, Malabar and Southeast Asia. The

---

[19]Cosmopolitanism in its traditional interpretation endorses a trend of theorizing reflective distance from one's cultural affiliations and a belief in universal humanity. It used to hold a promise of solidarity that was necessarily opposed to the exclusivity and particularism. But in its post-positivist versions there is a scope or possibility for analyzing cosmopolitan communities in which individuals from varying locations enter relationships of mutual respect subscribing to their differing affiliations and beliefs. The concept has now been broadened to accommodate a wide-range of experiences of people around the world but not reflect in a standardization of cultural and social expressions. Kwame Anthony Appiah, *Cosmopolitanism: Ethics in a World of Strangers,* (New York: W. W. Norton & Company, 2006).

[20] Dilip M Menon, "Houses by the Sea: State-Formation Experiments in Malabar, 1760-1800", *Economic and Political Weekly*, Vol. 34, No. 29 (Jul. 17-23, 1999), pp. 1995-2003.

[21]M.H. Ilias, *Hadrami Sancāṛaṉaḷude Dēsāntara Calanaṉal, Teḷicam* (15th Anniversary Issue), 2013,pp.44-47.

translation and publication of texts from Arabic and Persian to this language greatly influenced the speed and range of their dissemination and contributed to the creation of cosmopolitan consciousness and to the making of 'imagined communities' across the Indian Ocean region. *Mohiyuddin Māla,* the first known work in Arabi-Malayalam, for example, owed its inspiration to two Arabic texts, namely *Bahja* and *Takmila,* which were in wider circulation in these regions. The scope of such interconnectedness can be extended to the literary networks connecting Muslim communities across boundaries of space and culture. [22] This was a common phenomenon in the Indian Ocean region where such networks helped introduce, popularise and sustain certain texts which were well accepted in one region in others.[23]

In the context of Malabar, literary networks comprised mainly of poets from the coastal towns of Tamil Nadu and Karnataka, Sufi sages from the Northern states of India and scholars from Hadhramawt and various parts of Southeast Asia.[24] The activities of such networks included sharing of texts (stories, poems, treatises on a broad range of topics, travel writings etc.), translating and transmitting them in other places. It was Sheikh Nisamuddin, a Farsi scholar from Kalyan region of Maharashtra served at the court of *Kondotty Taṉal*, who popularised the plot of the Persian novel *Hussanual Jamal-Badrul Muneer* that became the major inspiration for Mappila poet Moinkutty Vaidyar to write a poem based on the same theme.

Performative traditions too were complemented and enriched within the context of this cultural and literary exchange. *Kolkkaḷi* or the stick dance, for instance, shows close resemblance to Gidda or sword dance of people of the Arabian Peninsula.[25] A close semiotic study of two popular art forms among Mappilas-*Dafmuṭṭu* and *Oppana*-also would reveal such a cross-cultural basis in their genesis and spread. While Oppana shaped the traditions borrowed from Yemen, *Dafmuṭṭu* traces its roots partly to Medina and Basra.[26]

With the nationalist discourse gaining momentum in the middle of twentieth century, mainstream literature in Kerala underwent a lot of transformations. Malayalam literature written mostly in stylistically finished and highly Sanskritized Malayalam became a master narrative. Since the conventions of it linguistically governed the state's creation, Malayalam was regarded as the most perfect expression of the national self. Literatures in other language varieties were conveniently sidelined as a part of broader re-conceptualization of literature in national terms.

One of the most significant developments of this period was the prevalence of national culture in public discourse and literary texts. Malayalam language became the most important marker of national identity and a central element of the national political imaginations of Keralites.[27] By

---

[22] Ronit Ricci, *Islam Translated: Literature, conversion and the Arabic Cosmpolis of South and Southeast Asia,* (Ranikhet: Permanent Black, 2011), p.1.

[23] Ibid., pp.1-2

[24] See M.H. Ilias, "Mappila Muslims and the Cultural Content of Trading Arab Diaspora on the Malabar Coast", *Asian Journal of Social Science,* Vol. 35, No. 4-5, 2007, pp. 434 – 456.

[25] Ibid.

[26] Interview with Backar Edakkazhiyur, a trainer of *Dafmuttu*.

[27] The concept of the nation became redefined as a community with a common cultural heritage and the members of the other social/religious groups were excluded from it.

embedding Malayalam literature in modern-national discourse, certain literary texts came to be regarded as representations of national identity. Literature emerged as a necessary corollary of emerging national consciousness from the nineteenth century and the linking of language, literature and the nation found a warm reception. The bulk of works under the label of Kerala literature had the national language (Malayalam) as their most basic organizing principle in common, which, in turn, was closely tied up with the national imagination. At the same time, Mappila linguistic and literary traditions were completely set aside right from the beginning, attributing lack of national coherence and having cross-regional linkages.

In the process of constructing a new 'Malayali/Keralite' identity in the 1950s and 60s, 'standardized' Malayalam became a political instrument for enhancing national sentiments. In that nationalistic frenzy emphasizing the 'particular', the culture of Kerala stripped of its 'cosmopolitan' content, molded itself into a more parochial national pattern. Secular-national historical narratives invented new ways of looking at old stereotypes and disseminated new images of Kerala culture on an unprecedented scale. There are several studies that testify to the search for 'authentically national' traditions that became a ubiquitous characteristic of the twentieth century Kerala.[28] The concept of nation was used in a restricted sense, referring only to the people who were sharing a 'common' cultural memory and invoking the legacy of a 'common' cultural heritage.

The cultivation of specific national cultural markers was not limited to constructing literary identity. Music that had particular stylistic features or associated with ethnic or cultural groups but not linked to a particular nationality was also completely sidelined. There was even less legitimacy for the musical genres developed by Arabi-Malayalam language as many approached them and studied them as instances of folksongs. Because of the tender themes-of love, lust and separation-incurring in the songs, they were gingerly accepted by the lyricists and musicians and were held out at an arm's length by the cultural theorists. Romance, fantasy and wild imaginations made these musical compositions unappealing to 'serious' listeners of music.

There was also a time when only religious institutions were the promoters of popular culture of Mappila Muslims as the 'secular' ones seldom furnished opportunities. And it was understood that Mappila popular culture which otherwise had an important role in creating and shaping the public sphere of the early twentieth century was much too lowbrow to warrant the attention of the 'cultural theorists.' Blame often went around their alleged attempt to dilute literary 'standards.'

From the traditional leftist view also, Mappila songs are considered to be a part of non-secular culture, produced for the consumption of a particular community, though Marxists in the state have successfully utilized the popularity and immense potential of it for mass mobilization. The religious content in the Mappila cultural traditions came under severe criticism. The everyday construction of such genres, according to the left scholars, did not just operate within the realm of pleasure, but functioned as the most important instrument mobilizing people along religious lines. The traditional analysis of Mappila culture by the left scholars is profoundly grounded in both colonial and national-secular interpretations. This has been echoed clearly in the observations of C. Achutha Menon, noted left literary critic and former Chief Minister of Kerala:

---

[28] Udaya Kumar, "Shaping a Literary Space", pp.19-24.

> Some notables from the community (Mappila Muslims) approached the government[29] with the purpose of establishing an exclusive centre for the studies of Mappila songs. The centre was meant to establish in memory of a Haji Hydrose[30]. As far as my understanding is concerned, Haji's genuineness as a poet is highly disputable. He has written some stuff ridiculing the Indian national movement and Gandhi's 'dubious' role in it in particular...[W]hat we need is integration, not disintegration...Haji is an icon of polarization.[31]

There is perhaps a lot in taking these comments seriously as the author himself has written extensively on the silence of authors on the contribution of marginalized groups including Muslims to the culture of Kerala. Whereas in recent years many of left scholars have come to the conclusion that culture of Mappila community has to be taken seriously in debates about the formation of modern culture in Kerala and the public sphere, such was not the case with many modern social theorists. They either ignored it completely or paid little attention to it, treating it as completely religious-driven one. Menon was probably alone in his consistent interest in taking up the issue of exclusion of Muslims from the cultural field.

Besides the religious content, popular Mappila songs have come under heavy criticism from various corners for being superficial, consumerist and sensationalist.[32] Some argue that Muslim society, as any other society, is constantly creating and circulating new elements of popular culture for massconsumption.[33] Mappila songs as a major ingredient of popular culture replace high art and authentic folk culture by tasteless commercialized artifacts. Working in the realm of pleasure, they do not pay much attention to the aesthetic side. But there is a newly emerging trend among the scholars to see Mappila songs as a site of struggle between the resistance of subordinate groups and the interests of dominant groups.[34] As a form of popular culture, Mappila songs, according to them, serve as a barometer for assessing the health of the society concerned.[35]

Investigating the power relationships and hierarchies in culture, some of them have identified Mappila cultural traditions as something akin to or represent the perspectives of downtrodden mass.[36] The secularist worries over the religious content of Arabi-Malayalam and its cultural homogenization have widely been challenged by a group of scholars. Mappila culture now appears to be closely related to identity and has been the ideological driving force for many young organic intellectuals from the community. To quote Kunjimohammed, a film maker turned left politician: "scholars from the left group reluctantly admit that the genres Mappila literature produced have something to say to them,

---

[29] The Government of Kerala while C. Achutha Menon was Chief Minister from 1970-77.

[30] The person referred in this comment by all probability is Pulikkottil Hyder, a popular and well-liked poet among the Mappila Muslims of Kerala. Hydrose was famous for his ardent advocacy for social reforms and for his criticism of the then prevailing social and political structure.

[31] See C. Achutha Menon, 'Māppiḷa Pāṭṭukaḷ', Souvenir published by Yuva Kala Sāhiti, 1982.

[32] Aboobacker, *Malayāḷatile Eṣal Vazhi*

[33] Ibid.

[34] AP Ahmed, scholar of Mappila Artforms in a conversation with the authors.

[35] Ibid.

[36] In an interview with T.K.Hamza, the scholar of Mappila songs held on 8th March, 2013.

even if they chose to do so unwittingly."[37] Criticizing the pessimism of left school, this group rejects the monolithic concept of mass culture and emphasizes on liberating and democratizing function of Arabi-Malayalam literature. The earlier generation of scholars from the community accepted the secularization thesis that, with modernization, religious influence on Mappila culture and literature would inevitably decline and hence there was little point in investing research effort into a field that was going to disappear.

The cross-cultural expressions of Arabi-Malayalam are also under attack from the puritans within the Muslim community. Major part of the worry is about the imaginations applied to it while narrating events in Islamic history. It is important to see how authors in Arabi-Malayalam literature interpret the text and how they create their religio-cultural symbols according to the context. Arabi-Malayalam literature interprets Islamic history, telling stories about the community under threat or victoriously, looking at great figures of the past, implying a contrast with the present. The past in Arabi-Malayalam literature is often used to serve the purpose of the present. The past depicted in the literary works can then tell more about the present than the present itself can. The histories may not necessarily be the official versions based on facts. The past narrated in such works belongs to another kind of history-a popular view of the past orally transmitted from generation to generation through myths and folktales. The power of this history is that it often replaces 'standard' versions of history in the public imagination. It is not about facts or truths but a representation of the past built on imageries, words and imaginations. It is interested mainly in popular tales wherein facts are subsidiary. So is the case even with the works in history in this language which are more subjective-subjective accounts and popular narrations.

Thematic Setting

Arabi-Malayalam continues to be a window to understanding linguistic and cultural orientations of Mappila Muslims of Kerala though certain inconclusiveness persists in regarding its evolution and the terrain of its spread. However, all or most of the of works which attempted in writing the history of Malayalam literature has knowingly or unknowingly failed to acknowledge the contribution of Arabi-Malayalam works. The works of Abu and Ubaid seem to have been pioneering and the most important effort to integrate Arabi-Malayalam texts and authors into a general and unified narrative of Malayalam literary history. This work offered a fillip to study the language in detail when this tradition was neglected for want of patronage and encouragement.[38]

Abu, Kareem, Moulawi, Mohamedali, Shamsuddin, Karaserry and Vallikunnu have contributed further to the development of the studies in Arabic-Malayalam language. Maulawi and Kareem in their work, *Mahatāya Mappila Sāhity Pārambaryam* further widened the scope by including the literary attempts made by Mappilas even in Malayalam language to the rubric of Arabi-Malayalam literature.[39] The rationale for such an argument is that any text, it hardly matters whether it is written using Arabi-Malayalam script or not, but with vocabulary from this language, in principle, can be considered to be a

---

[37] In a telephonic interview with PT Kunjimohammed held on 26th July, 2014.

[38] K.K.N.Kurup, *The Legacy of Islam: A study of the Mappila Muslims of Kerala,* (Kannur, Samayam Publications, 2006), p. 19.

[39] C.N.Ahmed Moulavi and K.K.abdul Kareem, *Mahatāya Māppila Sāhitya Pāṟambaraym,* (Calicut: Authors, 1978)

part of Arabi-Malayalam literature. The works of Shamsuddin[40] and Karassery[41] deal mainly with the literary, linguistic and semantic aspects of Arabi-Malayalam language.

Today, the number of publications in Malayalam dealing with different aspects of Arabi-Malayalam language and literature is large. These works range from the popular ones to academic writings, from large-scale surveys to studies of individual texts. Such studies are now a respectable part of the research agenda of a number of scholars and dissertations at universities.

Similarly, there is a popular attempt, in contrast to the general portrayal of Mappilas as a community which contributed very less to the development of literature in Kerala, by a large number of authors, who have ventured out to explain the contribution of Arabi-Malayalam authors to the literary history of Kerala. There is a corresponding move among a group of young Muslim scholars too. This group, constituted by scholars from Malabar affiliated to the universities in Kerala and outside,[42] recognizes the essential 'oriental' as well as 'nationalist' character of mainstream history- writing based mainly on colonial records.

The academia has already begun to resonate with the changing status of Arabi-Malayalam in the literary discourse. There is a huge cache of doctoral theses, which attempts to refocus history of Muslims away from the traditional domains of 'modern', 'national' and 'secular', towards the issues like 'identity' and 'resistance.' Malabar rebellion of 1921 has spawned at least hundreds of academic works with apparent signals of placing the voices previously unheard of and Islamic texts (in Arabic, Arabi-Malayalam and Malayalam) which were excluded from the traditional preview of 'standard' history writing.

There is also a significant attempt to draw attention to the differently situated experiences of a historically oppressed group, Mappilas of Malabar, within the framework of subaltern theory.[43] Closely adhering to the subaltern approaches in Indian historiography, there is an attempt to retell the history of Kerala from the counter-hegemonic standpoints of Muslims. Giving more importance to the multiple and diverse experiences, these studies encourage a refocusing of culture away from the traditional domains of high culture and aesthetics. Much importance has thus been given to Mappila culture as the expression of the under-represented, yet unheard voices of the others. The study of Arabi-Malayalam is presented in such studies as a dialogue with voices previously excluded from the mainstream. This discussion is more pertinent with Mappila art forms which have historically been a theatre of culture and aesthetics and of course a barometer to understand the thinking processes of the community. The song and dance traditions especially are well-accepted because of their specific roots in lived cultures of the ordinary people. They represent a subsection of the culture of Kerala appropriated by people in their daily lives and are created by people from their own experiences, imaginations and artistic resources.

---

[40] K.O.Shamsuddin, *Mappila Malayalam,* (Trivandrum: Author, 1978).

[41] M.N.Karaserry, "Arabic-Malayalam", in Asghar Ali Engineer (ed.), *Kerala Muslims: A Historical Perspective*, (New Delhi: Ajanta Publications, 1995), pp. 169-170.

[42] Mainly national institutions like Jawaharlal Nehru University, Hyderabad Central University, Jamia Millia Islamia, Aligarh Muslim University.

[43] M.T. Ansari, "Refiguring the Fanatic: Malabar 1836-1922" in Shail Mayaram et al (eds.) *Subaltern Studies XII: Muslims, Dalits, and the Fabrications of History*, (New Delhi: Permanent Black, 2005).

Mappila art forms have now made deep inroads into popular festivals, films and television shows. Yet at no point has Mappila songs occupied a more important place in the popular and scholarly imaginations as it does today. They are widely used in Malayalam films to communicate ordinary people's emotions, feelings and worldviews. The demand for lyrics that capture the daily life of people, particularly at the lower end of the spectrum, is high. There is a subsection constituted by Mappila musical albums visible on the television channels. Mappila Music albums telecast on television channels are repositories of imaginations and imaginary worlds showing ways in which change in the community is visualized in songs. Internet also has emerged as a major locale for Mappila cultural forms to spread.

An argument has been advanced that Mappila songs are increasingly turning to the diaspora for their listeners as well as for their themes and lyrics. The scholars see Mappila songs as the form that has become particularly expressive of Mappila migrants to the Gulf countries; their sensibilities and aspirations. A renewed interest in Mappila songs grows in this environment and gets identified as a major creative outlet to express their feelings and emotions. It is very important in this context to study how Mappila songs in turn shape the way the Muslim migrants to the Gulf imagine a new world and interpret it-how its imageries, words and music affect generate or regenerate images of the community across many media forms.

The largely undocumented history of Arabi-Malayalam deserves many more books devoted to it, but this one aims at making an investigation of Arabi-Malayalam language, the analysis of which seems to be the most reliable guide to understanding Mappila Muslim's linguistic and cultural traditions. Most obviously, the history of Arabi-Malayalam is more divergent and more fragmented, marking the mosaic-like appearance of several socio-cultural phenomena. There is significance in an in-depth study of indigenous Muslim communities, cultural as well as linguistic specificities they possess and of course of immunities they have acquired in a more globalized world. The present work is set in the context of a 'clash' that characterizes the cultural life of Muslims of Kerala, between the traditions of pan-Islamism and local tradition.

However, the aim of this book is not just to offer an understanding of Arabi-Malayalam language and its importance for the study of the cultural traditions of Mappila Muslims of Kerala, but to study this language as a product of cultural contacts and exchanges in the Indian Ocean region. Taking cues from the trajectory of evolution of Arabi-Malayalam literature, one can suggest it opens up an alternative way of conceptualizing the history of literature in Kerala. The major intention of this work is to describe particular cosmopolitan moments in the history of Kerala, characterized by the evolution of Arabi-Malayalam language which has not been written about adequately by colonial or local scholarship. Obviously to many historians of Kerala belonging to the 'left' and the 'right' spectrum, these slices or fragments of history and the strategies adopted to narrate them will be anathema. So the major argument of this book hinges on the idea that, the public reluctance to accept Arabi-Malayalam literary traditions and modern forms of nationhood / national subjectivity are profoundly related.

This work, on its part, asserts that a rethinking is inevitable and calls for a new historical approach, in which the unit of study should be the Indian Ocean region in its entirety. A sincere attempt to retell Kerala Muslim history in general and histories of Arab/Islamic diasporic groups in particular within the light of new frameworks should also address the cultural continuities and cosmopolitan moments they represent. Islam in Kerala is part of a larger 'cultural unit' characterized historically by the constant interchange of cultures and religious ideas. Looking at the life of people in Southern Arabia (Yemen, Oman and some parts of Saudi Arabia), Swahili Coast, Malabar and South East Asia, one can see there are some material and cultural commonalities across regions. This cultural uniformity unites Eastern coast of Africa, South western coast of India and some parts of South East Asia especially, Malaysia and Indonesia. Travel, faith-based diasporas, networks of scholars, *da'wa* or preaching etc have created elements of cohesion among the Muslims living in these regions.

There are works in abundance on different aspects of Muslim community in Kerala, but the academic literature on Arabi-Malayalam is very scanty. Most of the works are engaged in conventional characterization of it in terms of basic choices between 'modern' or 'traditional' and 'secular' or 'religious' that fails to measure the extent of dynamism and creative interplay of various interesting processes involved in it. Similarly, there are not many studies that adequately dealt with this language and its evolution from the socio-linguistic point of view. It is in the context of this literary gap, remaining portion of this work is attempted to make an enquiry into the linguistic aspects, literary traditions and the construction of knowledge in this language.

This work set forth, the following broad objectives:

1. To make a detailed socio-linguistic study on the origin, evolution and spread of Arabi-Malayalam language.
2. To acquire a basic understanding of the historical, social as well as cultural context in which Arabi- Malayalam gained wider popularity among the Mappila Muslims of Kerala.
3. To make an enquiry into the cross-cultural and linguistic influence on Arabi-Malayalam and trace out the cross-philological base of some of the widely used terms in this language.
4. To document art forms and cultural performances in which the oral literary tradition finds its expression.
5. To study how Arabi-Malayalam constituted a parallel way to understand the reality and knowledge production among the Mappilas.
6. To conduct a research so as to develop a comprehensive classification method for the literary texts and oral compositions considering their structure, language register and literary and stylistic features.
7. To analyze the translations of basic Islamic texts in Arabic to this language with the purpose of understanding the extent of freedom that the translators enjoyed, while interpreting the texts.

This work was done on the basis of a field work documenting Arabi-Malayalam language and its multitude of literary and cultural expressions. Simultaneously, an audio-visual documentation of Mappila art forms, cultural performances, rituals and liturgical practices, which are the theatres of various literary and cultural expressions for this language, was also carried out. The field documentation included transcription, translation and transliteration of literary works in Arabi-Malayalam disseminated in both oral and written forms.

The scope of the field work was to create audio, video, graphic and text documentation material covering the use of Arabi-Malayalam language in a variety of social and cultural contexts. The field study covered many art forms, rituals and life-cycle events among Mappila Muslims; the most prominent among them were *oppana, Vaṭṭapaṭṭu, kollkaḷi, nērcca, kaimuṭṭukaḷi* and *paricamuṭṭukaḷi.* This work has made a detailed study of such art forms and cultural performances in which the oral literary tradition of Arabi-Malayalam finds its expression. The scope of this work also included the study of *Mappiḷapāṭṭu* which makes up the large chunk of literary corpus. The work involved transcription, translation and transliteration of *malappāṭṭu, padappāṭṭu, kissapāṭṭu, kalyānapāṭṭu or wedding songs, madhu pāṭṭukal, Vaṭṭappāṭṭu* being disseminated in written and oral forms.

A cross-disciplinary method was used to undertake this study as this work transgressing the boundaries of many disciplines like history, philology, and cultural studies. Different types of sources were identified, used and analysed during this work. With regard to methodology, the effort was trifurcated to:

(a) Material collection leading to the preparation of a monograph

(b) On the spot audio-visual documentation

(c) General field research

As the material related to this language is often not available on secondary sources, data on the evolution of Arabi-Malayalam literature was constructed mainly through using primary sources and empirical work. The priority was given to primary materials, like memoirs, published and unpublished song books, colonial government records, travelogues, unpublished manuscripts, family histories, etc. This work has used a very rich but largely unutilized collection of journals, magazines, pamphlets, biographies and autobiographies published in Arabi-Malayalam and made optimum use of the vast but hitherto neglected private possessions such as, letters and diaries of ordinary women. The materials collected also include audio cassettes and video footages of various cultural performances and songs. The secondary sources included the books and other materials dealing with the history of Kerala Muslims. In addition, some off-beat texts of stories, myths, narratives, personal and family histories, speeches and other literary forms, were also collected from the field.

Major task of this work was to document songs and performances, transliteration and translation of Arabi-Malayalam used in both. Ethnographic method had to be employed for the field work since the purpose was not simply to document oral tradition or to collect texts in Arabi-Malayalam language, but also to present and preserve the cultural heritage of the community which is expressed through this language. Documentation also covered the use of language in a variety of social and cultural contexts. Malappuram and Calicut districts of Kerala were the major locations of field work, because of the regular occurrence of rituals and life cycle events in these places. In order to document in authentic setting, the performances which occurred alongside rituals and life-cycle events were given primacy.

The core of the field work involved documentation and creation of a corpus of audio and video materials on the very occasion of the performances, life cycle events and rituals with time-aligned transcription. There were regular (at least once a fortnight) documentation of performances and art forms. The documentation was carried out by recording sounds or other naturalistic usages and expressions using sound and video recorders and transcribing them (with phonetic notations). Special attention was given to documenting seasonal performances and festivals happening infrequently.

The field research carried out during the study employed methods like focused interactions and interviews. Interviews with artists, traditional performers, composers, lyricists, experts in the field, etc. were conducted to collect and gather opinions. Their performances were recorded on the spot. The focused discussions included are mainly with the elders in the community. These helped not only in collecting opinions but also in giving us a sense of the changes that have occurred in time, and the transformation undergone with regard to the development of certain art forms. Focused discussions with the people who have experienced change, revealed whether the transformations were negative or positive and what all were to be sustained.

2

Community, Text and Territory

The Mappila Community

The term Mappila is a generic one referring to all foreign communities of Semitic origin who came to Kerala for various purposes, including trade and propagating faith, and later on settled in the land. However, the scope of the term at least in some parts of Kerala is limited to Muslims only. The etymological base of this term is still a subject of debate with a variety of theories about its origin and semantic domain in circulation. According to a prominent one, the term Mappila appears to have been basically a title of nobility and respect in all the Dravidian languages.[1] Historically, Mappila as an honorific term had been conferred upon Jews, Christians and Muslims who trace out their origin to foreign lands. The Christians in certain parts of Kerala were known as *nasrāni*[2] Mappilas, the Jews as *yahŪda* Mappilas, while the Muslims were called as *jōnaka*[3] Mappilas.[4] But use of the term sometimes restricted to Muslims, who have been described in all the European colonial documents as Mappilas. Mappila, a diminutive of two Malayalam terms, *mahā* (great) and *piḷḷai* (child), denotes to the greatness of people came from outside.[5] The honorific nature of this term shows that such a term would very naturally have been applied by the natives of Kerala who respected and welcomed the travellers and immigrants from abroad.[6]

---

[1] Rolland Miller, *Mappila Muslims of Kerala: A Study in Islamic Trends,* (Madras: Orient Longman, 1971) & M. Gangadharan, *Mappila Padanangal*, (Calicut: Vachanam Books, 2004).

[2] The term refers to people originated from Nazareth, the birth place of Christ. See, JBP More, *Origin and Early History of the Muslims of Keralam 700 AD-1600 AD*, (Calicut: Other Books, 2011), p.32.

[3] More finds the origin of the word Jonaka in *Sonagam*, which in Tamil literature signified Arabia. Mohammed takes it further to Greeks who were the predecessors of Arabs in Indian Ocean Trade and were referred in historical texts as jon, jonan, yonan, yonakan, chonakan, yavanan. People of Kerala, according to Mohammed, might have confused Arabs with Greeks. Arabian horses were also known as 'Chonaka Kuthira' or Greek Horses in historical records. See More, *Origin and Early History of the Muslims of Keralam* and T.Mohammed *Māppiḷa Samudāyam: Cariṯram Samskāram* (Malayalam), (Kozhicode: Islamic Publishing House, 2013), pp.13-14.

[4] Miller, *Mappila Muslims of Kerala,* p. 31 and P.A. Saidumohammed, *Kerala Muslim Caritram,* (Thrissur: Current Books,1961), pp. 2-8.

[5] C.Gopalan Nair, *Malayalatile Māppiḷamār* (Manglore: Author, 1917).p.1 and Saidumohammed, *Kerala Muslim Caritram,* pp. 4-8.

[6] Miller, *Mappila Muslims of Kerala*, pp.31-32.

The use of this term had historically been extended to all communities (not necessarily Semitic) moved in through maritime linkages.[7] The oceanic trade in the Malabar region had necessitated frequent trade delegations from the Arab world, which used to sojourn for a shorter period and then returned to the region of origin. The sojourning nature of such visits led to temporary marriages with the local women. Since trading with the Arabs was the major source of revenue, the princely states in Kerala had encouraged such marriages even if they last only for a few months or years.[8] Mappila community finds its origin mainly in such marital linkages to the trading between the Arabs and the locals. As per another version, the term 'Mappila' which literally means the bridegroom, son-in-law or husband in all the Dravidian languages, has been used to denote the progenies of Arabs who were married to Malayali women.[9] When the Arabs reached south-western coasts and got married to local women, they became the bridegroom for the people of the Malabar who started calling them Mappilas.[10]

However, the first use of this term remains mysterious. Muslim historians like Sheikh al-Zaynuddin of 15th century had never used this term to designate the Muslim community of Kerala in their writings.[11] Similarly, no literary or epigraphic evidence to this appellation for the community is there before the 16th century. Scholars of Mappila history find a Portuguese connection in the first use of this term, though their application was confined to the local Muslims in order to distinguish from the *paradesi*[12] or foreign Muslims, who were said to have come from the Arab world.[13] The *Paradesi* Muslims of Malabar, which included the Arabs along with the other foreign Muslim groups like Persians, Khorasanys and Kutchi Memons of Gujarat, with their expertise in seafaring and trade, occupied a special position in several coastal towns where they were settled.[14]

The Portuguese author Duarta Barbosa in his work the *Land of Malabar* has consistently used the term *Mapuleres* to refer to the Muslim population in Malabar.[15] Barbosa's accounts of the community reflect the prosperity and pivotal role of Mappilas in the oceanic trade; "they (Mappilas) are rich, and live well, they hold all the sea trade and navigation in such sort that if the King of Portugal had not discovered India, Malabar would have been in the hands of them."[16] The Muslim population of Malabar, except some immigrants from other states of India, is generally called Mappilas. The non-Mappila population include a few Urdu speaking Muslims migrated from Gujarat (composed mainly of

---

[7] Mohammed *Māppiḷa Samudāyam,* p. 13.

[8] T. Mansurali, "Arabi-Malayalam Charitravum Sahityavum" in T. Mansurali (ed.), *Arabi-Malayala Sahityava Padanangal* , (Kozhicode: Lead Books, 2014), p.13.

[9] Saidumohamed, *Kerala Muslim Caritram,*pp.6-8 & Gangadharan, *Mappila Padanangal,*p.12.

[10] Balakrishnan Vallikkunnu, *Mappila Sahityavum Navodhanavum*, (Calicut: Yuvatha Book House, 2008), p. 12.

[11] More, Origin and Early History of the Muslims of Keralam, p.31.

[12] The word means foreigner in Sanskrit and some of the Dravidian languages including Malayalam.

13 Abu-Lughod has clearly described about this bifurcation: "Some of these merchants originally came from the Middle East but had settled, married, and generally assimilated to their new home (Malabar); others, however, were indigenous to the region but, through the prolonged contacts of trade, had converted and adopted Muslim culture and language." Janet Abu-Lughod, *Before European Hegemony: Th e World System Ad.1250 –1350,*(New York: Oxford University Press, 1989)p.251.See also More, *Origin and Early History of the Muslims of Keralam*, p. 32.

[14] Sinnappa Arasaratnam, *Maritime Indian in the Seventeenth Century* (New Delhi:Oxford Univeristy Press, 2004), p. 40.

[15] Joao de Barros, *Decadas da Asia I*, part 11, (Lisbon, 1563), p.324 as cited in Duarta Barbosa, *The Land of Malabar,* M.Gangadharan (ed.) (Kottayam: Mahatma Gandhi University, 2000), p.73.

[16] Ibid.

Memons from Kutch) and Karnataka (Nawayats from northern Canara region), Muslim traders from Tamil Nadu called Rawther and a miniscule few population of Shias from Western coasts of India.

Mappilas are mostly converts from the locals, especially from the 'lower' castes. The major reason for the massive conversion was the Arab connection and the arrival of Islam which offered the lower castes a relief from the caste-based suppression.[17] The growth of the community received an added encouragement through the conversion of a Malayali ruler, Cēramān Perumāḷ in the 7th century.[18] The story of the conversion, which has been discussed in detail below is found in both Hindu and Muslim local narratives. This conversion, according to some scholars, offered a major morale booster for the 'upper' and 'lower' caste alike to embrace Islam.[19] The other reason seems to be the attraction of influential and wealthy Arab Muslims and their immunity from the then prevailing caste system. The Mappila community's primary identification, however, was with the lower castes as they grew as a foreign community relatively free from the local caste system.[20] The lower castes found refuge in the Mappila community as a means to bypass caste hierarchies.[21]

With this hybrid composition, Mappilas could successfully plant their identity in tune with the local one and at the same time maintain an identity of privileged intermediaries of Arab culture. The community has been subjected to diverse influences; both external and internal. Arasaratnam notes:

> Mappilas are the product of a cultural mix, Arab and Malayali descent, they acquired an identity of their own, distinct from local society by their firm adherence to Islam and Arab language, but retaining many elements of social customs and legal practice of the local society, from which they emerged. [22]

As Miller points out, "the religious identity of Mappilas offers a peculiar mix of the indigenous (prevailing in the complex Kerala Muslims society of which they are a part) and pan-Islamic."[23] Their faith remains strictly within the framework of Islam, though they inherit two different traditions; Islam and the local. The pan-Islamic part of identity traces its genealogy to the Arabs, who came to Kerala

---

[17] Authors' conversation with Ummar Tharammel, a scholar of Arabi-Malayalam literature.

[18] Shaykh Zainuddin Makhdum, *Tuhfat al-Mujāhidīn*, translated by S.M.H.Nainar, **(Kuala Lumbur:** Islamic Book Trust, 2006), pp.29-35 & Miller, *Mappila Muslims of Kerala*, pp.46-51.

[19] Syed Mohideen Shah, *Islam in Kerala,* (Thrissur: Muslim Educational Association, 1972), p.p.16-30. Saidumohamed, *Kerala Muslim Caritram*, pp. 12-20.

[20] Unlike in North India, caste system in Islam in Kerala was poorly developed. The social stratification, with a few exceptions, remained horizontal based on social status, family and clan. The caste system represented mainly by two social groups, namely, *Ossan* and *Pusalan*. Ossans are Muslim barbers engaged in circumcision, besides hair-cutting, while *Pusalans* are mainly converts from the fisherman caste of the Hindu community. Both constitute the lowest sections of the Malabar Muslims on account of their traditional occupation and on others' unwillingness to establish matrimonial relations with them. Due to their status as descendents of the Prophet, Taṉaḷ or Sayyids from Hadramawt enjoyed special status and possessed sanctity. They occupy the upper strata of the hierarchy with unique spiritual power endowed thanks to their Sayyid lineage. See M.K.H. Siddiqui (ed.), *Marginal Muslim Communities in India*, (New Delhi: Institute of Objective Studies, 2004), pp. 493 & 501 and Stephen Dale, *The Mappilas of Malabar 1498 –1922: Islamic Society on the South Asian frontier* (Oxford: Carendon, 1980).

[21] The lower castes found a liberative potential in Islam (same was the case of Christianity) as a chance to overcome the castiest rules and thereby to win some degree of social freedom denied to them on account of the rigid caste system.

[22] Arasaratnam, *Maritime Indian in the Seventeenth Century,* p.266.

[23] Miller, *Mappila Muslims of Kerala*, p.36.

and mostly married local women. As Asgar Ali Engineer observes, "...they (Mappilas) imbibed native culture, customs and manners, making certain variations to the newly accepted religious faith and on the paternal side the Muslim faith, predominantly a local variation of it."[24] An especially striking feature, therefore, is that there are some beliefs of partly with local origin, but at the same time strengthened by the Arabian influence.

Cultural Fabric

The culture of Mappila Muslims, of course, represents a notable difference to the general Indian Muslim situation.[25] It stands apart having very little in common with their pan-Indian counterparts. Mappila community's isolation from Indo-Persian Islam is more significant as they have by-passed not only the political sway and tradition of it, but also the cultural heritage and theological affinity.[26] Even for the Mughal-Urdu traditions which determined the cultural being of Muslims up north, there are only a few takers in this part.[27] In its place, Mappilas uphold a peculiar cultural hybrid of Arab and Malayali descendents. The way in which Islam flourished in this part of India remains to be the prime reason for this exclusiveness. All available historical information show that Islam, like Judaism and Syrian Christianity, came into Kerala through merchants and scholars.[28] The Arab Muslims in Kerala were well-received on their arrival by the rulers who found in them a substitute for the Syrian Christians and Jews, whose influence in the Indian Ocean trade was declining.[29] So, Islam had a relatively slow but lively spread here through the trade and religious missions mostly from Arabia.

There is one more reason for the exclusiveness – perhaps this may be the strongest one among all. It is the direct relation of Mappilas with the other Muslim communities scattered around the Indian Ocean region that resulted in the lesser influence of the Indo-Persian brand of Islam in Kerala. The Mappilas historically maintained an eclectic mix of cultures that while hanging onto many elements of social and legal practices of the local society, differs from it by firm adherence to Islam. This cultural blend has also been the hallmark of their art and literature.[30] So is the case of Arabic-Malayalam, an indigenously developed language of the Mappilas of Malabar, overwhelming presence of which caused the poor growth of Urdu, which otherwise is considered to be the pan-Indian Islamic language.[31] This language, which has primarily been used as a language of trade and eventually become a vehicle of both religious and creative expressions among Mappilas, can be considered as a special achievement of the cross-cultural interface that Mappila life represented for centuries.[32]

---

[24] Asghar Ali Engineer (ed.),*Kerala Muslims: A Historical Perspective*,(New Delhi: Ajanta Publishers, 1995),p.6.

[25] V.C.Harris, "From Structure to Communitas and Back:Notes on the Arts and festivals of the Muslims of Kerala ",in Asghar Ali Engineer (ed.),*Kerala Muslims: A Historical Perspective*,(New Delhi: Ajanta Publishers, 1995),p. 201-201.

[26] Stephen Dale, *The Mappilas of Malabar 1498 –1922: Islamic Society on the South Asian frontier* (Oxford: Carendon, 1980).

[27] Harris, Ibid. , pp. 201-202.

[28] M.G.S. Narayanan, *Cultural Symbiosis* (Trivandrum: Kerala Historical Society 1972), p.5.

[29] Ibid., p.6.

[30] Harris, "From Structure to Communitas and Back", p.202.

[31] Except in Kerala, Urdu has widely been used among Muslims of India, not only as the language of religious services but also as the language of trade.

[32] M.N.Karaserry, "Arabic-Malayalam", in Asghar Ali Engineer (ed.), *Kerala Muslims: A Historical Perspectives*, (New Delhi: Ajanta Publications, 1995), pp. 169-170.

Thanks to the *globality* that the Kerala society possessed for many centuries, Mappilas might have more in common with the Muslims of far-flung Hadramawt or Sumatra than those of North India. Looking at the life of people live in the Indian Ocean region, one can see that there are some material and cultural commonalities across regions. This cultural uniformity with its lively spread sans borders unites Eastern coast of Africa, South western coast of India and some parts of South East Asia especially, Malayasia and Indonesia.[33] Cultures from these areas that often seem so widely divergent were in fact in constant contact and exchange with each other. As an atypical mix of having absorbed Arabian and local elements, there was, of course, a creative interplay of varied cross-cultural basics in the formation of Mappila culture and its customs and rituals.

The Arab-Malayali cultural blend has also been reflected in material culture. The jewellery and the wedding dress of Muslim women in Malabar display the fusion of Keralite and Arabian cultures and, perhaps the influence of other cultures that had contacts with Kerala such as Persia.[34] Mappilas maintain a peculiar sartorial identity which sometimes relives the life of forefathers came from the Arab world. The alternative ways of Muslim dressing always makes specific cultural statements through clothes.[35] Muslim women used to wear *penkuppāyam* or waist-length top and *kacimundu* or waist-cloth, and with a shawl they cover their head fully or partly (Plate 1.1). Later on, many in the community switched over to *sari* and *churidar* and covered their heads using the end of *sari* or separately bought *mafta or* head scarf.[36] The active Islamization in the 1990s--a process induced largely by Gulf migration--contributed in emulation of Islamic style of dressing. Burgeoning practice of wearing *abaya* and *purdah* is generally seen as a clear indication of Kerala women's new interpretation of the faith, which they define as liberating rather than constraining. By choosing to wear *purdah*, young Muslim women are reproducing the life of those Muslim women from 'the land of Islam.'

Mappila men's traditional attire bears a rendition of clothing of Muslim sailors of Southern Arabia (especially Yemen and Oman) and Southeast Asia (Plate 1.2). Wearing, knee-length *lungi* or waist cloth and a thick green belt on it and the tradition of keeping knife are said to have borrowed from Omani culture.[37] Wearing turban also bears the sartorial influence of Arabs. Long *kurtas* with round neck, and shall, *akal* are also put on certain occasions. The turban and flowing beard are also likely to resemble this tradition (Plate 1.3). Ulemas and clergies in the community enliven the Arab Islamic tradition by wearing white knee-length gowns similar to *kandŪra* or the cover-whole gowns of Arabs (Plate 1.4).

Mappila ulema of the modern age wear ankle-length plain or checked *mundus* or waist-cloths, white long shirt and a head-gear (Plate 1.5), while the younger generation shows inclination to trousers and coloured shirts. The popularization of trousers is attributable largely to the migration to the Southeast Asian countries at the initial period and then to the Gulf countries in the later phase. Though

[33] From an interview with Hussain Randathani, a scholar of Mappila Muslim History.

[34] Ibid.

[35] Caroline Osella and Filippo Osella, "Muslim Style in South India," *Fashion Theory*, vol. 11, no. 2-3, pp. 1-4.

[36] Ibid., p.4.

[37] V. P. Mohamedali, *Mappila Pattukal Noottandukalilude*, (Kottayam: Current Books, 2007), p.20.

the tradition of wearing *mundus* and *pants* are common among all the religious communities, the Muslim style of wearing them is visually distinguishable from Christians and Hindus in a subtle way.[38]

Many other cultural symbols being circulated among the Muslims in Malabar are taken directly from the Arab tradition. *Bakhur, Oud* and *Lubān* are smoked at home on special occasions.[39] Many of the Muslim houses in Malabar have courtyards meant for men folk to sit together bearing striking resemblances to *Majlis* in southern Arabia. Every household keeps hookahs for collective smoking. A group of four or five people sitting together and eating from a big plate called *suppara* kept in front of them. *Khahva,* the favourite drink made of cinnamon, ginger and coffee beans, is also popular among the Muslims of Malabar.

Malabar Muslim cuisine maintains an affinity with Arabic cuisine-- snacks and other food items served during special events and everyday life are borrowed from the Arabic cuisine. The Arabian influence on Malabar Muslims is also seen in the architecture of mosques, houses and buildings especially in coastal towns (Plates 1.6 & 7). There are couplets and small haiku-like compositions in Arabic inscribed on walls and wooden doors of these buildings (Plate 1. 8). Kerala Muslim architecture is reflective of Southern Arabian influence though they are structurally depended on the indigenous style. The Arabian influence is seen mainly with the domes of the mosques. Likewise, the Arab diaspora stimulated the development of urban centres in Malabar. The early diasporic groups lived collectively in settlements, where they introduced goods and services needed for a highly urbanised society.[40]

Matrilineal structure among Malabar Muslims, especially in lower class fisherman community and mariners in the coastal towns also bears testimony to the strong Arab influence. The matrilineal structure, marked by the presence of a system in which inheritance goes to women, is otherwise rare in Kerala confining to upper caste Hindus. It was due to the 'temporary marriage' system, *muta'* in which a spouse is ensured for the trading Arabs in every harbour, which they frequented, that the matrilineal system had a wide acceptance among those who inhabited the port towns.[41] Such marriages were short-lived and would often end when the Arabs return to their native place or move on to the next destination. D'Souza points out that these women, with whom such marriages were very often, if not always, were mostly from fisherman and mariner Muslims.[42] Though their offsprings multiplied in the harbours in conformity to the matriarchic custom, they were raised in accordance with the rules of Sunni Islam.[43]

1. Kerala's Arab Connection

Kerala's Arab connection pre-dates even the birth and spread of Islam in the 7th century. There were frequent Arab sailings back and forth since the 1st century, though the major diasporic drive from the

[38] Osella and Osella, "Muslim Style in South India,"p. 14.

[39] Sayyid Abdulla Munafar, *Ahlu Baith: Carithra Sangraham*, (Calicut: Vachanam Books, 2002).

[40] M.H. Ilias, "Mappila Muslims and the Cultural Content of Arab Trading Diaspora on the Malabar Coast", *Asian Journal of Social Sciences*, 35 (2007), p. 450.

[41] V.D. D 'Souza,"Status Group Among the Mappila Muslims on the South-West Coast of India",in Imtias Ahmed (ed.),*Social Strati .cation among Muslims in India* New Delhi:Oxford University Press, 1995), p.45.

[42] Ibid.

[43] Andrei Wink, *Al-Hind: The Making of the Indo-Islamic World* ,Vol.1, (New Delhi:Oxford University Press., 1995),p. 72.

Arabs merchants on the Malabar Coast came only during the 7th and 8th centuries.[44] Recent archaeological excavations at Pattanam in central Kerala have brought forth a variety of tangible evidences for Kerala's ancient trade links with different ports of Arabian Peninsula from the 1st century.[45] There is evidence for West Asia's trade interaction with Malabar and other parts of India from 2nd century onwards through the accounts of Ptolemy.[46] When Islam spread over Arabia in the 7th century, its impact was felt immediately in Kerala through the faith-based diaspora of Arab Muslim scholars who took up missionary work and strengthened their contacts with the people of Kerala, which led to the propagation of their faith, culture and language in Kerala.[47] It is important to note that Islam was brought to Kerala not by Kings or soldiers but by friendly merchants.[48] Muslim intellectuals, Sufi sages, clerics and missionaries joined this bandwagon in great numbers along with the frequent traders. Kodungallore (the ancient port of Kerala known otherwise as Muziris and Craganore in historical documents) is the place, where Islam, Judiasm and Christianity are believed to have come first in the region. Malik ibn Dinar along with an army of Sufis, and scholars were instrumental in bringing Islam to Kerala (more on this later).

However, according to Narayanan and Shah, the earliest historical evidence to the presence of Arab Muslims in Kerala is from the *Terisāppaḷḷi Cēppēdu* (*Terisāppaḷḷi* Copper Plate) of Ayyan Atikal of Venad, a subordinate of the then ruling *Cēra*[49] Emperor Stanu Ravi of Cranganore in the 9th century.[50] This copper plate issued in the year 849 AD, granting special mercantile rights for a Christian group, provides significant substantiation to demonstrate the presence of affluent Arab trading communities in the port towns of Kerala during this period. The names of all ten witnesses who signed in this document are of Arab Muslims. Arab-merchant witness to the grant must be people of considerable influence and importance during that period.[51] A tomb inscription at Pantalayini-Kollam provides vital clues to the presence of Arab Muslims from 8th century.[52] However, earlier references to the presence of Arab Muslim traders and scholars were mainly in the notes of Arab travellers and geographers.[53] In the absence of major epigraphic inscription related directly to Kerala Muslim history, travel writings in Arabic remain to be the major sources shedding light on the early period.

Further evidence on the presence of Arabs in the later period comes from the accounts of Ibn Batuta[54], the famous Arab traveller. He was the first writer to give detailed description of the Arab-

---

[44] See Narayanan, *Cultural Symbiosis,* p.82 & A.P. Ibrahim Kunju, *Mappila Muslims of Kerala,* (Thiruvananthapuram: Sandhya Publications, 1993), pp. 14-16.

[45] P.J. Cherian, *Pattanam: South India's Mohanjedaro* (Trivandrum: KCHR, 2006)

[46] S.M. Sasthri (ed.) Mc. Crindle's Ancient India as Described by Ptolemy, (Calcutta, 1927), pp. xiii, 22,29, 50.

[47] Kunju, *Mappila Muslims of Kerala,* pp.198-199 & Saidumohammed, *Kerala Muslim Caritram,* pp.8-12.

[48] Shah, *Islam in Kerala,* pp. 3-15.

[49] A dynasty ruled South India as Kodungallore as its seat.

[50] The purport of the inscription is the gift of a plot of land to the Terisappalli (Terisa Church) at Quilon of south Kerala along with several rights and privileges. The grant was made in the presence of the important officers of the state and representatives of the trading communities. See Seyd Mohideen Shah, *The Islam in Kerala*, p.8.

[51] Kunju argues, "It is evident that to be called up on to witness such an important document the Arab Muslim community must have been residents of Quilon for a pretty long time", Kunju, *Mappila Muslims of Kerala*, p.20.

[52] Miller, *Mappila Muslims of Kerala, p.* 42

[53] S.M.H.Nainar, *Arab Geographers Knowledge of South India*, (Madras: Madras University Press, 1962).

[54] Quoted by H.A.R Gibb, *Ibn Battuta : Travels in Asia and Afirca*, (London: Robert M. Mc. Bride and Co., 1929)

Muslims in various parts of Kerala in the late 14th century. The major impetus of settlements, according to him, was from Arabian Peninsula including Yemen, Oman, Bahrain and Baghdad. Batuta has recorded the presence of Arab merchants and settlements of sojourning Arab traders in most of the major ports of northern and central Kerala in his travel writing. "At all halting places on this road (Malabar), there were houses belonging to Arab Muslims... they were well honoured for their trustworthiness", writes Batuta.[55] His notes bear ample evidence for the presence of affluent Arab traders, who were settled more or less freely in every major port towns of Malabar.[56] Batuta has also given a vivid account of non-trading groups comprising Arabs and Persians who were engaged mainly in Islamization of people in the coastal areas.

2. Cēramān Perumāl Episode

The most popular view about the advent and spread of Islam in the early period is connected with 'the well-known legend of the conversion of Cēramān Perumāl into Islam'[57] and his departure to Mecca and subsequent arrival of Malik Ibn Dinār mission [58] in Kerala.[59] There has been much of mention in books of ancient history about Cēramān Perumāl, a king of Kerala, who became the first known convert to Islam from the Indian subcontinent, went to Mecca to meet the Prophet Mohammad and finally settled down in Dofar province of Oman and sent messengers who established the first ten mosques on the West Coast of South India. Though there is a rich and myriad repository of local narratives and other oral traditions that provide evidence to Cērmān Perumāl's conversion to Islamic faith and his journey to the Arabian Peninsula, the first written reference to this conversion and the partition of his Kingdom into eight princely states is found in *The Book of Duarte Barbosa: An Account of Countries Bordering on the Indian Ocean and Their Inhabitants*[60] composed in the middle of the second decade of the 16th century. Barbosa accounts go as follows:

> They (people of Kerala) say in ancient days there was a heathen king whose name was Cirimāy Pirimāl (Cēramān Perumāl), a very mighty Lord. And after the Moors of Mecca had discovered India they began to voyage towards it for the sake of pepper, of which they began to take cargoes at Coulam (Kollam), a city with a harbor where the King ofttimes abides. This will not be less than six hundred years ago...and continuing to sail to India for many years they began to spread out therein and they had such discussions

[55] Ibid.

[56] During his visit in 14th century, Ibn Batuta has noticed, every town in Malabar had its lot of rich Arab merchants and their places of worship.

[57] The last representative of the ruling line of the Cēramān Perumāl, the titular rulers of middle Kerala embraced Islam on the basis of an unusual dream.

[58] Malik Ibn Dinār arrived at Cranganore (also known in the historical documents as Musiris) with the purposes of preaching religion among the peoples of Malabar. Cranganore was the major port of Malabar and a place where all the other Semitic religions were (Judaism and Christianity) believed to have landed first in the sub-continent. Thanks to its close contact with Arabia, Egypt and the west, Cranganore had a wide acclamation among the Arabs. According to *Tuhfat ul-Mujāhidīn*, Malik Ibn Dinār at first landed in Cranganore. He brought with nine disciples who were well-read in Koran. They were made to reside at various port towns of Kerala and provided with all facilities to propagate Islam by the local rulers.

[59] Makhdum, *Tuhfat al-Mujāhidīn,* pp. 46-51 & Shah, *Islam in Kerala,* p. 16.

[60] Translated into English from Portuguese original by Mansel Longworth Dames and first Published in 1918. See Barbosa, *The Land of Malabar*, pp. 13-15.

> with the King himself and he with them, that in the end they converted him to the sect of Mafamede (the Prophet Mohammed), wherefore he went in their company to the house of Mecca, and there he died, or, as it seems more probable, on the way thither; for they say that Malabarese never heard any tidings of him.

Somewhat similar version has been shared by Joao de Barros, the first official historian of the Portuguese in the 16th century in his *Decada de Asia* (2000). His account on the conversion of 'Sarama Pereimāl' (Cērmān Perumāl) sounds as follows:

> ...[T]he King (Cērmān Perumāl) was so powerful that in memory of his name, they used to make a reckoning of the period of his reign...making it the starting point of an era[61]...in his time the Arabs now converted to the sect of Muhammed began to trade with India...when they were settled in the country, this king, Sarama Pereimāl, became a Moor and showed them great favour...then they persuaded him that for his salvation he ought to end his life at the House of Mecca. He agreed...and determined...to make a partition of his country among nearest kindred."[62]

Louis de Camoes, the Portuguese poet who was in Malabar in the fifties of the 16th century, mentions in his epic poem, *Lusiad*, the story of the conversion to Islam of a 'Perumāl' and division of his country among "servants he loved best."[63] Later in the century Sheikh Zaynud-Din, a scholar of Arab origin, gave a detailed account of the tale about the conversion to Islam of "a monarch of the whole of Malabar, and the division of his country among "governors."[64] *Keralōlpatti* Chronicles, a native work of the 17th or 18th century (perhaps an oral tradition of earlier times later on compiled during this period) also has a detailed reference which sounds as follows:

> Cēramān Perumāl, the last Cēra ruler of Kerala, who became enamoured of Islam, partitioned the Kingdom and secretly left for Mecca with some Arab traders and lived for a few years in obscurity and peace in Arabia. There he visited the Prophet and embraced the new faith. On his return, Perumāl died and was buried on the Arabian coast.[65]

There are different versions of the story of conversion of Perumāl in circulation through the oral history in Kerala. The prominent one among them says that Perumāl embraced Islam on the basis of an unusual dream.[66]

> He saw in a dream that the full moon appeared on the night of the new moon, and that when at the meridian it splits into two, one half descending to the foot of the hill, where the halves joined and then set. He shared this bizarre dream with a few Arab Muslim

---

[61]According to another tradition, the partition of own Kingdom by Cēramān Perumāl marked the beginning of Kollam era which belied to have started in the year 825 A.D. See Herman Gundert, *Kerlolpathiyum Mattum* (Kottayam, NBS 1962).

[62] Joao de Barros, *Decadas da Asia I*, part 11, as cited in Kunju, *Mappila Muslims of Kerala*, p. 180.

[63] Louis de Camoes, *Lusiad*, translated by Richard Franshawe (Harvard, 1940), as cited in Barboas, The Land of Malabar, pp. 14-15.

[64] Makhdum, *Tuhfat al-Mujāhidīn,* pp. 46-51.

[65] Raghava Varrier, *Keralolpatti Chronicles* (Calicut: University of Calicut 1984), pp.56 & 60.

[66]P.P.Mohammed Koya Parappil, *The History of Calicut Muslims,* (Calicut: Focus Publications, 1994)

> pilgrims to Adam's peak in Ceylon, who visited Cēramān Perumāl at Muziris (Kodungallore) on their way. In an audience given by the King, one of the pilgrims, Sheikh Sooriji al-Deen, interpreted the dream by connecting it with the story of the Prophet Mohammed splitting the moon up his sleeve in Arabia. The King was much interested in the interpretation given by them and secretly informed the Sheikh of his desire to embrace the faith and to go to Arabia to meet the Prophet.

Miles writes:

> ...[O]n his return journey, the Sheikh was secretly instructed by the King to have a ship prepared for a voyage, and after eight days embarked in the vessel with the Sheikh and his companions for Shihr on the Arabian coast.[67]

Another tradition has it; "the King Perumāl landed first in Shihr from there he proceeded to Dhofar, where he settled for a while. After some years, Perumāl wished to return to Kerala in order to invite his own people to the new faith he embraced, but the deteriorating physical condition seized him and finally died and buried in Dhofar."[68] Perumāl on his return from Arabia was accompanied by the family and friends of Malik ibn Dinār. Before the king died at Dhofar on the Arabian coast, Perumāl had instructed Dinar and his companions to proceed to Kerala, to take over his mission and spread the new faith in Malabar.[69] In Omani local records Cēramān Perumāl is known by another name-Abdul Rahiman *al-Sāmiri*. He is believed to have accepted this name on his arrival in Arabia. The name Sāmiri may be derived from the word Zamorin a Sanskrit word means the custodian or caretaker of the sea.[70]

There are numerous theories in circulation over the arrival of Malik ibn Dinar in Kerala. The most prominent one is that following Perumāl's instructions, Malik ibn Dinar and his associates landed at the ancient port of Kodungallore. On arrival, they were welcomed by the close associates of Perumāl and the first mosque in the Indian subcontinent was, thus established in Kodungallore.[71] Logan in *Malabar Manual* writes:

> ...[T]hey (Malik ibn Dinar and his companions) were well received in accordance with the instruction of Perumāl and were given land to build a mosque, and suitable endowments were also given. Malik ibn Dinar himself became the first Kazi of Cranganore (Kodungallore).[72]

From Kodungallore, Dinar and companions moved to different parts of Kerala and established ten mosques in various port towns. Dinar appointed *Qazis* in each mosque with a view to propagate Islam in Kerala and each mosque became instrumental in spreading Islam in the respective localities. The

---

[67] S.B.Miles, *The Countries and Tribes of the Gulf,* (London: Harrison & Sons, 1919), pp. 553-54.

[68] As per another local narrative, Perumal was buried in Shahar Mukhalla in Yemen. See Shah, *Islam in Kerala,* pp. 17-29.

[69] Miles, *The Countries and Tribes of the Gulf,* pp. 553-54.

[70] This appellation was conferred on a set of rulers in Calicut who championed the maritime trade of the region. It has been confounded with the word Zamorin, the title given by the Portuguese to the King of Calicut, but the latter word is of Sanskrit derivation. The word signifies 'calf' and is applied to the worshippers of the cow, and it probably has reference to Perimal being of the Hindu religion before his conversion. See Miles, *The Countries and Tribes of the Gulf,* p 554.

[71] The first mosque according Zaynud-Din was established by a group of missionaries from Arabia under the leadership of Ibn Dinar in seventh century.

[72] William Logan, *Malabar Manual I*, Pt.1&2, P.J. Cherian et al. (eds.), (Thiruvananthapuram: KCHR, 2008) pp.91-96.

work of these missionaries resulted in large-scale conversion of people into Islam in different parts of Kerala.

Although there are ample evidences to the Perumāl episode in the oral history, the period of these occurrences appear to be not fairly well established. Opinions of those who compiled such oral traditions vary, though their findings converge on two points-Cērmān Perumāl's conversion and his journey to Arabia-with near-total unanimity. The most important point which has been thoroughly debated, relates to the date and the probability of meeting the Prophet Mohammed. Kunju sums up: "there are at present three differing versions regarding the period of occurrence of this event: (i) during the lifetime of the Prophet (i.e. between 622 and 632 A. D) (ii) during the 8th century and (iii) during the 9th century."[73] However, Pillai, a historian known for his reading of early *Cēra* inscriptions, has inferred that the ruler who took to Islam might have been the last Perumāl of Mahodayapuram of early 12th century.[74] Making a point further, Narayanan, another scholar, on the basis of circumstantial evidence from inscriptions and literary works, endorses Pillai's argument that the story of the conversion of a King of Malabar might be a reflection of what happened in the case of Rama Kulasekhara, the last Cēramān Perumāl of Mahodayapuram (Kodungallore) in the early 12th century.[75]

The inscriptions from Mādayi mosque in north Kerala furnishes a hint that this mosque was built by Mālik Bin Dinār, the companion of Cēramān Perumāl and the first Sufi missionary in Kerala, who moved to Malabar with the instruction of the latter after his death. After going through many local narratives in Dhofar, Miles has come to another conclusion that King Cēramān Perumāl left India in 210 A.H. (A.D. 825), remained at Shihr two years, reached Dhofar in 212 A.H. (A.D.827) and died there in 216 A.H. (A.D. 831).[76] The inscription at Perumāl's tomb at Dhofar also reads that "Abdur Rahiman Samiri arrived in Arabia in Hijara 212, died 216 A.H." Fard ud-Din Attar (1966)'s work *Tadhikirat ul-Auliya* presents another version with different dates which he tries to prove by relating it to the period when Hassan ul-Basri, the famous Sufi sage lived.[77] Malik ibn Dinar who died in 748 A.D., according to him was a disciple of Hassan al-Basri. Since these sources are almost unanimous in their accounts about the conversion and migration to the Arabian Peninsula, the Perumāl tradition in Kerala history cannot be dismissed as mere fiction or figment of imagination.

3. Trading Arab Diaspora on the Malabar Coast

Malabar holds an all-important position on the trading map of the ancient and medieval world. Being pivotal in the exchange of goods between the east and the west, Malabar had a greater role in this wide network of Indian Ocean trade, not only in terms of its geographical advantages, but also in terms of high-value goods it possessed and exchanged. Malabar's fame came from both its strategic location on the trade routes as well as its production of pepper and spices.[78] The importance of Malabar further increased as it was in the direct supply line between Arabia and China.

---

[73] Kunju, *Mappila Muslims of Kerala,*p. 16.

[74] Elankulam Kunjan Pillai, *Keralacharithrathile Iruladanja Edukal,* (Kottayam: NBS, 1933).

[75] Narayanan, *Cultural Symbiosis,* p.185.

[76]Miles, *The Countries and Tribes of the Gulf,* p.554.

[77] Fard ud-Din Attar, *Tadhikirat ul-Auliya* (1966) as cited in Randathani, *Mappila Muslims,* pp.28-30.

[78] Arasaratnam, *Maritime Indian in the Seventeenth Century*, p.39.

Malabar had played a crucial role within this Afro-Asian led global economy (oriental globalization)[79] for many centuries.[80] The cultural results of these economic linkages also varied enormously. The long-distance trade in essentially high-value goods (like spices) spurred a number of factors that operated in promoting cultures among the participating regions.[81] Within the framework of trade-based oriental globalization, Malabar had been the melting pot of many cultures. The traders from Rome, China, Arabia etc., paid voyages to Malabar coasts in search of spice. Malabar had absorbed the best of all of these influences and became a perfect repository of diverse cultures for long centuries.

Another salience of the development of trade in Malabar was the migration of substantial merchant communities from widely dispersed lands. The trading diasporas were actually universal phenomena throughout the Indian Ocean region since the long distance trade necessitated a situation in which the trading communities had to settle for long periods of time at the terminal points of trade.[82] The pre-modern trade that flourished throughout the Indian Ocean, needed on-site agents to represent the interests of traders sending goods from far away, and everywhere they moved to, those on-site agents established diaspora[83] communities.[84]

The rise and expansion of Islam must perhaps be the most critical of those factors that fostered the Arab trade in a big way. There is, of course, a cultural element in it. To quote Arasaratnam:

> Among the several elements of dynamism and growth brought out by the expansion of Islam was commercial ethics and commercial practice, which spread through the Islamic land like a wildfire, generating an economic growth in this and neighbouring lands, which sustained itself for several centuries.[85]

Hourani observes:

> With the newfound faith for several centuries the Arabs had showed an unusual energy extended to warfare, trade and commerce, travel, as well as to literature of travel, geography and history.[86]

In Malabar also one of the most significant aspects of Islam was its penchant for trade and establishing trade-based settlements. The diasporic communities of merchants that formed throughout the eastern reaches of the Indian Ocean did not consist of a single diaspora but a diverse

---

[79] John Hobson in his book *The Eastern Origins of Western Civilzation* traces the existence of the oriental globalization to a global economy that Persians, Arabs, Jews Chinese, Africans and Indians had created and maintained till around 1800. Major political and economic forces of the world at all times were interlinked in this system. John M Hobson, *The Eastern Origins of Western Civilization* (Cambridge: Cambridge University Press, 2004), pp.138-139 & Janet Abu-Lughod, *Before European Hegemony: The World System Ad.1250 –1350*, (New York: Oxford University Press, 1989).

[80] Hobson, *The Eastern Origins of Western Civilization*, pp. 138-39.,

[81] Arasaratnam, *Maritime Indian in the Seventeenth Century*, p.33

[82] Arasaratnam, *Maritime Indian in the Seventeenth Century*, p.36.

[83] Clark defines the trade Diaspora as "a community of merchants of common origin gathered in a foreign city or culture in order to conduct trade". See Hugh R. Clark, "Maritime Diasporas in Asia Before Da Gama: An Introductory Commentary ",*The Journal of the Economic and Social History of the Orient* ,Vol.49,No.4, 2006,p.391.

[84] Arasaratnam, *Maritime Indian in the Seventeenth Century,* p. 391.

[85] Ibid.

[86] George F. Hourani, Arab Seafaring in the Indian Ocean in Ancient and Early Medieval Times (Beirut: Khayats, 1963), p. 53.

one with a number of overlapping communities. It included Jews, Persians, Syrian Christians, Gujaratis and Memons of Kutch. Arab communities, however, constituted a major part of the broader diaspora occupying important nodes in the diasporic network. Early Muslim success furthered the expansion of the Arab diaspora out of the region and into a large expanse of territory belonging to different continents. Later, trading brought Islam to India, South East Asia, parts of China along with European territory. The process of Arab migration and establishment of trading settlements have served to bring all these places, where the Arab traders moved, closer into the commercial networks of the world trade. As the trading Arab networks amplified its proximity with the world commercial economy, Malabar too had benefited a lot from the presence of diasporic Arab communities.

Major salience of Malabar's trade linkages with the Arab world was migration of substantial Arab merchant communities from widely dispersed lands. Although some of these Arabs may have come from Hijaz, Oman and Bahrain on religious missions in the earlier period, the later diasporas in the 18th and 19th centuries represented Arab scholars and traders from Hadramawt[87] in Yemen. They brought with them several innovative practices and traditions, leaving tangible imprints upon the religious domain of Malabar. Each expatriate community became an integral part of local social life, as they were vital to further Islamization of Malabar.

The Portuguese advent, however, brought a situation wherein a violent destruction of Arab trading interests was taken place. By this time, the situation in the Indian Ocean had slipped out of control of the Arab merchants. When they landed in Kerala, right from the start, the Portuguese came up against the *Paradesi* Muslims, whom they wanted to eliminate from the Indian Ocean and they declared war on Calicut, which was the main centre of *Paradesi* activities.[88] The Portuguese advent itself had reduced the number of foreign Muslims coming to Malabar.[89] Arab sailing to Malabar was also badly affected by the consistent attack of the Portuguese force on them both in Malabar and in the Red Sea entrance.[90] The blockade of the Red Sea also prevented the Egyptian merchants from having trade relations with the port of Malabar. Thus by the second decade of 16th century, Arab Merchants, who were settled at Malabar Coast temporarily for the purpose of trade, returned in large numbers to Cairo and a few of them to Hormuz.[91]

4. Hadrami Sayyids and Religious Orientation of Mappilas

Any attempt to trace the evolution of the Mappila Muslim community in the Malabar Coast must begin with the medieval Arab trading diaspora of maritime Asia as these Arabs were the chief progenitors of them. Malabar, from the earliest times, has been in direct contact with the seafaring peoples of the Arab world.[92] As discussed earlier, the advent of Islam fostered the Arab sailings back and forth

---

[87] Hadramawt is a historical region of South Arabian Peninsula along the Gulf of Aden in the Arabian Sea, extending from Yemen (proper) to the Dhofar region of Oman. The society is still highly tribal, with old Saiyid aristocracy, descended from Prophet Mohammed. R.B. Serjeant, *The Saiyids of Hadramawt*, (London: School of Oriental and African Studies, 1957), 24.

[88] K.M. Panikkar, *Malabar and the Portuguese* , (New Delhi: Voice of India, 1997),pp.93-98.

[89] Ibid.

[90] Panikkar, *Portuguese and Malabar,* 93-98 & Arasaratnam, *Maritime Indian in the Seventeenth Century,* p. 42.

[91] O.P. Mayankutty, "The Portuguese Advent and the Decline of Arab Trade in Malabar " in M.H.Ilias, *India West Asia Relations: Understanding Cultural Interplays* ,(New Delhi: New Centaury Publications, 2007), pp. 90-95.

[92] Arasarthnam, *Maritime Indian in the Seventeenth Century*, p. 395.

between Arabia and Kerala. The Mappila community finds their origins in the process of trade and people-to-people cultural interactions between Arabia and Kerala. The main impetus of Arab settlements, however, came in the 18th century from the activities of Hadrami Sayyids who in particular were known to have been more active in preaching Islam and in proselytising local Muslims.[93] The spread of the *Ṣhāfī* School in Malabar traces back to Hadrami Sayyids who, in fact, had a particular mission of propagating this school against the encirclement of *Hanafism* and *Shīsm* from northern parts of India. Hadrami Sayyids tried to convert Muslims of Malabar from semi-pantheist mysticism which was in wider circulation thanks to the presence of Sufi sages, to the orthodoxy of Mecca and Medina, inculcating *Ṣhariah*.[94]

Hadramawt in the first half of the 18th century was a rather improvised region, once flourishing agricultural economy of which had been severely damaged by internal warfare. This region also had a long history as an important centre of Islamic learning. Its educational centre of Tarim was perhaps the most highly regarded in South Arabia and the intellectual and religious life has been very well developed in a number of Sayyids, Sufis and *ulema* whose influence extended overseas.[95] It thus came as no surprise that the more enterprising of its youth contemplated migration, either to India and further South East Asia, or to the East African coast. In the 18th century, it was India, the prime destination of Sayyid emigration eastwards though there was parallel movement of a substantial number of Sayyids from Hadrami centres like and Tarim and Mukhalla to East Africa and Southeast Asia as merchants and missionaries. Among the Indian destinations, Malabar with *ulemas* and religious leaders from Hadramawt were given special power to run religious institutions, became a prominent port of call.[96]

Due to their successful networking, the Hadrami Sayyids played a much greater role in Malabar. They were found dispersed all over the coastal and interior locations as religious leaders or as merchants and sometimes they combined both religious and commercial activities.[97] With the patronage of Zamorins, they exercised varying degrees of spiritual and political influence over the local Muslims. The Hadarami Sayyids were further divided into a few prominent houses of *kabilah* or clans, some of which emerged to claim notable status especially in religious affairs. But the differences among the groups were more sectarian based on the Sufi order they followed than ethnical in character. *Idid, Ṣhihabuddin, Jamalullail, Musawa, Hibsi, Sakhāf, Idrus, Bā-Alawi, Bā-Hassan, Bā-Fakhi* and *Jifri*, were some of the major clans that reached and settled in Malabar with the mission of preaching Islam.[98]

---

[93] The *Barahami* clan of Mukhallah and *Thameems* were the other major groups from Yemen who landed with the mission of trade.

[94] Dale, *The Mappilas of Malabar 1498 –1922, pp.* 115-16

[95] Omar Khalid, "Sayyids of Hadramawt in Medieval and Modern India", *Journal of the Gulf and Arabian Peninsula Studies*, no.127, pp.11-15.

[96] They moved in large number towards the Indian Coast and settled in important commercial, cultural and political centres like Bijapur, Surat, Calicut, Hyderabad and Ahmadabad. See Khalidi, "Sayyids of Hadramawt in the Medieval and Modern India," 11-13 and Serjeant, *The Saiyids of Hadramawt*, 24.

[97] LRS Lakshmi, *The Malabar Muslims: A Different Perspectives*, (New Delhi: Cambridge University Press India Ltd, 2012), 22.

[98] Although innumerable number of kabeelas have reached and settled here for the missionary works, many of them are either endangered or on the verge of extinction. Many moved further to Indonesia, Malaysia, Burma of South East Asia

Hadrami Sayyids enjoyed a peculiar position in religious affairs and the Mappila theology of modern times, to a large extent, is dependent on their teachings.[99] They brought in many changes in the pattern of religious consumption and integrated an indigenous Muslim community into a wider Islamic world by reconfiguring their rituals and practices within a strict Sunni-*Shāfīte* code. The Mappilas generally show a strong proclivity to this combination as far as their theological orientation is concerned. The *Shīte*-Persian influence, however, continues to find expression in certain rituals and cultural performances. A complete departure, therefore, did not happen, despite concerted efforts of de-Persianization by Hadrami Sayyids.[100]

Due to their status as descendents of the Prophet, Hadrami Sayyids enjoyed special status and possessed sanctity. As a result of their lineage, the Sayyids were well accepted with huge sphere of influence and endowed with unique spiritual power. Being considered superior to other Muslims, they were entitled to issue *fatwas* on several religious issues.[101] The key sign of grace and authority was their acts of wonder, power and miracles. Mappilas turned to such figures, dead or alive, to have solutions for most of their daily life problems.[102] At times of need or special undertakings, devotees visited their shrines.[103] Dispute settlements in many places in Malabar were entrusted in this community. People from other religious communities also gave them due respect and local chieftains were obedient to them.[104]

The *Mambram Taṉaḷs*, a family established by Sayyid Sheikh Jifri who arrived in Calicut in 1755, were the most prominent group among the Hadrami Sayyids. On his arrival Sheikh Jifri was welcomed warmly by the Zamorins of Calicut with a gift in land and recognition as a dignitary.[105] His later seat at Mambram became a sacred shrine to a large number of devotees in Malabar. Throughout his life, Sheikh Jifri engaged in preaching *Alawīyya tariqa*, an influential Sufi order of Southern Arabia. Besides the religious positions they occupied, *Mambram Taṉaḷs* were very active in anti-British agitations and became the spirit behind several of Mappila outbreaks in 19th century. Several of their sheikhly miracles and *karāmats* or indications of divine power have found expression in many of the popular anti-colonial narratives.

---

and others to the African countries like Ethiopia, Tanzania, Somalia, Sudan Ghana, Nigeria and others. Munafar, *Ahlu Baith* and Parappil, *The History of Calicut Muslims*.

[99] Dale, *The Mappilas of Malabar 1498 –1922,* pp.115-16.

[100] Some of the devotional rituals like Nercha, observed to commemorate the saints or martyrs cannot be connected to Sunni tradition. Similarly, in their preaching Mappilas praise Ali and his sons Hasan and Husayn, yet they balanced it with typical Sunni criticism of those who denounce the first three Caliphs. See Dale, *The Mappilas of Malabar 1498 – 1922,* pp.115-16.

[101] Dale, *The Mappilas of Malabar 1498 –1922* & K.N.Panikkar, *Against Lord and State: Religion and Peasant Uprisings in Malabr 1836-1921,* (New Delhi, 2001).pp.61-62.

[102] Miller, *Mappila Muslims of Kerala: A Study in Islamic Trends,* p.230.

[103] Ibid.

[104] Munafar, *Ahlu Baith*

[105] Kunju, *Mappila Muslims of Kerala,* p. 26.

5. Kondōṭṭy-Ponnāni Factional Feud

Shite Islam in Malabar from the eighteenth century onwards has been represented largely by *Kondōṭṭy Taṉaḷs*[106] another diasporic Muslim group claiming descent from the Prophet's family. The *Kondōṭṭy Taṉaḷs* have always been under attack by the Hadrami Sayyids for their alleged *'Ṣhīṭe-Sufi'* connection. They were an exceptional group forming the only known Perso-Islamic *Sufi* order in northern Kerala.[107] The Persian speaking *Ṣhīa* Muslim Sheikh Muhammed Shah, who was the founder of this group, therefore, had an alien stature among the Muslim scholars.[108] Some of his practices like the celebration of the *Muharram* festival and the insistence for the prostration of *murids* or disciples before him often invited popular suspicion of his Sayyid lineage.[109] Hadrami Sayyids and *Kondōṭṭy Taṉaḷs* engaged in de-legitimating the claims of each other with *fatwas* and counter *fatwas*. Each group managed to get rulings and scholarly opinion on matters of Islamic law from recognized authorities inside and outside India for the purpose of validating their claims.

While Sayyids of Hadramawt enjoyed a huge sphere of influence, Kondōṭṭy faction gained consistent political support from the colonial rulers. When the British took over the rule of Malabar in 1792, they confirmed the position of Muhmmad Shah as *Ināmdāṛ,*[110] the position which was originally granted by Tipu Sultan of Mysore. In return for this, *Kondōṭṭy Taṉaḷs* were always loyal to the British and were successful in preventing their adherents from participating in the periodic Mappila outbreaks in which *Mampuram Taṉaḷs* actively participated and taken the leadership role. So, there was an obvious political angle to the dispute between these two groups which came to be known as *Kondōṭṭy-Ponnāni Kaitaṛkkam* or *Kondōṭṭy-Ponnāni* factional feud.[111]

As the keepers of Perso-Islamic tradition and with loyalty to the British, Kondōṭṭy faction was able to attract only a miniscule few population in Malabar. Adhered closely to the teachings of Hadrami Sayyids, Mappila *ulema*, anathematized Muhmmad Shah and his disciples as heretics. It was their alleged *Shia* practices that attracted the wrath of Hadrami Sayyids who succeeded in damaging the legitimacy of *Kondōṭṭy Tangaḷs* through a series of *fatwas*. Inclination of Shah towards *Shīsm* met stiff opposition from Makhdūmis of Ponnāni,[112]another group of diasporic scholars of Arab origin who had maintained strong ties with Hadrami Sayyids. This dispute gained further religious significance with the pronouncement of heresy against Muhmmad Shah by Sheikh Jifri.[113] He criticized Shah and his disciples for their *Shia* connection though the latter denied it, and claimed himself a Sufi belonging to

---

[106] Though the term *Tangaḷ* in Malayalam language refers to noble persons in general, it in certain contexts has been used mainly to denote noble ones with lineage tracing to the family of the Prophet.

[107] Kunju, *Mappila Muslims of Kerala*, p. 112

[108] Ibid.

[109] A.P. Ibrahim Kunju, *Mappila Muslims of Kerala,* (Thiruvananthapuram, Sandhya Publications, 1993), pp.26-27.

[110] The state dignitary who has been given rent free lands as gift. See Randathani, *Mappila Muslims*, p.51.

[111] *Kai* refers to faction or order and *taṛkkam* means dispute in Malayalam Language.

[112] Ponnāni, a coastal town in Malabar was the centre of Sunni Orthodoxy led by Makhdūms a group of scholars believed to have come from the Arabian Peninsula.

[113] A prominent Hadarmi Sayyid scholar reached Malabar Coast in the year 1746.

Sunni sect.[114] In his work *Kanz-al Barahin*, Sheikh Jifri called Muhammad Shah a pseudo-Sufi with an agenda of misleading Muslims of Malabar.[115]

On his part, Muhammad Shah established a *takiya* or commune at Kondōṭṭy with the purpose to propagate his views and to give religious instructions to disciples. Though Muhammad Shah himself rejected a connection with *Ṣhīsm, Ṣhīte* rituals and ceremonies were reported to have followed at Kondōṭṭy.[116] The way, *Muharram* was observed with a procession bearing close resemblance to *Aṣhura* along with other practices like the prostration of *murids* or disciples before *Taṉaḷ*, invited the displeasure of the Sunni group.[117] The most objectionable practices which provoked the Sunni *ulema*, according to Alikutty Musliyar were abstinence from compulsory prayers, women taking pledge by seizing the hands of the Sheikh and using intoxicants like hashish and alcohol by Muhammad Shah and his disciples.[118] Kondōṭṭy faction had given up obligatory prayers during *dikr* or litany and gone to the extent of considering *zakat* and *hajj* not compulsory.[119]

As Muhammad Shah and his disciples were found infidels and apostates by the *ulema* at Ponnāni, religious and social boycott was imposed up on them. The boycott has been elevating to the extent of not allowing Kondōṭṭy faction to enter into local mosques. The *ulema* adhered to Ponnāni faction including those from the Arab World issued several *fatwa* against the *Ṣhīte* practices followed by *Kondōṭṭy Taṉaḷs.*[120]Their dead bodies were not allowed to bury in the graveyards and eating the meat slaughtered by them also was made *harām* or forbidden by various *fatwas*.[121] The *ulema* decreed that the disciples of Mohamed Shah should not be appointed as imams in the mosques. Another *fatwa* was issued asking Sunni Muslims of South Malabar to refrain themselves from dining with the disciples of Mohamed Shah or eating the food prepared by them and not to marry from their families. [122] Regular public debates between the two factions were held in this regard and a large number of judicial cases were filed by both the parties in various courts in Malabar. Hadrami Sayyids insisted people of Kondōṭṭy to abstain from what is forbidden, repent for such practices and stick to the laws of *Ṣhariah*.[123]

Sayyid Alawi of Mampuram depicted Shah as Shia belonging to the Bohra sect falling under an extremely heretic group called *Rawafiz.*[124] Following the line of his predecessor, Sheikh Jifri, Sayyid

---

[114] Randathani, *Mappila Muslims,* p. 53.

[115] Sayyid Sheikh Jifri, *Kanz al Barahin,* (MS, 1784).

[116] Interview K.K. Mohamed Abdul Sathar, a scholar of Mappila history. For further details of this issue see, K.K. Mohammed Abdul Kareem, *Hazrat Muhammed Shāh Taṉal,* (Kolathur: Islamic Da'wa Centre, 1964).

[117] Kunju, *Mappila Muslims of Kerala*, p.26.

[118] See Alikutty Musliyār, *Fatwa* (MS, 1891) and Cōlayil Ahammed et al., *Fatwa al-Radd Kondōṭṭy* (MS, 1861).

[119] Randathani, *Mappila Muslims*, p.57.

[120] Apart from the prominent ulemas in Malabar, *ulema* from the Arab world like Ibrahim al Bajūri, the Mufti of Al-Azhar University, Cairo, Shaikh al Islam Muhammad Abu al Saud of Hejaz, Muhammad al Bali of Madinah, Mufti Ahmad Dakhlan and Mawlawi Hizbullah also have issued fatwas in support of Ponnāni faction. The manuscripts of all these fatwas are well-preserved in the personal collection of Edatōḷa family in Malappuram district of Kerala.

[121] A set of fatwas issued by Putiyakat Kammukuṭṭy Musliyar in 1860. See Ahammed et al., *Fatwa al Radd Kondōṭṭy*, p.20 and Randathani, *Mappila Muslims*, p.57.

[122] Ahammed et al., *Fatwa al-Radd Kondōṭṭy,* p.20.

[123] Randathani, *Mappila Muslims*, p.59.

[124] A fatwa issued by Sayyid Alawi on 13th Ramzan 1256. See Ahamed et al., *Fatwa al-Radd Kondōṭṭy*).

Alawi launched virulent attacks on practices of Kondōṭṭy Taṉaḷs. His teachings, actually, initiated a process of revival among the Māppiḷas and his sermons were having the potential to re-orient the community along the line of reform by abandoning Perso-Islamic tradition.[125] Urging strict compliance with the tenants of Islam, Sayyid Alawi inculcated the need to stress more on the importance of unity among Muslims against the ill-effects of 'shiaziation' of Islam in Malabar.

6. Community in Transition

Thanks to the overwhelming Hadrami Sayyid influence, majority of Muslims of Kerala are with *Ṣhāfi/Sunni*[126] orientation.[127] In respect of Ideology, majority follow a traditional version of Sunnism as against Salafism though the latter has a fast spread in Malabar because of Mappila migration to the Arab Gulf countries. Salafism in Kerala unlike the other parts of India had a different history of origin leading to the Egyptian connection of Islamic scholars in the early Twentieth century. The Egypt connection also led to a lively spread of *al-safiyya wal-tanwiriyya* or enlightenment Salafism among the pioneers of this movement like Vakkam Moulavi. The Mappila migration has now brought an increasing popularity of a puritan *Wahhaabi* version of *Salafism* among a section of Malayalee Muslims in the Gulf. As Gardner and Osella observe, "the current religious practice and consumption tend to be reflective of this transformation".[128] The 'original ' Islamic practices and traditions imported from the Gulf often receive wide acceptance as they elevate the status and efficacy of an average Muslim in the community in Kerala. This is more visible among Malayalee Muslims returning from Saudi Arabia --the place which is considered to be the cradle of Islam.

The interventions of contemporary *Salafism* (which is otherwise known locally as *Gulf Salafism*) have a profoundly transformative affect in the social and political fields. People start looking at Islam with a new perspective and the experience of living there becomes a validation of 'original Islam'. Endorsing 'original Islam' often creates a different understanding of 'Indian Islam' and people begin to see the cross-cultural mingling in the past as an aberration, not an asset. Experience of living in the Gulf, along with the adoption of practices and dress culture borrowed from the region become a means of establishing moral and religious superiority over fellow-Muslims.[129]

Historically, the *Salafi* tradition in Kerala has been simultaneously pan-Islamic taking inspiration from a multitude of strands popular in the wider Islamic world and also local with roots in Kerala specific social and historical contexts. A cursory glance through the history of it seems to confirm the diversity of the contexts and various streams coexisted within the movement. This diversity had been well reflected in the political positions of the early *Salafi* leaders who were keenly aware of the difference between themselves and the puritan *Wahhabi-Salafi* reformism in Saudi Arabia. Though they had greatly valued the contributions of Saudi *Salafi* scholars like Muhammed ibn Abd al-Wahhab

---

[125] Panikkar, *Against Lord and State*, p.62.

[126] Those who follow traditions in this context, nothing to do with Sunni-Shia divide)

[127] Sunnis who represent almost seventy per cent of Kerala Muslims are characterized by orthodox theology and *Ṣhāfī* School of jurisprudence.

[128] Katy Gardner and Filippo Osealla, "Migration, Modernity and Social Transformation in South Asia: An Introduction", in Filippo Osealla and Katy Gardner (eds.), *Migration, Modernity and Social Transformation in South Asia,* (New Delhi: Sage, 2004), p. xxiii.

[129] Osella and Osella, " Muslim Style in Kerala" p.8

and translated their writings in Malayalam, politically they kept a safe distance from *Saudi-Wahhabi* tradition because of its anti-Ottoman ideology. Endorsing *Wahhabism* theologically did not mean that they were unaware of the perils that their Saudi counterparts created politically. Rather, they maintained close ties with the Egyptian reform-oriented *Salafi* tradition called *al-Salafiyya al-tanwiriyya.*

The movement also displayed a remarkable adaptability to the political circumstances existed in Kerala. The brand of *Salafism* that flourished in Kerala combined *Wahhabi* and *Tanwiṛi* traditions though both seemed mutually conflicting with each other. Though the Arabic word *tanwiriyya,* meaning enlightenment in English, the *Salafi*-inspired Islamic reform movement in Kerala parted away wholly from the European project of enlightenment based on the ideals of 'universalism' and 'rationality'. While similar initiatives in other communities in Kerala took inspiration from colonial modernity, the Islamic reform in the state did not have any engagement with it. In place of it, one can see Islamic world-wide strands of reform, which had often been brought into Kerala by the translated works of West Asian and North African Islamic reformist scholars like Jamal Al-Din Afghani, Mohammed Abdu and Rashid Rida. Politically, many *Salafi* scholars were a part of anti-colonial movement and nurtured an inclination towards Turkish *khilafat* that continued to exert a key role in framing their anti-British ideology. But for another section, nationalistic orientation of the movement seemed unappealing; criticizing it overtly, they maintained a strong leaning towards pan-Islamist ideology.

Things, of course, changed for the *Salafi* movement in the 1970s and 80s. The Saudi sponsored puritan version of *Wahhabism* started making deep inroads into the community with massive migration of Kerala Muslims to the Gulf countries. The Gulf connection also culminated in the creation of a huge army of Saudi-educated scholars who were assigned officially to popularize *Saudi-Wahhabi* brand of *Salafism*. The physical sign of *Saudization* was explicit in the construction of large *Salafi* mosques in remote corners of the state, rapid development of market for *Salafi tafsirs* (interpretations of the Quran) published from Saudi Arabia and easy availability of popular materials on *Salafism*. *Gulf Salafism* stresses the superiority of the *Salafiyyat* and maintains an intolerant attitude toward other Islamic movements especially Sufis, casting doubt on their beliefs. They are also intolerant of other *Salafi* groups for latter's alleged dilution of the ideology in order to adjust with specific cultural and political context of Kerala and hold a critical view of prevailing practices either for being inclined to secular traditions or for adopting local customs. Jama't Islami al-Hind, an organization adhered to the doctrines of Abul Ahla Maududi and Islamic Brotherhood in North Africa (Egypt and Tunisia) also has a considerably huge number of takers in Kerala.

Electronic media also play a key mediatory role within an expanding arena of popular Islamic argumentation and deliberation among the Muslims of Kerala.[130] The potential of the new media to influence the Muslim Societies lies not simply in its contribution to disseminate different ideas but its ability to form a virtual 'public sphere', where the attitudes and interests of different sorts of Muslims

---

[130] M.H. Ilias,"Ulema and the Internet: A Case Study of Muslim Scholars' Engagement with New Media in Kerala" paper presented at the International Seminar on "Time for Medialization: Integrating Media and Transcultural Communication Research Within Islamic and Areas Studies" held on April (8-10), at Humboldt University, Berlin.

in Kerala are increasingly defined and shaped. New means of communication have provided many Muslim groups in Kerala with an intermediate space and new means of sharing experiences on a "virtual space" beyond their limited conceptual and physical spaces. The Traditional *ulema's* engagement with new technology is the most significant and interesting phenomenon. Perhaps, more striking is the newfound popularity of websites and blogs among them for variety of purposes like religious (sometimes political also) mobilization, opinion building and even for fund raising. The increasing popularity of new media has, of course, brought a change in pattern of religious discourses and the ways in which they have been received among Kerala Muslims.

Parallel to this, there is the emergence of a new class of politically motivated preachers distinct from those of the classical *ulema* with target audiences (mostly the educated classes). The traditional means of massive indoctrination lost its charm with a more effective mode of political preaching that adapted topics and technologies appealing to the educated public. The rapid development of a market for inexpensive Islamic books, easy availability of popular materials, tutor CDs and magazines also exemplified this heightened public interest in Islam. Perhaps, more striking is the new-found popularity of social media among the Muslim organisations for a variety of purposes like religious mobilization and opinion building.[131]

7. Origin of Arabi-Malayalam Language

It is in the context of great traffic of goods, scholars and ideas between Malabar and the Arab world that one can find the origin of Arabi-Malayalam. There are two major theories in circulation regarding the origin and spread of this language. The first one attributes the credit of it to the Arabs who reached Malabar Coast with the purpose of trade and promotion of Islam.[132] Arab Muslim traders and scholars who moved in such a way to different parts of the world embarking on the mission of trade and preaching Islam had maintained an offbeat habit of recording their instructions in the vernacular tongue using Arab script.[133] Preaching Islam making use of Arabic, or the languages of the localities where they reached, seemed difficult for them. That necessitated the service of a new language capable enough to create smooth and hassle-free communication and indoctrination of Islamic principles and practices among the locals. This sort of a synthesis cannot be seen as a unique one; Arabs devised such religio-lect wherever they moved for the purpose for trade and the spread of faith. Arabi-Tamil in neighboring Tamil Nadu was developed when the Arabs used their own script system to write and learn Tamil language.[134] Likewise, the interactions of Arabs with people in coastal Karnataka had culminated in the formation of Arabi-Kannada language. There is an argument that Arabi-Tamil originated long before Arabi-Malayalam. It was from Arabi-Tamil and Centamil[135] that Arabi-Malayalam

---

[131] Ibid.

[132] Mansurali, "Arabi-Malayalam Caritravum Sahityavum", p. 16.

[133] Ibid.

[134] Tayka Shu'ayb Alim, Arabic, Arwi and Persian in Sarandib and Tamil Nadu. A Study of the Contributions of Sri Lanka and Tamil Nadu to Arabic, Arwi, Persian and Urdu Languages,Literature and Education, (Madras: Imamul Arus Trust, 1993),pp.98 as cited in Basheer Ahamed, Arabu-Tamil (Unpublished Manuscript).

[135] Centamil is the classic variety of Tamil language used generally in formal writing and speech now a days. It is the language of textbooks, literary texts and public speech.

had borrowed its vocabulary than Malayalam.[136] Arabi-Malayalam's closer ties with Arabi-Tamil dialect illustrate this connection well.

The dispersion of Arabs throughout Malabar Coast and their early movements into the countryside had made the ascendancy of Arabi-Malayalam a major trade language of trans-regional use. Arabs, who came mostly as traders, adopted Arabi-Malayalam language when they settled down in mainly in port towns of Kerala and married local women. Arabi-Malayalam was, thus, developed as a local lingua franca for trading and preaching Arabs to communicate with the natives and vice versa. The next many generations of preachers recognised the effectiveness of Arabi-Malayalam as a medium to instruct the moral lessons among those who embraced Islam recently.[137] Malayalam then was not capable enough to translate the Quran and *hadith* from Arabic language to it. Furthermore, writing religious related material in Malayalam or in any other Dravidian script was considered blasphemous among a larger section of Muslim population.[138] So, the clergies found it essential to devise a separate script for overcoming this dilemma. Mohamedali sees Arabi-Malayalam script system was further developed as a result of this search.[139]

Some scholars of Islam in Kerala trace out the genesis of this language to an unintentional attempt of first many generations of Arab traders who reached Malabar coasts before the advent of Islam in the region. "Arabi-Malayalam might have been there, if there was the presence of Arabs before the arrival of Islam in Kerala...when Arabi-Malayalam had its genesis, the script system of Malayalam was poorly developed. *Vaṭṭazhetu* and *Kōlezhutu*[140] were the ones used to write the proto-Malayalam language", argues Ahamed.[141] The scholar of Arabi-Malayalam language, Abu traces its origin to the end of 9th century and the beginning of 10th century.[142] When they came to Malabar, Arab traders felt the pressing need to interact with the locals in their language. They began to write the name of people, goods and places in Kerala in their mother tongue.[143] They eventually turn to write words in the local language they learnt so far in Arabic language.[144] On account of regular interaction between the Arabs and the local merchants, it was elevated to the status of the major trading language of the Malabar Coast. Since the first use of this language came from the maritime traders (Arab and the local), many Arabic words especially to describe trade, travel and warfare thus had spread into this language.[145]

Lately, the language percolated beyond the merchants, who lived principally in the costal belt, to the countryside. The decline of maritime trade, frequent invasions and colonial conflicts for

---

[136] C.N.Ahmed Moulavi and K.K.abdul Kareem, *Mahataya Mappila Sahitya Parambaraym* (-Calicut: Authors, 1978).

[137] Mohamedali, *Mappila Pattukal Noottandukalilude*, p.20.

[138] Ibid.

[139] Mohamedali, Mappila Pattukal Noottandukalilude, p.20.

[140] Two writing systems originated from the ancient Tamil used to write the Proto-Dravidian languages including Tamil and Malayalam.

[141] Jameel Ahamed, "Arabi-Malayalatil Ninnu Malayala Islāmilekku" in T. Mansurali (ed.), *Arabi-Malayala Sahityava Padanangal* , (Kozhicode: Lead Books, 2014), pp. 88-89

[142] O.Abu, *Arabic-Malayalam Literary History,* (Kottayam: NBS, 1976), p 22.

[143] K.O. Shamsuddin, *Mappila Malayalam,* (Trivandrum: Author, 1978), p.12

[144] Ibid.

[145] Abu, *Arabic-Malayalam Literary History,* pp. 22-24.

resources from 16th century onwards made Mappilas to move from the coastal belts to hinterlands and engage in agriculture.[146] Not just to the hinterlands in Malabar, but to where all they moved in further, Mappilas had carried over the tradition of Arabi-Malayalam and preserved its literary legacy intact.[147] The presence of Arabi-Malayalam in Lakshadweep and Andaman Nicobar Islands, where Mappilas either migrated in or deported to, validates this argument.

The historian of Arabi-Malayalam Shamsuddin puts forward a different theory with regard to the origin of Arabi-Malayalam. The Muslims in Malabar, earlier times, knew only Arabic script and later, by the 14th century, had learnt and started using Arabic as the liturgical language.[148] The frequent visits of *ulema* from the Arab world also fostered this process. The knowledge of Arabic was considered to be essential for all Muslims as they recited the Quran as well as their daily *du'as* or prayers in Arabic. The children first learnt Arabic script in an attempt to master the verses of the Quran and this recital was considered to be a religious ritual at that time. And it is important to note that many in the community learned Arabic not just as a liturgical language but a language for communication in its classical form. Classic Arabic literature was also taught in curriculum as a part of larger approach to the study of language. So, it became necessary for a large chunk of Muslims then to acquire Arabic language for the religious purpose. Nevertheless, the ideas which were unable to express using Arabic were continuously interpreted in Malayalam using the same script. So, knowing Arabic letters and certain words through the Quran, Mappila Muslims attempted to extend the usage of Arabic script to their mother tongue. Though initially, attempts were made to write all Malayalam letters in Arabi-Malayalam script, the script system was modified in order to accommodate Malayalam letters which have no corresponding ones in Arabic.[149] Since Mappilas wanted both Arabic and their mother tongue, they retained Malayalam for written discourse but rendered it in Arabic script.[150]

Taking cues from the popularity of Persian words in Arabi-Malayalam language, Moulawi and Kareem extend the source of origin of this language to Farsi language also.[151] The presence of influential Persian scholars widely noted in the earlier documents dealing with the history of Kerala Muslims, has been used by them to substantiate this theory. Many local mosques in Malabar had *Imams* recruited from Persia and many Persian scholars had great fan-following across the region. Through them, the Persian religious and literary texts were also in wider circulation in Malabar.[152] *Meezan*, a text read widely at the Madrassas in Malabar is a Persian one. Similarly, Persian scholars like Imam Bukhari, Imam Gazzali, Abu Haneefa, Tirmudi, Ibn Maja, Abdul Kader Jeelani and Moulana Rumi enjoyed wider acceptance among the Mappila Muslims.[153] Arabi-Malayalm has borrowed a considerably large set of vocabularies from Farsi language. The Persian word *Ṣirni* had widely been used to refer to the sweet items prepared in the kitchen. While *azān* is widely used to denote the

---

[146] Dilip Menon, "Houses by the Sea: State-Formation Experiments in Malabar, 1760-1800", *Economic and Political Weekly*, vol. 34, no. 29 (1999), pp. 1995-2003 & K.K.N.Kurup, *The Legacy of Islam: A study of the Mappila Muslims of Kerala*, (Kannur, Samayam Publications, 2006), p. 14.

[147] M.N.Karasserry in an interview by the authors.

[148] Shamsuddin, *Mappila Malayalam*, p. 12.

[149] Shamsuddin, *Mappila Malayalam*, p. 12.

[150] P.P Abdul Razak, Arabic-Malayalam and the Cultural Lansdcape of Muslims of Malabar (Unpublished MS), pp.3-4.

[151] Moulavi and Kareem, *Mahataya Mappila Sahitya Parambaraym*, p. 35.

[152] Ibid. pp. 35-36

[153] Dale, *The Mappilas of Malabar 1498 –1922* & Moulavi and Kareem, *Mahataya Mappila Sahitya Parambaraym* p. 36

routine call for prayer, the Muslim community in Malabar has a Farsi word, *banq* for the same.[154] The term *mullaka* being used for religious scholars is, by all probability, derived from the term with similar meaning, *mulla* in Farsi. Most of such words are having no corresponding ones in both Arabic and Malayalam.[155]

However, many recent studies reveal that the development of Arabi-Malayalam happened only towards the beginning of 16th century.[156] The argument of Ahamed regarding the origin of Arabi-Tamil is significant in the context of Arabi-Malayalam also. "If these languages were from Arab initiative, the period should have been traced back to seventh and eighth centuries", argues Ahamed.[157]The theory considering the development of these languages as a contribution of locals alone seems to be logically sound.

Anyway, right from the beginning, the verse tradition enjoyed supremacy over the other literary genres in Arabi-Malayalam.[158] Before the advent of printed texts, copying religious texts manually in a massive scale seemed difficult for the local scholars. They, instead, resorted to the practice of imparting the principles of Islam, *sharia, fiqh* and *sunna* or the teachings of the Prophet Mohammed in the form of verse prepared using locally popular artistic resources.[159] This practice eventually led to express human feelings and emotions using the same genre. The development of verse tradition takes inspiration partly from the Arabs who had maintained the habit of learning important texts in Islam in verse form. Memorizing the names of forefathers in a family or clan by tracing it through composing poems using their names in genealogical order, was also a prominent tradition existed in the Arabian Peninsula. [160]

The first reference to the use of Arabi-Malayalam in Malabar is seen in Francis Buchanen's travel writings published in the early 19th century. "Though the Malayalam as described by the Europeans was the language of Muslims of Kerala, the spoken language was a crude mix of Arabic, Malayalam and Tamil", notes Buchanen[161] This mix indeed refers to Arabi-Malayalam. At the initial stage, the written expression of this language was in circulation mainly among the Mappilas of coastal region who were in constant interaction with the Arabs came for trade and the propagation of Islam in Malabar.[162] Non-Muslim communities in Kerala did not show much of interest in the development of literature in this language since the script was in Arabic and the vocabulary was an admixture of Arabic, Persian, Tamil and Sanskrit. Many, outside the community, had nurtured a wrong perception that the basic literary activity of Mappilas was confined to the translation of the Quran and other basic texts.[163]

---

154 Moulavi and Kareem, *Mahataya Mappila Sahitya Parambaraym*, p. 35.
155 Ibid., p. 35.
156 Mohammedali, *Mappila Pattukal Noottandukalilude,*pp.20-22.
157 Basheer Ahamed, *Arabu-Tamil* (Unpublished Manuscript) p.2
158 Moulavi and Kareem, *Mahataya Mappila Sahitya Parambaraym*, pp. 37-38.
159 Ibid.
160 Moulavi and Kareem, *Mahataya Mappila Sahitya Parambaraym*, pp. 37-38.
161 Francis Buchanen, *A Journey from Madras: Through the Countries of Mysore, Canara and Malabar* (-originally published in 1807 in three volumes), (New Delhi: Asian Educational Society, 1999).
162 In an interview with Hussain Randathani.
163 Vallikunnu, *Mappila Sahityavum Navodhanavum*, p. 15.

Burnel's work *Specimens of South Indian Dailects* published in 1873 gives a detailed account of rich literary tradition in Arabi-Malayalam in the 18th and 19th centuries. The Mappilas, according to him, were by no means destitute of literature. The publication of treatises, songs, religious and historical texts during this period contributed a lot to the richness of literature in this language. Brunel writes:

> All these are vastly superior to the miserable strings of conceits which pass for poetry in South India and are remarkable for a manly tune which must have come from Arabia. Except Mappilas of Thalasserry, people all over the South-Western coast, are using a modified Arabic script for writing their dialect of Malayalam. There is no clue of who and when introduced this language.[164]

The development of Arabi-Malayalam literature was partly governed by trade and cultural proximity to Southern Arabia. In part also, they were the result of some specific social developments taken place in Malabar in which religion played an important role. Mappilas' resistance against the European powers, which initially, was very fragmented and scattered, but continued to occur at regular intervals throughout the 19th and early 20th centuries and culminated in the *Malabār Kalāpam* or Malabar Rebellion of 1921. This rebellion was the major one among the socio-political developments that shaped the literary landscape of Arabi-Malayalam language.[165] The leverage that anti-colonial agitations had on engendering a vast body of literature has been discussed in a comprehensive manner in the third and fourth chapters.

The anti-colonial feeing, according to Sheikh Zaynuddin Makhdum whose work *Tuhfat al-Mujāhadīn fi b'ad ahwal al-Purtukaliyyin* pioneered indigenous writing of Mappila history, was first developed in response to the Portuguese.[166] All attacks against the colonial forces by Mappilas prepared a ground for Arabi-Malayalam literature to flourish when the Mappilas carried them out in service of their faith. South Malabar with an overwhelming domination of Mappilas became the major theatre for the anti-colonial agitations. The strained relations of Mappila peasants with the colonial administration on one side and with the Hindu landlords on the other resulted in a series of Arabi-Malayalam works to instil 'revolutionary spirit' among Mappilas in South Malabar.

Another seminal event in the Mappila history that spawned enormous amount of literature in Arabi-Malayalam language was the Islamic reform movement in Kerala which came to prominence towards the end of 19th century. Though there is strong argument that there was a massive production of Arabi-Malayalam texts in literary-knowledge field initiated mainly by the traditional scholarship even before that,[167] the Islamic reform movement in Kerala and the consequent development of 'modern'

---

164 A. C. Burnell, *Specimens of South Indian Dailects*, No.2, 1873

165 Dale, *The Mappilas of Malabar 1498-1922*, p.1.

166 Zaynuddin Makhdum's is considered to be the most valued work as its sheds light on the turbulent history of Mappilas during the colonial period. Mappilas continue to regard it as the most authoritative recording of their own past by an organic intellectual within the community. Several of their encounters with the Portuguese and the suffering of the Mappilas with inculcation of the necessity of *jehad* have been narrated in this work. *Tuhfat al Mujāhidīn* which has primarily been taught in madrassas had a great relevance in fostering the ideology of anti-colonialism and in cultivating an element of resistance against the European hegemony. Makhdum, *Tuhfat al-Mujāhidīn*.

167 Salahuddin.C.T., "Arabi-Malayalatile Vaidya Kritikal", in T. Mansurali (ed.), *Arabi-Malayala Sahityava Padanangal* , (Kozhicode: Lead Books, 2014), p. 133.

Muslim press (both have been covered in detail in chapter 5) had triggered a literary explosion with works from both those who advocated reform and those who opposed it.

When the press gained wide popularity in the early 20th century, Muslims of Kerala successfully utilized the possibility of it in disseminating reform ideals among a wide section of population. Mappila migration to different parts of the world (especially to the Arab Gulf countries) started in a massive scale around the middle of 20th century also ignited a revolution in the literary production in Arabi-Malayalam. The process, with newfound elements from diasporic life, affected the pattern of cultural and literary consumptions of the community and brought a radical change in aesthetic realm and artistic imagination.

The religious education at *madrassas* with Arabi-Malayalam as the chief medium of instruction also contributed to the further growth of Arabi-Malayalam. Balakrishnan traces its history back to the establishment of the first *dars* by Imam Mohamed Ibn Abdullāhil Hadrami at Juma' Masjid at Tānur in 1290 AD.[168] Following it another *dars* was established at Miskal Masjid, Kutticira by Shiekh Zainuddin Rahmānul Sāliyāti in 1404 AD.[169] Off late Kazi Fakruddin Aboobacker made it a renowned institution with students from far flung places in the Indian Ocean region.[170] It took almost another half a century for Ponnani *dars* which became a hub of Islamic knowledge in Malabar to emerge.[171] The position of Ponnani had been elevated to the Mecca of Kerala with the establishment of this *dars*.

[168] Vallikkunnu, *Mappila Sahityavum Navodhanavum*, p. 19.

[169] Ibid, p.19.

[170] Ibid p.19-20.

[171] See Hussain Randathani, *Makhdumum Ponnāniyum* (Ponnani: Ponnani Juma Masjid Committee, 1998) & Vallikkunnu, *Mappila Sahityavum Navodhanavum*, p. 19.

3

Structure and Linguistic Features

Arabi-Malayalam is neither Arabic nor Malayalam in the purest sense but a crude mix of both.[1] As has already been mentioned in the earlier chapter, there exist many linguistic cleavages between Arabi-Malayalam and these languages. In terms of grammatical base and syntax, Arabi-Malayalam follows Malayalam while it depends Arabic for the script system as its base. The vocabulary, however, consists of words from a wide variety of languages.[2] Many words and usages, which are alien to both Arabic and Malayalam, can be seen while going through the literary texts in this language. In addition to its basic indebtedness to Arabic and Malayalam, the vocabulary of Arabi-Malayalam, characterizes a strong influence of Dravidian languages like Tamil, Kannada and Tulu as well.[3] The combination is amazing with words loaned from the West Asian languages like Farsi and from other Indian languages like Urdu and Sanskrit.

There is a widely-held tendency to describe Arabi-Malayalam and the *Mappila Malayalam,* which is considered to be a dialect of Malayalam that Muslims in southern parts of Malabar used for their daily needs and for cultural purposes as coterminous ones.[4] Because of the specific social and historical reasons like Sanskritization of Malayalam, *Mappila Malayalam* has been elevated to the common dialect of South Malabar with wide acceptance cutting across the religious lines.[5] The use of Arabi-Malayalam, despite its myriad repository of literary works, on the other hand has been limited to Mappila community.[6] Needless to say, because of the Arabic script system, this language bred alienation among the non-Muslim communities in Malabar. It is, to a great extent, true that like Arabi-

---

[1] M.N.Karaserry, Arabic-Malayalam, in Asgar Ali Engineer (ed.), *Kerala Muslims: A Historical Perspective,* (New Delhi: Ajanta Publications, 1995), pp.168-69.

[2] Krishna Chaithanya, *A History of Malayalam Literature*, Hyderabad: Orient Longman, 1971, p. 195.

[3] Udayakumar, "Shaping a Literary Space: Early Literary Histories in Malayalam and Normative Uses of the Past", in Hans Harder (ed.) *Literature and nationalist Ideology,* (New Delhi: Social Science Press, 2010), 19-50, p.31.

[4] M.N.Karaserry, *Kurimānam* (Kozhikkode: Malayalam Publications, 1989), p.78.

[5] K.O. Shamsuddin, *Mappila Malayalam,* (Trivandrum: Author, 1978), p. 4.

[6] T.Mansoorali, "Arabi-Malayalam Sāhityavum Caritravum", in T.Mansoorali (ed.), *Arabi-Malayala Sahitya Padangal*, (Kozhicode: Lead Books, 2014), pp. 14-15.

Malayalam, *Mappila Malayalam* also possesses a rich vocabulary with words borrowed from languages like Arabic, Farsi, Tamil and Kannada, but there is a slight difference that lies in latter one's over dependence on Malayalam language for semantics and syntactical structure. This dependency has been reflected in *Mappila Malayalam*'s inherent confinement to oral expression with no separate script, grammar and a rich cache of literature.

Arabi-Malayalam may be defined as a religio-lect fused with Arabic lexemes and possibly other Arabic language peculiarities (phonemes, morphemes, syntactic constructions, etc.). Besides many interesting linguistic issues concerning the daily usage of Arabi-Malayalam, the usage of this religio-lect conveys a vast array of oral and written traditions, ranging from folksongs and classical poems to travelogues and philosophical writings. Though Arabic alphabets are the basis for Arabi-Malayalam letters, this language is a rich storehouse of vocabularies, phrases and usages loaned selectively from various languages. This diversity was essential for a language, which accommodated a vast range of linguistic influences thanks to Mappila community's trade linkages with far-flung places in the Indian Ocean region.

The influence of Arabic language has always been strong in Arabi-Malayalam, but the tempo of its evolution was not same in all the phases. The linguistic composition varied in each phase with changing nature of constituting South Indian languages. Most of the features of the first phase of evolution were oriented towards early Tamil as it was a link language for Aarabi-Malayalam in the nascent stage. *Mohiyuddīn Māla* (Plate 3.1), the first known work in this language written in the 17th century represents this orientation with many of the morphological features used in this work derived from early Tamil.[7] Imageries and metaphors lavishly used in this work also are indicative of a strong Tamil influence.[8]

The second phase marked a period in which the literary tradition was dominated by Malayalam with increased influence of Sanskrit. According to Shamsuddin, this phase came into existence in the late 19th and early 20th centuries, characterized by an eclectic mix of many linguistic fusions though Sanskritized Malayalam maintained domination over others.[9] This phase, in which vocabularies from a wide array of languages such as Arabic, Persian, Tamil, Malayalam and Sanskrit had been incorporated, also maintains some resemblance to the evolution of *Manipravāḷam.*[10] This blend can be seen in most of the early works of Arabi-Malayalam in which Arabic, Malayalam and Tamil words mix up in interesting linguistic amalgams with no fixed rules.[11] The opening line of *Mohiyuddīn Māla*, for instance, contains words from five languages.

Allah tirupērum tutiyum salawātum,

atināl tudaṉuvān aruḷ ceyta bedāmbar.

---

[7] P.K.Mohammedkunhi, *Muslingalum,Kerala Samskaravum,* (Thrissur: Kerala Sahitya Academi, 2008)

[8] Thoppil Muhammed Meeran, "Arabitamizh", in T.Mansoorali (ed.), *Arabi-Malayala Sahitya Padangal*, (Kozhicode: Lead Books, 2014), pp.63-64.

[9] Shamsuddin, *Mappila Malayalam,* pp. 95-96.

[10] Manipravāḷam is a literary style which had been of wide use in mediaeval South India. This was an admixture of Tamil and Sanskrit. Shamsuddin, *Mappila Malayalam* pp. 95-96.

[11] Abdullah Abdul Hameed, *Naduthoppil Abdulla's Akbar Sadaqa Pakshipattu,* (Translation & study), (Kasargod: Central University of Kerala, 2012), p.12.

(Since the Prophet ordered to start
in the name of God, praise to him and his prophet,
I start this with the same)[12]

Arabic : Allah, swalat
Persian : bedambar (Vedambar)
Tamil : tiru
Sanskrit : tuti (stuti)
Malayalam : perum, atinal, arul, ceyta

Anyway, literary conventions of all these languages coexisted in a crude synthesis though the effects of it had seldom been uniform in all the works of this period.[13] Over a period of time, this language evolved to the current phase accommodating considerable vocabulary from many linguistic fusions, but within a strictly basic Dravidian structure and Malayalam grammatical base. Most of the morphological features are still related to those of Tamil and early Malayalam and many of the words are derived phonetically from Early Tamil.[14] Almost all lexical items of Arabi-Malayalam can, thus, be related to corresponding ones in Arabic, Tamil and Malayalam. But for some, finding equivalent ones in these languages becomes a futile exercise.

Currently, Arabi-Malayalam language, especially its spoken expression, is moving along a different trajectory thanks to the process of Gulf migration. Migration of Mappila Muslims to the GCC states has been one of the greatest social changes over the last four decades. The Gulf migration has produced several dynamics complicating the old pattern of social life among Mappila Muslims. The process has incorporated the indigenous Muslim community of Kerala into a wider Islamic world and has helped reconfigure every day religious practices within a unified pan-Islamic code of conduct. With its instant realization, Arabi-Malayalam language is a handbook to understand how these diaspora-induced changes have affected the cultural life of Mappila community. 'Shattered dreams' of the unsuccessful migrants, the stresses they face at the work place and the breakup of relationships have become the major themes for many Mappila songs. Linguistically speaking, the diaspora, on its part, also has popularized some Arabic vocabularies and generated a variety of interesting literary expressions[15] among the Muslims of Kerala.[16] Following are some of the examples:

arbāb (boss)

kafīl (sponsor)

---

[12] See G.P.Muneer Hudawi, *Spiritual Leadership in Anti-Colonial Struggle: A Study of Life and Works of Qazi Muhammad Al-Kalikuti* (New Delhi: Writers Choice, 2014) for the full translation of Mohiyuddīn Mala in English.

[13] Ibid. pp.63-64.

[14] C.N.Ahmed Moulavi and K.K.abdul Kareem, *Mahataya Mappila Sahitya Parambaraym*(Calicut: Authors, 1978).

[15] Two recent bestsellers in Kerala, namely, *Adujeevitam* and *Barsa* revolve around the poignant stories of Malayali Muslim expatriates in the Gulf. While *Adujeevitam* depicts the story of an ordinary labourer caught up in the vortex of traumatic experiences of diaspora, inhumane laws and monarchic insensibilities, *Barsa* narrates the predicaments of migrant women through the story a lady doctor who has been appointed in the Holy city of Mecca.

[16] Interview with M.N.Karasserry, a scholar of Mappila literature during the field trip in 2012.

tartīb (arrangement, adjustment)

mudīr (manager)

kubbūs (Arab bread)

kurūj (exit pass)

vāsta (brokerage)

khaddāma (female servant)

Geography of Spread, Dialects and Slangs

Though there are no documented evidences to the evolution of Arabi-Malayalam script, some scholars are of the view that the history of it is five hundred years old.[17] Scholars like Kareem hold the view that it could be as old as one thousand and five hundred years while Miller shortens the span to five hundred years.[18] The Arabi-Malayalam script was in wider circulation in Malabar[19], Lakshadweep and southern parts of Karnataka. Arabi-Malayalam is apparently in use among some of the Muslim communities of Andaman Islands, most of who were deported from Malabar during the anti-British Mappila Rebellion of early 20th century.

Abu argues that Arabi-Malayalam is a regional language with its locale of spread confining to northern Kerala, between Kodungallore and Kasargod.[20] This argument seems to be untrue as there is evidence to the existence of Arabi-Malayalam works in southern districts of Kerala like Ernakulam (Cochin) and Alapuzha. The spread of Arabi-Malayalam in these areas was characterized mainly by publication of books, pamphlets, journals and news papers. Similarly, it is no less incorrect to consider Arabi-Malayalam as a unified entity as various local expressions and slangs of this language (mainly Ponnani, Calicut, Eranadu, Canannore and Kasargode) contribute to its richness and diversity within. The language has undergone several transformations due to the interaction with the other South Indian languages. Dialects were developed mainly because of the influence of such languages on Arabi-Malayalam, and each dialect of Arabi-Malayalam carries certain number of colloquial forms in terms of vocabulary and pronunciation.

Some scholars consider Arabi-Malayalam not as a separate language but yet another dialect of Arabic written in Semitic script with more sophistication given to the letters in order to accommodate Malayalam phonetics.[21] Say, for example, normally there is no letter *pa* in Arabic, but Arabi-Malayalam has devised the letter پ (*pa*) by modifying and giving additional signs to the letter ب (*ba).* The letter *pa* is in fact loaned from Farsi language. The lack of *pa,* had earlier been compensated by the letter *fa.*

[17] Karaserry, M.N., "Māppiḷapāṭṭu", in Raghavan Payyanadu, *Kerala Folklore,* (Payyannur: Folklore Fellows of Malabar, 1997), p. 49.

[18] C.K.Kareem, *Muslim Samudāyawum Samskārawum* (Trivandrum: Charithram Publications, 1983) and Roland E. Miller, *Mappila Muslims of Kerala,* (Hyderabad: Orient Longman, 1992)

[19] Geographically, Arabi-Malayalam had a spread all over Malabar except in two *taluks* (Palakkad and Chittur).

[20] Kodungallore is the place where Islam believed to have landed first in the Indian sub-continent. Kasargod is the northern most tip of Kerala sharing border with neighboring Karnataka. O.Abu, *Arabic-Malayalam Literary History,* (Kottayam: NBS, 1976), p.11

[21] M.N. Karasserry, " Arabic-Malayalam", in M.H. Ilias, India-West Relations: Understanding Cultural Interplays, (New Delhi: New Century Publications, 2007).

Similarly, there are no corresponding characters for Arabic ones خ (ḵha) and ض (la) in Malayalam. The letter ഴ (ẓha) is absent in Arabic. Arabi-Malayalam has incorporated both خ (ḵha) and Ž (ẓha) along with the vowel 'o' which is also absent in Arabic.[22]

Almost thirteen letters in Arabic language have no corresponding ones in Malayalam. Similarly, thirty nine characters in Malayalam which include both vowels and consonants find no match in Arabic. Arabi-Malayalam that way becomes a place where the phonemes of two different languages meet.

Malayalam vowels with no matching ones in Arabic

ഋ	എ	ഏ	ഐ	ഒ	ഓ	ഔ
r.	e	ē	ai	o	ō	au

Malayalam consonants with no matching letters in Arabic

ഖ	ഗ	ഘ	ങ	ച	ഛ	ഝ	ഞ	ട	ഠ	ഡ	ഢ
Kha	ga	gha	ñ	ca	cha	jha	n̰	ṭa	ṭha	ḍa	ḍha
ണ	ഥ	ധ	പ	ഫ	റ	ഷ	ള	ഴ			
ṇa	tha	dha	pa	pha	ra	ṣa	ḷa	ẓha			

There is a diverse view considering Arabi-Malayalam as a dialect of Malayalam written in Arabic script with suitable changes made in order to accommodate local phonetics.[23] For scholars like Karassery, "absence of own grammar" becomes a major point to substantiate this argument. "Basically, a language has to have, not just script and vocabulary, but a grammar. Arabi-Malayalam does not have a grammar. It always depends on Malayalam for one, argues Karassery."[24]

Anyway, Arabi-Malayalam flourished primarily on account of its use for the religious purpose. The use of this language as the medium of instruction in *madrassas* underlines its importance in the religious life of Mappilas. Knowledge of Arabic was, of course, considered to be essential to Muslims as they used it in reciting Quran as well as in daily prayers. Nevertheless, for many centuries, it was mandatory for Mappila students to learn Arabi-Malayalam alphabets by heart simultaneous to knowing those of Arabic.[25] Mappilas wanted to keep Arabic (the language of religious texts), Malayalam (the language of the land) and Arabi-Malayalam (their local lingua franca) together, but for written discourse they retained Arabi-Malayalam only.[26]

As a 'bridge language', the use of Arabi-Malayalam was initially confined to religious instructions alone. However, in the course of time, this language began to move along a different trajectory and gained popularity, especially when the Mappila population began to express their thoughts and imaginations in it. With this, Arabi-Malayalam acquired a literary dimension also.[27] The

[22] Arabic has only six vowels; the vowel 'O' is absent in this language.
[23] Karassery, "Arabic-Malayalam",pp. 107-9.
[24]Ibid.
[25] Shamsuddin, *Mappila Malayalam,* p. 14.
[26] P.P Abdul Razak, Arabic-Malayalam and the Cultural Landscape of Muslims of Malabar (Unpublished MS), pp.3-4.
[27] Ibid. p.3.

18th and 19th centuries marked a discernable shift in the orientation of this language.[28] The works in Arabi-Malayalam also gradually began to reflect some of the issues and stresses that the community passed into.

The language found fame chiefly among the Mappila women, whose education has largely been confined to *madrassas*. Arabi-Malayalam became the primary medium of routine communication and many of them used it even for writing letters. Arabic for Mappilas remained to be the language of the sacred book and liturgical practices while Sanskritisation of Malayalam language furthered their alienation with that language. The education in Arabic was limited to the study of the Quran and *fiqh.* The study of the meaning and contexts of the religious texts was a scholarly exercise confined to a few as the great majority seldom had a chance to learn Arabic as a language with its classical literature.[29] This situation necessitated the need of fostering Arabi-Malayalam further as the local lingua franca with which the ordinary Muslims of Malabar could express their emotions and creativity. It was not an exaggeration to say that there were only a few among Mappilas who did not know how to read and write Arabi-Malayalam. Though the total literacy rate in Malabar during the early 1940s was less than ten percent,[30] Mappila community had a considerably huge number of youngsters who acquired literacy in Arabi-Malayalam[31] but ironically, census reports did not consider them as literate due to the lack of official recognition of this language by the British Administration.[32]

Parallel to this, the use of Arabi-Malayalam as an alternative to Arabic in the religious realm also continued. The Mappilas had even made efforts to translate the Quaran to this language, which was otherwise considered an act of irreverence among tradition-oriented Muslims. All such efforts initially met stiff oppositions from the conservative *ulema* (see Chapter 4 for details). Following it, other texts related to religious belief and jurisprudence were also translated and that eventually constituted the bulk of writings in the Arabi-Malayalam prose.[33]

Arabi-Malayalam Alphabets

Arabi-Malayalam uses a script which is basically Arabic with some additional symbols incorporated. While Arabic alphabet forms to be the basis of the characters used by Arabi-Malayalam, the additional symbols function in accommodating certain Malayalam consonants which have no equivalents in Arabic.[34] But, it is too certain that this language had a script even before the evolution of Malayalam script. This is evident from the fact that there were books in this language that provided instruction to learn *vaṭṭeẓhutu* and *kōleẓhutu,* two *Brahmi*-based writing systems prevalent in Kerala during the medieval times before the advent of Malayalam script. [35]

---

[28]C.N.Ahmed Moulavi and K.K.abdul Kareem, *Mahataya Mappila Sahitya Parambaraym*(Calicut: Authors, 1978).
[29] Ibid.
[30]Ajmal Khan, "Gulf Migration and Development of Malabar: Revisiting the Development of Muslims and Malabar", http://www.muslimsocieties.org, (Accessed on 28th June, 2013).
[31] Shamsuddin, *Mappila Malayalam,* 15.
[32] Ibid.
[33] Karassery, " Arabic-Malayalam", pp.107-9.
[34] Chaithanya, *A History of Malayalam Literature*, p. 195.
[35]Ulloor S. Paramesvarayyar, Kerala Sāhityacaritram, vol. 1, pp. 427-28 cited in V. P. Mohamedali, *Mappila Pattukal Noottandukalilude*, (Kottayam: Current Books, 2007)

Arabic is written mainly in two script systems-*kufic* and *naṣkhi*-both are derived from *nabātaean*[36] cluster belonging to Aramaic language. The use of *kufic* script (originated from the Kufa region of Arabian Peninsula), however, has historically been restricted to the ornamental or calligraphic writing. The *naṣkhi* script, on the other hand, is used widely and Arabi-Malayalam script appears to be a Kerala variant of *naṣkhi* script.[37] Writing from right to left and vowels given above or below the consonants are the two peculiarities of Arabic script. Arabi-Malayalam also follows this tradition intact. However, there are some additional orthographic signs in order to record the letters alien to Arabic language.

The *naṣkhi* script has twenty eight letters, but there are only twenty characters to write all these letters. Arabi-Malayalam alphabets are made of these twenty characters. Other letters are created by giving additional signs to the existing ones. In its earlier stage, Arabi-Malayalam alphabet had only 35 letters and for many Malayalam letters had no corresponding signs. On account of standardization, Arabi-Malayalam now contains fifty letters that can transcribe most of the Arabic and Malayalam letters. Malayalam, in total, has fifty six alphabets while Arabic has only twenty eight alphabets. So, not just in form, in structure also Arabi-Malayalam maintains some distinctiveness. Malayalam has corresponding letters only for letters like ا, ب, ت, ج, ر, س,, ش,, ك, ل, م, ن, و, ه, ي in Arabic language. Arabi-Malayalam cannot be considered as a scriptural cousin of Malayalam since what remains after removing Arabic letters from this language, is not Malayalam.

Phonetically, certain Malayalam characters do not have matches in Arabic characters and vice versa. In order to get matching phonemic sounds, the Mappila Muslims have made up at least twenty eight special characters in Arabi-Malayalam. Similarly, Arabic language has no vowels. But for accommodating Malayalam sounds, Arabi-Malayalam has devised vowel sounds by making minor orthographic changes to the Arabic letters.

Let us first deal with the vowels and consonants and then proceed to some of the special characters developed by Arabi-Malayalam in order to accommodate letters which are having no corresponding ones in Arabic and Malayalam. For the vowels and consonants which are already present in Arabic language, same signs are in use in Arabi-Malayalam also.

Letters denoting vowels in Malayalam and Arabi- Malayalam

Malayalam	അ	ആ	ഇ	ഈ	ഉ	ഊ	ഋ	എ	ഏ	ഐ	ഒ	ഓ	ഔ	അം	അ:
Arabi-Malayalam	اَ	آ	اِ	اِي	اُ	اُو	اِرْ	ا	ا	اَيْ	ا	او	اَوْ	اَمْ	أ
English	a	ā	i	ī	u	ū	ru	e	ē	ai	o	ō	au	am	a:

Of these, *Sukūn* (ْ), *ḍammu* (ُ) and *fataḥ* (َ) are used in Arabi-Malayalam to create vowels specifically to meet the requirements of Malayalam.

[36] Group of languages of the Nabataeans of the Palestine, Jordan and Egypt.

[37] Arabi-Tamil and Arabi-Kannada also use the same script systems. Shamsuddin, *Mappila Malayalam*, p.11.

Kasrah (ِ◌) *ḍammu*(ُ◌) *fataḥ* (َ◌)

Short Vowel Markers

Short vowels in Arabi-Malayalam are taken directly from Arabic without making any changes.

Fataḥ اَ	a	in AT	بَ
Kasrah اِ	i	in IT	بِ
ḍammu اُ	u	in CUT	بُ
Zadd اّ		in bba	بّ

Long Vowel Markers

Long vowels are indicated by additional *alif, yā* and *wāw,* respectively and the diphthongs are written with *fataḥ* (a) plus *yā* or *wāw*.

آ	_	بَ	+	ا= bā
اِي	_	بِ	+	ي= bī
أو	---	بُ	+	و= bū

These signs are called *harkats*. *Sukūn* in Arabic is used mainly to arrest a word or a sentence. The letter 'a' is created by putting the sign *alif maddi* (آ).

a	ā
ا	آ
അ	ആ

The vowel 'o' is formed by putting the sign to denote *ḍammu* in a slightly slanting manner. Long vowel of it is made adding the character و in Arabic.

O	ō
ا	او
ഒ	ഓ

While *SukŪn* serves the purpose of full stop in Arabi-Malayalam, use of it here is to indicate nasal sounds.

اَيْ	اَوْ	اَمْ
ഐ	ഔ	അം
ai	au	aṃ

SukŪn (ْ◌) is also used for making ....

نْ	ضْ	لْ	نْ
ൻ	ൾ	ൽ	ൺ
nu	ḷu	lu	ṇu

Consonants in Malayalam and Arabi-Malayalam

In addition to the basic Arabic letters, several characters have been introduced to write Malayalam sounds that are not found in Arabic.[38] All such letters used for denoting Malayalam letters do not match with the Arabic script system. While going through the Arabi-Malayalam alphabet, one can see that Arabi-Malayalam, though being represented in the Arabic script, follows Malayalam orthography to a certain degree to make additional sounds.

Malayalam	ക	ഖ	ഗ	ഘ	ങ	ച	ഛ	ജ	ഝ	ഞ
Arabi-Malayalam	ك	كه	گ	گھ	غ	چ	چھ	ج	جه	ڠ
English	k	kha	Ga	gha	ṅ	ca	cha	ja	jha	ňa

Malayalam	ട	ഠ	ഡ	ഢ	ണ	ത	ഥ	ദ	ധ	ന
Arabi-Malayalam	ب	ب	ٹ	ٹھ	ڹ	ت	تھ	د	دھ	ن
English	ṭa	ṭha	ḍa	ḍha	ṇa	ta	tha	da	dha	na

[38] Some Malayalam letters can be written with more than one Malayalam or Arabi-Malayalam letter or one of these Arabi-Malayalam stands for more than one Malayalam letter.

Malayalam	പ	ഫ	ബ	ഭ	മ	യ	ര	ല	വ	ശ
Arabi-Malayalam	پ	پھ	ب	بھ	م	ي	ڔ	ل	و	ش
English	pa	pha	ba	bha	ma	ya	ra	la	va	śa

Malayalam	ഷ	സ	ഹ	ള	റ	ഴ
Arabi-Malayalam	ڜ	س	ه	ض	ر	ژ
English	ṣ	sa	ha	ḷ	ṛa	ẑa

Cross-Linguistic Influences

Arabi-Malayalam words are formed mainly from the words taken from Arabic, Malayalam, Tamil, Kannada, Sanskrit and Persian. It is deserved to be noted here that most of the Arabi-Malayalam words correspond to Early Middle Arabic and Tamil ones. The verbal-bases are also mostly directly allied to the verbal bases of these languages.[39] There are, however, a number of bases which have no direct counterparts in Arabic or Tamil. Some of the words are taken directly from theses languages. Arab, Farsi and Hindustani words are sometimes used as such without much structural and syntactical changes or even changes in pronunciation.[40] So is the case with some of the words taken from languages like Tamil and Kannada. Following are some examples:

Tamil	**Arabi-Malayalam**
pēśuka (to speak)	pēśuka (to speak)
āndavaṇ (God)	āndavaṇ (God)
uṇgaḷ (you)	uṇgaḷ (you)
aruḷ (to tell)	aruḷ (to tell)

Kannada	**Arabi-Malayalam**
erudu (two)	erudu (two)
ēḷu (seven)	ēḷu (seven)

[39] Abu, *Arabi-Malayalam Literary History*, pp. 7-10
[40] Ibid., 7.

Arabic	**Arabi-Malayalam**
adāb (punishment)	adāb (punishment)
adab (politeness)	adab (politeness)
agnāṃ (goats)	agnāṃ (goats)
kabīr (big)	kabīr (big)
jabal (mountain)	jabal (mountain)
nāja (face to face)	nāja (face to face)
naśīda (song)	naśīda (song)
mahbāy (disappeared)	mahbāy (disappeared)
murād (intension)	murād (intension)
Persian	**Arabi-Malayalam**
āfat (disaster)	āfat (disaster)
kanōt (wedding)	kanōt (wedding)
maja (nobility)	maja (nobility)
mast (intoxication)	mast (intoxication)

Some of the Tamil, Kannada and Sanskrit words are being used with greater amount of changes to their meaning and pronunciation. Some of them have undergone structural and semantic transformations over a period of time. Change of first, second or some other letters in a Tamil or Malayalam word sometimes leads to the formation of a new word in Arabi-Malayalam. Following are some of the examples for such word formation:

Malayalam	**Arabi-Malayalam**	
*i*raci (meat)	*e*raci (meat)	i:e
*i*la (leaf)	*e*la (leaf)	I:e
*u*rumbu (ant)	*i*rumbu (ant)	u:e
*i*da (space)	*e*da (space)	i:e
samma*t*aṃ (consent)	samma*d*aṃ (consent)	t:d
*bh*avana (imagination)	*p*avana (imagination)	bh:p
Tamil	**Arabi-malayalam**	
u*y*ir (life)	u*ś*ir (life)	y:s
vānaṃ (sky)	*bā*naṃ (sky)	v:b
uṇma (truth)	uṇma (truth)	ṇ: ṇ

Kannada	**Arabi-Malayalam**	
bīdar (wife)	bīdar/vīdar (wife)	b:v
Sanskrit	**Arabi-Malayalam**	
*bhā*sha (language)	*pā*sa (Language)	bh:p
anyāyaṃ (injustice)	annināyaṃ (injustice)	n:nn
vēda (scared text)	*bē*daṃ (sacred text)	v:b

There is another argument that most the words taken from Tamil and Kannada are not taken from these languages but are borrowed from the Dravidian prototype to which Tamil, Kannada and Malayalam trace their origin.[41] Similarly, some words taken from Tamil and Kannada have several variants in Arabi-Malayalam. The word unkaḷ (you), for example, has got almost five variants:

umay (you)

umate (you)

umatil (among you)

umatu (you)

umaykaḷe (you)

Grammatical Structure

A commonly held misconception is that Arabi-Malayalam does not have its own grammar and the language depends on other languages, mainly Malayalam and Sanskrit for its grammar. That is not true. Arabi-Malayalam grammar maintains some uniqueness which one can never find in Malayalam and Arabic.

Arabi-Malayalam has developed some special features that seem to challenge grammatical rules in both Arabic and Malayalam. This language always shows a tendency to transcend the boundaries of the parent languages and develops a sort of immunity from the conventions. Arabi-Malyalam, in most of the case, does not loan a word from Arabic, Malayalam or any other languages as it is. Making some morphological changes, it sometimes presents such words as completely new. Some alterations are made to represent phonemes which are not present in other languages to which Arabi-Malayalam has a great deal of indebtedness. The loaned words get a new form, so, one cannot say that a particular word has to be used in a particular situation as it has been used in Arabic or in Malayalam in the same way. The context in which a loaned word is used becomes significant regardless of its meanings in the language of origin. *Udayavaṇ*, a word taken from Malayalam to denote God, for instance, has got two alternate forms in Arabi-Malayalam, namely, *udayavaṇ* and *udayōṇ*.

A study of such features based on two major works in Arabi-Malayalam-*Mohiyuddīn Māla* and *Mariyakutty's Katupāṭṭu*- would demonstrate the things better.[42] *Mohiyuddīn Māla* published in 1607

[41] Moulavi and Kareem, *Mahataya Mappila Sahitya Parambaraym* and Abu, *Arabi-Malayalam Literary History.*

[42] For analyzing the salient features of Arabi-Malayalam grammar, the authors relied mainly on two works, namely *Mohiyuddīn Māla* of Qazi Mohammed and *Mariyakutty's Katupāṭṭu* of Pulikkottil Hyder.

is supposed to be the oldest work in Arabi-Malayalam song tradition while *Mariyakutty's Katupāṭṭu* composed in 1922 is a modern poem chronicling around a significant social issue. *Mohiyudhīn Māla* is a work, highly devotional in nature, representing the genre of Sufi literature in *Arabi-Malayalam.* This work was composed when Arabi-Malayalam literary tradition was still dominantly influenced by Tamil and Arabi-Tamil literature. This work, thus, contains a large number of Tamil words and imageries. The influence of Tamil, however, coexisted successfully with the Arabic literary conventions. The period of *Mariyakutty's Katupāṭṭu*, however, was marked by the phenomenal influence of a standardized Malayalam. The influence of Tamil and Arabic literary conventions was on gradual decline during this period. Analyzing these two texts, definitely, would reveal some of the peculiarities that Arabi-Malayalam language represents.

1. Phonological Features

The phonological features can broadly be bifurcated into following:

1. The application of new phonemes

These phonemes are the ones that evolved in Malayalam out of vocabularies borrowed from Arabic language and widely used in Mappila songs. Though there are no separate scripts to denote and minimal pairs[43] for them, such phonemes are popular thanks to their enormous use in both Arabi-Malayalam songs and normal discourse.

The letter *k* (ك) in Ak̲bar, for instance, is foreign to Malayalam language but is in wide use in Arabi-Malayalam language. Following are the most illustrative contexts in which the new phonemes are used.

ḳh (خ) in *ḳh̲utub* خطب [x]

ain (ع) in *va̲'lu* وحض [ʕ]

ḷa (ض) in *Aḷḷahu* الله [d̪ˤ]

2. Phonological variations

These variations are emerged in Arabi-Malayalam partly as a result of the extensive use of Arabic words. Peculiar oral expressions developed among Mappila Muslims also, in part, have contributed to these variations. In the cases given below, the sound *a* is replaced by *e* in most of the words while using it in Arabi-Malayalam language.

Malayalam	Arabi-Malayalam	
vanna (come)	- vanne	a:e
tinna (eaten)	- tinne	
Kariῆa (burnt)	- kariῆe	

[43] In phonology, minimal pairs are pairs of words or phrases in a particular language, which differ in only one phonological element, such as a phoneme, toneme or chroneme and have distinct meanings. They are used to demonstrate that two phones constitute two separate phonemes in the language.

ini (hence)	-	eni	i:e
parāti (complaint)	-	purāti	a:u
utaram (answer)	-	utiram	a:i
piẓha (fine)	-	pila	ẓh: l
bayaṃ (fear)	-	pasaṃ	b:p, y:s

De-Cluster Forms

Many words loaned from other languages have undergone some phonological and morphological changes while entered into Arabi-Malayalam language.

Malayalam		**Arabi-Malayalam**
swarnaṃ	സ്വർണം	سُورَنَمْSwaranaṃ (Gold)
Candraṇ	ചന്ദ്രൻ	جَنْدِرَنْcandiraṇ (Moon)
swād	സ്വാദ്	سُوادْ suwād (taste)
dukhaṃ	ദുഖം	دَوكّمْ dukkaṃ (sadness)

These changes highlight the peculiarities of Arabi-Malayalam language. They are made mainly for the convenience and hassle-free pronouncing.

Arabic words in various forms have been used in many of the Mappila songs. As discussed elsewhere, some words are taken directly without much of morphological changes while others are used adding Malayalam post-fix or suffix. In certain cases, some modifications have been made to the Arabic words according to the grammatical rules in Malayalam.

عالم +കൾ ālankaḷ (worlds) (آلَنْكَلْ)

جِنْ+ കൾ Jinnukal (Jihns) (جِنْكَلْ)

إبْلِيس + അവർ iblisavar (the devil) (إبْلِيسَوَرْ)

Use of Malayalam suffix to get plural is more significant in this context.

مَلَائِك + കൾ Malāikkathukaḷ (Angles) ((مَلائِكَتُكَلْ

أَوْلِيَاكَلْ+അൻ+മാർ Awliyākkanmaṛ (saintly figures) (أَوْلِيَاكَنْمَارْ)

Following are some of the recurring Arabic words used in the texts referred to in this context. These Arabic words enjoy a wide popularity in the oral expression also.

śankh (apprehension)	شَكْ
hubbu (love)	حُبْ
twalaq (divorce)	طَلَاقْ
eaman (belief)	يمَانْإ

towba (repentance)	تَوْبَ
barkat (blessing)	بَرْكَةْ

Some words have been borrowed from Arabic language with changes affecting the basic syntactical nature of them.

Arabic	**Arabi-Malayalam**
vuzu (ablution)شُوَال	suvale
zyada (excess) جَاسْتِ	jasti
dunya (universe)دُنِيَاوْ	duniyavu
kīs (pocket) كِيشَ	kīsa

Morphological Features

1. There is a host of special features of Arabi-Malayalam morphology which may be described with reference to Malayalam, Arabic and Arabi-Malayalam. Following are the examples of adding bound morphemes to the plural Arabic words in order to create Arabi-Malayalam words.

kitab (book -Arab) +pusthakaṉaḷ (books-Mal.) =kitabukaḷ (Books- Arabi-Mal.)

śhahīd (martyr-Arab)+rakthasākshikaḷ(martyrs-Mal.) =śuhadākkaḷ (MartyrsArab- Mal.)

2. The usages which do not use the link morph, *ath*

Malayalam	**Arabi-Malayalam**
tāḷatil (in a plate)	tāḷamil
vidhatil (in a way)	vidhamil

3. Using *nte* instead of *ude* in genitive cases

Malayalam	**Arabi-Malayalam**
kodiyude (...of the flag)	kodinte (...of the flag)
ammāyiyude (...of the aunt)	ammāyinte (...of the aunt)

4. When the word ends with nasal sound *mil* instead of *il*

Malaylam	**Arabi-Malayalam**
urakatil (in the sleep)	urakkamil
dinathil (on the day)	dinamil

5. Situations in which the accusative suffix *na* or *va* replaces *ya* when two vowel join together. In Malayalam, *ya* is used on such occasions.

Malayalam	**Arabi-Malayalam**
Tala+e = Talaye (Mal.) a+e=ye	Thalane (Ar.Mal) a+e=ne
Mala+e = Malaye (Mal.) a+e=ye	Malane (Ar.Mal) a+e=ne

6. *Var* is used to express reverence in plurals

Malayalam	**Arabi-Malayalam**	
kandavar (those who have seen)	kandovar	a:o
paranjavar (those who said)	paranjovar	a:o

7. Palatals become dentals:

Malayalam	**Arabi-Malayalam**	
mikaca (the best)	mikata	c:t
ayaca (sent)	ayata	c:t

8. The case-suffix condensed:

Malayalam	**Arabi-Malayalam**
mutukil ninnu (from the back of the body)	muthuvinnu
manasinuḷḷil (in the mind)	Manasuḷḷil

9. Arabi-Malayalam carries some of the features of old Malayalam language which cannot normally be seen in modern Malayalam. Following are the examples of such words with a distinctive process of nasal assimilation and palatilization.

Malayalam	**Arabi-Malayalam**	
teḷiṋu (became visible)	teḷintu	ṋ:t
mikaca (the best)	mikate	c:t a:e

10. Incomplete verbs adding to the complete verbs in order to create new words:

Malayalam	**Arabi-Malayalam**
ṋan kōrtu (I strung together)	kōrtēn (I strung together)
nī kēḷkkuka (you listen)	kēḷpine (you listen)

11. Application of some *puruṣa pratyas* or masculine suffixes which are no longer used in Malayalam.

Malayalam	**Arabi-Malayalam**
āṭṭiya āḷ (the one who did shake)	āttiyaḷ
mykaṇi āl (the one with beautiful eyes)	mykaṇiyāḷ

12. Some old Malayalam usages which are still in use in Arabi-Malayalam:

Malayalam	**Arabi-Malayalam**
kīẓhe (below)	kīḷe
piẓha (fine)	piḷa
mēle (above)	Mēyye
munpu (ahead of)	munnaṃ
parayuka (to say)	embiduka
undākki (built)	keṭṭi
athupole (similarly)	āndapole
oẓhike (without)	oyye
kuẓhi (trench)	kuyyu
avaḷ (she)	ōḷ
jayilil (in prison)	jēlil
avan (he)	ōn
veḷuta (white one)	beḷuta
udayavan (the creator)	udayōvan

13. Some unique features do exist in Arabi-Malayalam and some of these have been archaisms preserved in South Malabar Muslim colloquial. The overwhelming influence of Arabic language has been reflected in the way in which certain Malayalam words are pronounced.

ഴ (zha) / യ (ya)

The letter ഴ is almost absent or replaced by the letter യ in both oral and written expressions of Mappila Muslims.[44] It is because of the absence of the letter ഴ in Arabic, which would be the first language learnt systematically in Mappila Muslims' case. The incorporation of യ is common in the texts and in the South Malabar colloquial. Following are some of the examples for this.

Malayalam	**Arabi-Malayalam**
ma*zha* (rain)	ma*ya* (rain)
ko*zhi* (hen)	ko*yi* (hen)

റ (ra) / ല (la)

[44] Sabna Pari, "Mappila Vamozhiynum, Arabi-Malayalavum", in T.Mansoorali (ed.), *Arabi-Malayala Sahitya Padangal*, (Kozhicode: Lead Books, 2014)p.117.

റ (ra) is another Malayalam sound absent in Arabic which has only ര(ṛa). So, Arabi-Malayalam shows a tendency to pronounce റ (ra) as ല (la).[45] One would come across a host of such instances, where the old literary texts in this language. Most of the old generation Mappila song composers used the letter ല (la) in place of റ (ra). In Mappila Ramayana[46] ല (la) has substituted റ (ra) even in the case of pronoun Rama.[47]

Malayalam	**Arabi-Malayalam**
*rā*thri (night)	*la*thri (night)
*ra*ndu (two)	*la*ndu (two)
*Ra*ma	*La*ma

Likewise, Arabic possesses no *athikharaghoshangal* (voiced and voiceless aspirated stops). So the standardization of Arabi-Malayalam was done giving due consideration to all these limitations.

ശ (Śa) / ഷ (Ṣa)/ സ (Sa)

The letter ഷ (Ṣa), because of the absence of it in Arabic language, seldom finds place in Mappila Muslims' oral expression. Sometimes, ശ (Śa) / ഷ (Ṣa)/ സ (Sa) are used as conflating letters.[48]

Malayalam	**Arabi-Malayalam**
ka*sha*ṇam (piece)	ka*sa*ṇam (piece)
vise*sha*m (news)	vise*sa*m (news)
vi*sha*mam (difficulty, agony)	ve*sa*mam (difficulty, agony)

പ (pa) / ഫ (fa)

Similarly, there are many instances in which the letters *pa* and *fa* have been used interchangebly in the last century. There were no rigorours rules for that before standardization. The letter *f* in place of *p* for instance was widely used in the copies of *pakṣhipāṭṭu* printed and published from northern Malabar.

Arabi-Malayalam Dictionaries

Arabi-Malayalam is a rich mine of synonyms and homonyms and many attempts were made to compile them in book form. Some dictionaries, in part, dealt with grammar also. *Khawāsul Muslimīna* alias *Lakhan Nahvu* compiled by Kunjalli Hassan Abdul Qadir Vaidyar was the first ever dictionary published in Arabi-Malayalam language. This dictionary, published in the year 1899 (Hijra 1317) with almost two thousand synonyms for two hundred words in Arabi-Malayalam language, also served the function of

---

[45] Ibid., p.118.

[46] Presenting the story in the cultural milieu of Kerala Muslims and using their own artistic resources, Mappilas have prepared an alternative version of Ramayana in Arabi Malayalam. This Ramayana is composed strictly according to the poetic rules in Arabi-Malyalam with lots of funs and satirical references to plot in original Ramayana.

[47] Pari, "Mappila Vamozhiynum", p.118.

[48] Ibid.p. 118.

thesaurus and inspired many creative works. *Muajumul Mufarada'* published by Bayaniya Press, Parappanagadi and *Khawasul Muslimīn* authored by Kōdam Palli Narikunnu Kuṉ̂ali Hassan Abdul Qadir Vaidyar also add to the list of dictionaries. Chakkiri Moidheenkutty's *Bāshabōṣham* (Plates 2&3) was the first exclusive thesaurus published in Arabi-Malayalam. The recent attempt by Hassan Nediyadi to compile a dictionary with meanings for words taken from one hundred and fifty poems is a worth-mentioning effort in the history of this language.[49] This dictionary comprises around ten thousand words with meanings in Arabi-Malayalam and details of the source language from where each word is taken. Latheef's *Mappila śyli* published in 1994 is an endeavor to compile idioms and usages popular among the Mappila Muslims.[50] Following is a list of dictionaries and thesaurus published so far in Arabi-Malayalam.

1. *Khawāsul Muslimīna* alias *Lakhan Nahvu*- (Arabi-Malayalam-Malayalam) Kunjalli Hassan Abdul Qadir Vaidyar
2. *Muajumul Mufarada'*(Arabi-Malayalam-Arabic) - Bayaniya Press
3. *Khawāsul Muslimīn* (Arabi-Malayalam-Tamil)- Kodampalli Narikunnu Kuṉ̂ali Hassan Abdul Qadir
4. *Makhsanul Mufdarat* (Dictionary of Ayurveda) - K.T.Ibrahim Maulawi
5. *Bahubāṣha Nighandu* (Arabi-Malayalam-Arabic/Malayalam/Sanskrit)-Sayyid Mohammed Koya Thangal
6. *Arabi-Malayalam Urdu* Dictionary- P.P.Ubaidullah Mawlavi.
7. *Bāshabōṣham* (Arabi-Malayalam Thesaurus)- Chakkiri Moidheenkutty
8. *Arabi-Malayala Padakōsam* (Arabi-Malayalam-Malayalam) - Hassan Nediyadi.

Standardization of the Language

The efforts for standardizing Arabi-Malayalam scripts have been done by different people at different stages of Kerala Muslim history. The close of 19th century had witnessed many efforts leading to the standardization of the Arabi-Malayalam script and the restructuring of its grammatical rules. Prominent among them was the one which had been initiated by the pioneers of Islamic reform movement in Kerala during the early 20th century. The scholars, who spearheaded this effort, were Vakkam Maulavi, Chaliyakath Maulana Kunjahammad Haji and Makti Thangal. Presentation of letters in modern form matching with the Arabic and Malayalam language was done mainly by Vakkam Maulavi. *Kīmiya Sa'da* authored by Maulavi in 1919 was the first work that used standardized Arabi-Malayalam script.[51] But there is a criticism that Moulavi's works represented a transformation of the language from more unsophisticated vocabularies of indigenous synthesis to a more Sanskritized and stylistically finished Malayalam words. Haji's effort to standardize the language has been compiled in a work called *Tasvīrul Hurūf (Akṣharaniyama Śāstram).* His mission was manifold. Haji prepared textbooks in Arabi-Malayalam language with the purpose of carrying out reforms in *madrassa* system and added

[49] Hassan Nediyadi, *Arabi-Malayala Padakosam*, (Thrissur, Kerala Sahitya Academi, 2009).
[50] N.K.A. Latheef, *Mappila śyli* (Kottayam: National Book Stall,1994)
[51] Shamsuddin, *Mappila Malayalam*, pp. 12-13.

science and arts to the curriculum in addition to theology.[52] Maulavi and Haji together revised Arabi-Malayalam script as a whole and now the language has the capacity to accommodate most of the sounds from not only Malayalam and Arabic but also from a host of other languages.

Another initiative along this line was taken by Kulanaraveettil Moidu Musliyar alias Suja'i Musliyar.[53] The publication of *Al-Mui'n*, the first dictionary in Arabi-Malayalam language in the post-standardization period compiled by C.A.Mohammed Maulawi of Thirurangadi helped Mappilas get familiarised with the modified letters.[54] Sayyid Sanaulla Makti Thnagal attempted in popularizing the standardized version further by way of writing a booklet entitled *Tha'līmulikhwan* in it.

With the difficulty to accommodate some of the Arabic and Malayalam letters, the advent of printing made the standardization process necessary. So, it was no surprise that one among the pioneers of Arabi-Malayalam standardization, Chalilakath Kunhahammad Haji besides being a part of the Islamic reform movement, was also associated with Arabi-Malayalam printing industry through his family. This language consisted of only twenty eight and thirty five letters at various stages of its evolution. Initially, the sounds *a* and *o* were completely absent and *ya* and *va* were used in place of them. Similarly, the letter *ṛa* was introduced lately by putting a dot under the letter *ra* in Arabic.

Arabic	**Arabic Malayalam**
ṛa	ra
ر	ڔ

The fifteenth letter of Arabic ض has been modified slightly to accommodate the sound 'ള' in Malayalam.

'ള'	Malayalam
'ض'	Arabic
'ۻ'	Arabi-Malayalam

The standardization was done mainly through introducing additional orthographic signs to the Arabic letters. So the base letters were remained same in both Arabic and Arabi-Malayalam. On account of standardization, Arabi-Malayalam now contains fifty six letters that can transcribe all Arabic and Malayalam letters.[55]

Another interesting development took place parallel to this was the standardization of Arabic script. The script which has traditionally been used for writing Arabic in Malabar is known popularly as *khattufunnāni* or *Ponnāni*[56] style of writing[57] (Plate 4). Arabi-Malayalam printing industry flourished

---

[52] A.P.Ibrahim Kunju, *Mappila Muslims of Kerala: The History and Culture*, (Trivandrum: Sandhaya Publications, 1989) p. 232-33.

[53] Abu. *Arabic-Malayalam Literary History*, p.19.

[54] Aburaseeda, "Chalilakath Kudumbakkar", *C.H. Ibrahim Haji Smaranika-2001*, 187-199, p. 196.

[55] Kunju, *Mappila Muslims of Kerala,* p. 198 .

[56] Ponnani is a place in South Malabar, the seat of many diasporic Arab scholars historically occupies a pivotal position in Islamic learning and Arabi-Malayalam printing.

alongside the standardization of the language naturally culminated in reformation of Ponnani script system, which bears some similarity to the script system of the former, in the late 19th century. Use of additional *harakats* or signs developed to mark new sounds was one of the salient features of standardized Ponnani script system. Despite the rapid spread of Ottoman script due to the Turkish Khilafat, Ponnani style continued to dominate over others for many centuries and copies of the Quran were printed in this script system. New fonts were specially designed by the printing presses to accommodate the changes occurred in script system. Both Arabic and Arabi-Malayalam calligraphy also received a fillip as a result of this development.[58] Despite the easy availability of the copies of Quran distributed by Saudi-funded religious missions in Kerala, the publishing companies still depend largely on Ponnani script as the switch over to other script systems seems difficult for a large chunk of Muslims in Malabar.[59]

---

[57] The reformation of script in Arabic has led to the emergence of several styles of writing. SulŪsi, Fārisi, DĪvani, Ijāsa Naṣhki, Rukha', etc. are the most prominent ones widely received and practiced in the Muslim world. See Hussain Randathani, *MakhdŪmum Ponnāniyum,* (Ponnani: Ponnani Juma Masjid Committee, 1998), p.121.

[58] Ibid. pp.120-21.

[59] This information was shared by C.H.Mahboob, the proprietor of C.H. Press, Thirurangadi in an interview with him during the field research. This press, according to him, sells out thousands of copies of the Quran printed in Ponnani script annually.

4

Creative and Critical Interventions: The Prose Tradition

Besides invoking many interesting linguistic issues, Arabi-Malayalam boasts a vast array of oral and written traditions, ranging from folksongs and classical poems to recording of oral histories and writings on Islamic philosophy. A great chunk of this literature is in verse and the themes are predominantly religious. The literature in Arabi-Malayalam can, broadly, be bifurcated into prose and verse; the latter is otherwise known popularly as *Māppiḷappāṭṭu* or Mappila Songs.[1] *Mālappāṭṭu, padappāṭṭu* or war songs *kissappāṭṭukaḷ* or story songs*, kalyāṇappāṭṭukaḷ or wedding songs, madhupāṭṭukaḷ* or praise songs, *kattupāṭṭukaḷ* or letter songs, *kessupāṭṭukaḷ* or story songs, *dārśanika kāvyangaḷ* or philosophical poems are a part of the verse tradition in Arabi-Malayalam language.

The verse tradition revolves most importantly around the stories related to seminal historical events through which the Muslim community passed. The major compositions are narrative poems about Muslim scholars, martyrs, saints and Sufi mystics.[2] This genre includes renditions of life histories of ancient Arab and Persian sages and legends, hymns that eulogize the holy figures, mythical saints, martial songs, moral teachings, historical recording of holy events, epistolary verses and love lyrics, etc.[3] Malabar rebellion of 1921 itself has spawned an extraordinary amount of interesting Mappila songs.[4] The themes of such compositions are organized largely around the lives, struggles and martyrdom of people who were a part of anti-colonial agitations with great amount of wonder and admiration.

Similarly, there are number of life-cycle events in which the oral literary tradition in Arabi-Malayalam finds its expression. Chapter 4 contains a detailed discussion of such occasions. Among them, the most prominent one is *oppana* performance, which is widely popular among Muslim women across the region. Mappila women perform *oppana* accompanied by songs on the occasion of wedding.

---

[1] M.N.Karasserry, "Arabic-Malayalam: Interactions among Arabs and Mappila Muslims of Kerala", in M.H.Ilias and P. J. Vincent (ed.), *India-West Asia Relations: Understanding Cultural Interplays,* (New Delhi: New Century Publications, 2007), pp.107-112.

[2] Krishna Chaithanya, A History of Malayalam Literature, (Hyderabad: Orient Longman, 1971), p. 197.

[3] M.N. Karassery,"Arabic Malayalam",in Asghar Ali Engineer (ed.),*Kerala Muslims: A Historical Perspective* ,(New Delhi: Ajanta Publishers, 1995), p.169.

[4] Rolland Miller, *Mappila Muslims of Kerala: A Study in Islamic Trends,* (Madras: Orient Longman, 1971), pp.289-296.

The songs sung in such events are drawn out of a huge and dynamic corpus that reflects the linguistic and cultural fusion of the local Kerala culture with the culture of Arabia. *Kōlkkaḷi* or stick game, another occasion, where the verse tradition finds its place, has its own distinctive tunes to accompany Arabi-Malayalam songs as well as unique dance steps. The songs performed in this way are yet another medium surrogating the specific blend of Indian and Arab traditions. In addition to these, there are certain performative occasions that enliven the Arab influence on Mappila culture. They include: *dafmuṭṭu* and the *arabanamuṭṭu* which are, normally, performed along with rituals and collective prayers such as *rātib* and *dikr.*

Vaṭṭappāṭṭu literally means circle-song is a performance of devotional songs by men. The themes range from anecdotes from Islamic history to contemporary social issues like dowry system. The songs that accompany *vaṭṭappāṭṭukaḷ* are basically in Arabic Malayalam. With distinctive performance and linguistic features, *vaṭṭappāṭṭu* songs juxtapose the tradition of classical poems and tradition of folk songs in a single composition. Similarly, there are many regional performing arts like *muṭṭum viḷiyum* (instrumental musical performance), *kaimuṭṭukaḷi* (hand-clapping play), *paricamuṭṭukaḷi* (shield game), *kalyānappaṭṭukaḷ* (wedding songs), etc. and it is important to note that it is Arabic-Malayalam songs that create a musical ambience to such performances and their contents and their linguistic registers are specially designed to serve some artistic functions.

The prose tradition in Arabi-Malayalam in its teething stage consisted mainly of translations of the Quran and interpretations of *hadith.*[5] Two noteworthy works that energized an alternative genre to emerge were Mulāmbatu Kunhamu's *Iblīz Nāma* (various names of Iblīz) and *Kināvinte Ta'bīr* (interpretation of dreams).[6] The prose ranges from the simple re-entering of Arabian Nights to works on indigenous medicinal system, *Ayurveda*, astronomy, logic, *kissah* (genre of short stories and novels) and the like.[7] Mohamedkunhi has categorized Arabi-Malayalam prose into following genres:[8]

1. Translations and interpretations of the Quran
2. Interpretations of the Prophet's teaching
3. Islamic philosophy, works of Islamic jurisprudence and ethics
4. Texts of Islamic and local history
5. Short stories and novels
6. Texts on medicine, astronomy and other sciences
7. Literary criticisms
8. Dictionaries

A scrupulous reading of the history of Arabi-Malayalam literature reveals that its evolution spans across three distinct phases.[9] The first phase stretching back almost to three hundred to five

[5] P.K.Mohamedkunhi, *Musliṉalum Kerala Samskaravum,* (Thrissur: Kerala Sahitya Academy, 2008), p. 174.
[6] Ibid, 175.
[7] C.N.Ahmed Moulavi and K.K.abdul Kareem, *Mahatāya Mappiḷa Sāhitya Pārambaraym*(Calicut:Authors, 1978), pp. 50-51.
[8] Mohamedkunhi, *Musliṉalum Kerala Samskaravum,* p. 177.
[9] V. P. Mohamedali, *Mappila Pattukal Noottandukalilude*, (Kottayam: Current Books, 2007), p. 70.

hundred years contained mostly simple Malayalam and Tamil words which were a part of routine communication along with a few Arabic words. *Mohiyuddin Māla* exemplifies this tradition with extensive use of Malayalam and Tamil words and some essential Arabic words which were taken from Islamic texts. In the second phase, increased influence of Tamil language was apparent thanks to the presence of Tamil poets who popularized many words and rhyme schemes from Tamil in Arabi-Malayalam language.[10] At some point of time, Tamil had a monopoly over the works written by the Mappila poets.

The phase followed it, marked the presence of a rainbow mix of languages; Arabic, Tamil, Urdu, Malayalam, Farsi, Sanskrit and Kannada. Most of the works of Moinkutty Vaidyar and Chettuvayi Parikutty are reflective of this mix.[11] This phase lasted for almost one and half centuries from 19th century and generated a huge cache of interesting works which together formed a golden period in the history of Arabi-Malayalam literature.[12] The spread and development of a language or dialect at some stages sometimes requires the direct or indirect support of ruling elites. There is an argument that in some way, the use of Arabi-Malayalam as the official language by Arakkal dynasty offered a major boost for this language to flourish. [13] Arabi-Malayalam had also gained the backing of scholars from the community who consistently used this language for imparting Islamic knowledge.[14]

The prose tradition in Arabic-Malayalam includes a vast corpus of prose compositions such as novels, short stories and non-fiction literature.[15] The history of fiction writing in this language traces its history to the publication of *Akharul Muniss-Cāhr Darvēṣh* based on a Farsi novel with the title *Cāhr Darvēṣh* (four saints)written by Amir Kunsru. This work published in 1883 predates *Indulēkha* (published in 1889) a work considered to be the first novel in Malayalam language conformed to the standard by almost six years.

A well-received folklore in medieval Persian literature, *Cāhr Darvēṣh* was presented in the form of a story told by Amir Kunsru to his spiritual leader Hazrat Nizamuddin on the instruction of doctors treating him. [16] Around the end of the storytelling, Nizamuddin was cured from his illness, came back to normalcy and became able to indulge in routine works. This miraculous incident led to the spread of a belief that reading *Cāhr Darvēṣh* or listening to it brings healing to the sick persons.[17] This *kissa* or story which was originally composed and circulated orally was recorded later on in Farsi language and then translated to Urdu, Punjabi and Hindi.[18] Malayalam translation was done based on the original

---

[10] Ibid.

[11] Ibid, pp. 70-71.

[12] Ibid., p.70.

[13] K.O. Shamsuddin, *Mappila Malayalam,* (Trivandrum: Author, 1978), p.5.

[14] Ibid.5

[15] Shamsuddin divides the works in Arabi-Malayalam into vyghynama or interpretation, tarjama or translation, kadha or story and kavya or verse. Ibid., p. 92.

[16] Ramesh.V.K., "Arabi-Malayalatile Novelukal", T. Mansurali (ed.), *Arabi-Malayala Sāhitya Padanangal*, (Kozhicode: Lead Books, 2014), pp.143-48, p.144.

[17] Ibid.

[18] Ibid.

work in Farsi by Nalakath Kunhimoiddin, a polyglot with a good command over Farsi, Urdu, Arabic and Arabi-Malayalam language.[19]

The publication of *Cāhr Darvēṣh*, that happened six years ahead of *Indulēkha*, shows that Arabi-Malayalam language was capable of using even modern genres such as novel. It also reflects the popularity and wider acceptance of Farsi language and literature among Mappila Muslims. It is interesting to note that the Farsi language novels constituted a large share of early translated works in Arabi-Malayalam.[20] The publication of *Cāhr Darvēṣh* influenced many others to translate popular Arabic and Persian novels to this language. For instance, it inspired Kariydan Kunhimoosa to translate *Aliflaila O'Laila* (Thousand and one nights) to Arabi-Malayalam.[21] And what followed was a sudden inflow of such works. *Alāvuddīn, Qamarsamān, Śamsussamān, Umarayyār, Amīr hamza, Gulsanōsar, Subaida, Sainaba* and *Khiḷar Nabiyekkanda Nabeesa* (Nabeesa who saw the prophet Khilar) were the major ones belonging to this genre.[22] The first six novels in this slot were translated directly from Farsi language while others were based on indigenous plots.

Taking a perspective akin to modern feminism, the novels such as *Subaida, Sainaba* and *Khiḷar Nabiyekkanda Nabeesa* adopted an apparent strategy of telling the stories from women's point of view. One can also see a subtle attempt to make the Mappila women's self, which once embodied many limitations in individual and social life, a symbol with a keen desire to achieve freedom and liberty in these novels.[23]

Since a large chunk of works falling under the category of translation, Arabi-Malayalam texts were, at some point of time, called otherwise as *tarjamakal* or translations.[24] Many of them, though gained a wide popularity, were of unknown authors. Following are the major works appeared in this category during the initial period of evolution of Arabi-Malayalam language:

1. *Tuhfa* (The Gift, written in Arabic by Ibnhajar Haittima)-translated by Chalilakath Alihassan Moalawi in eight volumes.
2. *Failulmannār* (Source of Goodness)-translated by Thenveettil Abdul Qadir Musliyar
3. *Fathul Mannār* (Unveiling Virtue) and *Fathu Nnūr* (Unveiling Light)-translated by Noohukannu Musliyar
4. *Nibrāsul Ināya* (The Light of Destination) - translated by Adima Musliyar.

A rough estimate says that there are almost around two hundred prose works published in Arabi-Malayalam language.[25] Out of which, almost sixty percent are religious texts. The number of

---

[19] Ibid.,p.145
[20] Ibid., p.143.
[21] Mohamedkunhi, *Musliṉalum Kerala Samskaravum,*p. 175.
[22] Moulavi and Kareem, *Mahatāya Mappila Sāhitya Pārambaraym,* pp. 51-52.
[23] Ramesh, "Arabi-Malayalatile Novelukal",p.144.
[24] Mohamedkunhi, *Musliṉalum Kerala Samskāravum,* p. 177.
[25] Ibid.& Maulawi and Kareem, *Mahatāya Mappila Sāhitya Pārambaraym*.

songs published is around six hundred.[26] Apart from the historical texts, many books dealing with canonical laws in Arabic had been translated in this language. With a view to reach to Muslims of interior Malabar, European missionaries had published the translation of Gospel of Luke in Arabi-Malayalam language. This translation entitled *Injīl Luka* was brought out by Madras Auxiliary Bible Society in 1905.[27]

In the prose tradition, authors maintained a balance of Arabic, Malayalam and Tamil vocabularies. Nevertheless, the religious texts kept a difference from this pattern with Arabic words outnumbering the words from other languages. Songs represented a delicately balanced mix with words which were taken from Persian and Sanskrit in addition to Malayalam, Arabic, and Tamil. This composition made it difficult for non-Mappilas to follow the context of most of the works in the verse tradition. However, with the purpose of making them widely appealing, songs and stories were recited with detailed interpretations in special gatherings called *sīrapārāyana sadassu.*[28]

The non-fiction tradition includes writings on history, philosophy, entertainment, medicine, war, travel and trade. [29] Besides it, there were many journals and dailies brought out in Arabi-Malayalam; *al-Islam,* edited by Vakkam Maulavi and *al-nisa* (The Women), a women's magazine, *al-Irṣhād* published by Manappattu Kunjumohammed Haji of Kodungallore and *Swalāhul Ikhwān* and *Rafeeq-ul-Islam* published by C. Sadialikuuty Master of Thirurangadi being the most famous ones among them.[30]

> In those days, the chief medium of instruction was Arabi-Malayalam...ordinary Mappilas found Malayalam too difficult to read and grasp...Saidalikutty Master's choice of Arabi-Malayalam for publishing news papers (*Swalāhul Ikhwān* and *Rafeeq-ul-Islam*) was, thus, a deliberate one. *Swalāhul Ikhwān* started publishing in the year 1317 Hijra (1899 AD) quickly gained a wide acceptance. With a periodicity of two-three issues a month, it maintained high standard in layout and language on par with modern news papers...maintained a huge diversity in coverage also; issues ranged from administrative reforms of Ottoman Sultans to aesthetics of *Alif Laila* (Arabian Stories). [31]

However, *Rafeeq-ul-Islam's* concerns revolved mostly around the debates that characterized the Muslim society of Malabar towards the close of the 19th century. Following note on series of public debates taken place among various factions of Mappila Muslims illustrates the nature of content;

> Our Malayalam district (Malabar[32]), for long time, appears to be not immune from the conflicts along the sectarian-doctrinal lines. Allegations against Kondōṭṭy faction[33] set in

---

[26] Hassan Nediyadi, "Sāmūhika Navōdanatinte Māppilapattukaḷ", *Mujāhid Samstāna Sammēḷanam Souvenir 2008,* pp.231-32.

[27] http://shijualex.in/gospel_of_luke_arabi_malayalam_1905/

[28] Hassan Nediyadi, *Arabi-Malayala Padakōsam*, (Thrissur, Kerala Sahitya Academi, 2009), p.17.

[29] Shamsuddin, *Mappila Malayalam*, p.92.

[30] O.Abu, *Arabic-Malayalam Literary History,* (Kottayam: NBS, 1976) & Shamsuddin, *Mappila Malayalam*,pp.92-93.

[31] Maulawi and Kareem, *Mahatāya Māppiḷa Sāhitya Pārambaraym* pp.407-408.

[32] British Malabar was the only Malayalam speaking district in the State of Madras.

[33] A detailed note on Ponnani-Kondotty factional feud has been given in the first chapter.

motion from the time of Makdoumis of Ponnani seem to continue with no sign of end in the near future. Fissure over hand-clapping during religious processions in Calicut is not a thing of distant past.[34] Ahamadiyya community of Kannur spills alarmingly over to Calicut also. Dispute over the direction of Qibla[35] originated in Thirurangadi now gathers momentum all over Malayalam (Malabar). There is an appeal to everyone engaged in these rows to give up their parochial arguments and to work collectively for enduring peace in the community.[36]

There were a number of political magazines and weeklies in Arabi-Malayalam, dealing with the then contemporary social and political issues and some of them were even confiscated or banned by the British. Thus the Arabi- Malayalam language, throughout the history, had maintained a rich literary tradition and contemporized the debates through diverse set of works published in it. This diversity was also reflective of it hermetic nature, as far as the other linguistic fusions of Malayalam were concerned.[37]

With the purpose of reaching out to a large section of Muslim population, nationalist leaders and social reformers had taken out a strategy to capitalize the popularity of Arabi-Malayalam and published a plethora of pamphlets in this language. These works, as Shamsuddin observes, "represented an attempt to reform and unify Arabi-Malayalam by making it more close to Malayalam."[38] Though these journals were published in Arabi-Malayalam language and used Arabic words lavishly, they invariably followed the style and grammatical structure of Malayalam. With the increased use of standardized Malayalam vocabulary in place of Arabi-Malayalam one, these journals characterized a concerted move by the reformists to change the linguistic orientation of Mappila Muslims.[39] The eclectic nature of Arabi-Malayalam slowly gave way to Malayalam expressed in Arabi-Malayalam script.

An avalanche of travelogues was published in this language and some of them can appropriately be put under the genre of 'indigenous historiography' with a potential to become a counter-text to colonial mode of writing history with the inevitable 'oriental gaze.' Hajj writings--personal narratives of some early Hajjis from Kerala for certain specific reasons occupy a prominent position among them.[40] The scope of their memories of early Hajjis cannot limit to the personal exercise of telling the stories of past. It rather can be extended to a collective effort to re-tell the history in an alternative way. In fact the academic significance of such oral histories lies in their potential to form an alternative version of history of Hajj and the history of Saudi Arabia as well. They are especially useful for understanding ordinary people's accounts of travel and the places they have

[34]Use of music instruments and hand-clapping during the religious processions became a contentious issue among the Muslims of Calicut. Many fatwas for and against were issued by two conflicting Kazi groups of Calicut in the early twentieth century.

[35] See also Ain al-Qibla dispute referred in this chapter.

[36] *Rafeeq-ul-Islam, vol. 2, no. 4, 1909.*

[37]Chaithanya, *A History of Malayalam Literature*, p. 197.

[38] Shamsuddin, *Mappila Malayalam*, p.14.

[39] Ibid., p. 93.

[40] A detailed account of travel songs has been given in chapter four.

been to which are generally not available in the 'standard' records of history often written by the European scholars.

Though there are works in abundance in Malayalam, writing on Hajj in Arabi-Malayalam is relatively scanty.[41] The first known work belonging to this genre is the travel writing of Thithachumma Hajjumma, written in 1930. [42] This work written in the form of a diary revolves mainly around two things; traumatic experience of travel and life in Saudi Arabia. However, among the writings on Hajj, poetic forms dominate over others. P.T. Veeran Kutty Maulawi's travelogue on his journey to Mecca, *Hajj Yātra* is written in the form of song in a style close to ordinary speech. [43] The narratives in such works, generally, take shape in different forms; individual's memories, personal commentaries; recollections and narrative accounts of events and experiences during the journey. K.T.Manu Musliyar and K.V.M. Panthavoor also have shared their experience of performing Hajj in verse form. Clearly distant from the norms of 'standard verse' in Malayalam, these works can be seen largely as a part of Mappila Muslims' tradition of narrating each and every experience of life including travel in the form of poems or songs.[44]

Similarly, the Arabic Malayalam literature often contradicts the colonial sources and tries to undo the common notions set by the colonial history texts in registering the situations, societies and geographies of the east. *Al-Fathul Fatah*[45] authored by Sujayi Moidu Musliar is an illustrative example of such works employing an alternative narrative strategy in the history of rendering of Muslim society from Adam to the Ottoman period. Sujai's another work of Islamic history titled *Faiḷul Fayyāḷ*[46] narrating the history from the genesis to the rule of Abbasids can indeed be seen as a part of a collective effort by the scholars of Indian Ocean region to re-tell the history of the religion in the light of community-specific frameworks and resources. A new notion of past, which had a non-European provenance was put forward by them. The Islamic scholars of Malabar, East Africa and Southeast Asia were the leading proponents of this new discourse of community's history (The alternative way of telling history prevalent in the Indian Ocean has been discussed further in Chapter 5.)

Anyway, taking fragmented slices from history, these works generally adopted an uneven and non-linear pattern in recording developments in the Islamic history that questions the grand linear concept of historical progress. The insights and narrative strategies employed in these works speak of a different sensitivity that was previously unheard. This is quite evident from the divergent and fractious styles adopted by *Mohiyuddin Māla* of Khazi Mohammed in rendering the history of Islamic society of post-Prophet period.

Today, however manifold cultural expressions of Arabic Malayalam literature are struggling to survive. The steady increase in general education has culminated in eventual decline in popularity of

---

[41] Sheikh Zainuddin Makdum's work in Arabic Tauhtaul Mujahiddin is the first one shedding light on Mappila pilgrimage to Mecca for Hajj. In an effort to visualize the hardships that Mappila community suffered, Makdum has given a detailed account of the Portuguese attack on Mappila pilgrims on their way by sea in country crafts.

[42] The manuscript of which has been preserved in the personal collection of Edathola Gafoor.

[43] A.P.Kunhamu, *"Malayaḷatile Hajjezhutukaḷ"*, *Bodhanam,* January-March, 2013, pp. 5-15., p. 6.

[44] Ibid.

[45] This work was published from Thalassery in three volumes in 1903.

[46] As per the reference given in the text this work was published in the year 1887.

this language. The spread of modern education for the last four five decades has resulted in Mappilas switching over to Malayalam and English as the medium for knowledge construction. There is also the issue of Gulf migration and consequent integration of Malabar Muslim community to the wider Islamic world. As discussed in the earlier chapter, the process has aided in reconfiguring everyday life within a homogenous pan-Islamic framework. The cultural meaning of this shift is evident from the puritan attack on Arabi-Malayalam and its multitude of cultural expressions for being 'un-Islamic.' Around the same time, the *"hurries* or angels of paradise" genre, which were often discussed in Arabi-Malayalam texts gave way to topics such as indications of scientific truths in Quran.[47] Among the majority, traditional works which once acted a means for massive indoctrination lost its charm and replaced or abandoned for more advanced and effective mode of preaching. The publishers also turned to publish translations of old Arabi-Malayalam texts in Malayalam which brought a sudden decrease in the number of people who know this language.

Some believe that the relevance of Arabi-Malayalam is no longer there as the Mappilas are capable enough to learn Arabic and Malayalam without the help of a bridging language. Arabic has taken the role of liturgical language, while written expression has predominantly been shifted to Malayalam. The publication of popular and creative works in Malayalam language, mainly novels with indigenous plots and translations, made it more attractive to Mappilas. The modern Malayalam writers from the community like Vaikkom Muhammed Basheer and N.P. Mohammed were instrumental in promoting the use of Malayalam as the chief medium of creative expression. Kareem and Maulavi find the popularity that modern education gained as the major reason for the decline of Arabi-Malayalam language and literature.[48]

The switch over from Arabi-Malayalam to Malayalam was a well promoted move by the British who aided new generation of *madrassas* introducing 'secular' education in Malayalam and English. Even the moral science curriculum was designed by the colonial administration with the support of modern *ulema* who staunchly advocated for a complete transformation of religious education under the British aegis.[49] The scholars like V.Kunhimoyi Haji of Manchery were specially assigned for the successful execution of this thoughtfully designed project.[50] Hajji prepared a set of text books called *Hidāyutul Muslimin* in 1924 for the standards I to VIII. *Muslim Sanmārga Dīpam,* another set prepared by Abdul Gafoor Shah was also meant for the students of same level. Publication of these text books marked the beginning of a partial switch over of Mappilas from Arabi-Malayalam to Malayalam in learning 'religious' and 'secular' subjects in the centres of religious learning.

The establishment of Training schools for Mappila teachers with the purpose of imparting 'secular' subjects in Malayalam and English accelerated the process further.[51] But all the efforts meant to teach Islamic subjects in Malayalam met stiff opposition from the traditional *ulema* and the effort was considered by them as something blasphemous.[52] Compulsory modern schooling in the places

[47] T.K.Hamza, a scholar of Mappila songs in an interview with the authors.
[48] Maulawi and Kareem, *Mahatāya Māppiḷa Sāhitya Pārambaraym,* p. 75-6.
[49] Ibid., pp. 75-6.
[50] Ibid.
[51] Ibid., p.76
[52] Ibid., p.77 and Ummar Maulawi, *Ormakaḷude Tīṛatu,* (Cochin: Da'wa Books, 2009).

which were the hubs of Mappila Rebellion of 1921 implemented by the British administration as its policy also yielded a negative result with Mappilas seeing it as yet another cycle of colonial invasion.

The standardization of the script also is seen by some scholars as a partial reason for the decline of this language.[53] Though well accepted initially, the standardization on the basis of certain scientific principles made the language more difficult to use for the ordinary Mappilas.[54] The script became quite alien to those who were having mere literacy.[55] Another major issue that Arabi-Malayalam currently encounters is the lack of digitization of its scripts. As a language incompatible for typesetting, digital printing in this language is more or less impossible.

Nevertheless, Arabi-Malayalam in its oral form seems to withstand all such bitter times. Although the written tradition has lost its purchase considerably, Arabi-Malayalam continues to exist as the major medium of oral literary expressions. Most of the works in oral literary tradition still derive their inspirations from this indigenous synthesis. Mappila songs being used in popular cinema are well liked by people cutting across religious lines. Gulf migration, contrary to the situation discussed earlier, enriched the language by making meaningful contributions to enriching its vocabulary.

1. Arabi-Malayalam Manuscripts

The Arabi-Malayalam texts in manuscript form were in wide circulation long before the first printing press was established. The manuscript repositories in Malabar attest to rich and diverse nature of this tradition, containing a broad spectrum of works ranging from folksongs and classical poems to oral histories and philosophical writings. A great chunk of this manuscript is in verse and the themes are pre-dominantly religious. The manuscripts in Arabi-Malayalam cover a wide range of issues from simple renditions of the life histories of some influential Sufi scholars to serious political works chronicling the imperial designs of the Portuguese and British. However, one can see that two seminal events in the history Malabar Muslims-Ponnāni-Kondōṭṭy kaitharkam or factional feud and anti-colonial Māppiḷa Rebellion-have produced an extraordinary amount of manuscripts.

With regard to the content, these manuscripts can be put under the general rubrics of *fatwas*; *fiqh*-based discourses; anti-colonial dossiers and philosophical texts for massive indoctrination. Most of these manuscripts which initially belonged to a number of private family collections were later on donated to mosque libraries.[56] Among them, the translation of Holy Quran by Valiyapurackal Mayinkutty Ilaya of Thalaserry was the most popular one (Plate 4.1). [57] This manuscript in six volumes was considered to be the most-valued preserve by some of the mosques and wealthy families in Malabar. Being a rich merchant from north Kerala, Ilaya distributed his work at free of cost, though the

[53] Shamsuddin, *Māppiḷa Malayalam,*pp.14-16.

[54] Interview with M.N. Karassery, a scholar of Muslim literature in Kerala by the authors held on 2nd January, 2012.

[55] Interview with Hussain Randathani, a scholar of Kerala Muslim history by the authors on 22nd March, 2012.

[56] Codicologically speaking, most of them are preserved with in loose covers of paper and kept in stitched envelopes made of white fabric. This is the common method of preserving manuscripts and other rare materials in Malabar. These manuscripts are generally are penned using Ponnāni script, a locally devised script system giving additional orthographic signs in order to accommodate local phonetics and make it simple for Mappila readers.

[57] Quran had a translation first by Mayin Ilaya almost hundred years ago.

effort costing hundreds of thousand rupees that time.[58] Later on with the lack of confidence in his own ability to translate the Holy text, Ilaya himself withdrew the copies of this work from the mosque libraries and personal collections.[59] However, this work still remains in the manuscript form in many personal collections.

After Ilaya's landmark attempt, many scholars had ventured in translating the entire Quran or in portions with varied interpretations in Arabi-Malayalam. Konkanamveettil Ibrahim Musliyar, for instance, translated two *sūrahs- kahf* and *yasin*-from the Holy text. *Khairatul Muslimīna* – a work dealing with Arabic astronomy is another worth-mentioning contribution to his credit. The *sūrahs* like *hamma* (Plate 4.2) and *tabārah* have been translated by Thenparambil Abdul Qadir Musliyar while Eananveettil Mohammed Musliyar translated the *Sūrah, al-baqra,* P.K.Moosa Moulavi translated *iqlās* and C.H.Mohamed Moulavi translated *fatiha.* Following the translation of the Quran many seminal works from Arabic had been translated into Arabi-Malayalam language. There were translations for two major works from Arabic chronicling the life history of the Prophet Mohamed; *Aqbar Muhamadiyya* by Chalilakath Mohamed Musliyar and *Sīratunabawiyā* by Mulambathu Kunjamu respectively.

Among the *fiqh* or jurisprudence texts translated, *Attalhattulbahiyya: fil Ahkāmil Fiqhiyya,* a compilation of interpretations by various scholars given to *Shafi* Jurisprudence was the most significant one. This work based on a widely renowned work in Arabic *Tuhfa Tussaimīn* authored by Ibn Hajarul Haithami was published in two volumes respectively in Hijra 1311 and 1313.[60] The translations of seminal works in Islamic philosophy included two major works of Imam Ghazali- *Minhājul Ābiddīn* and *Ihyā Ulūmuddin*- by Chalilakath Abdulla Maulawi.

Some of the works published earlier were either dilapidated or destroyed prior to the advent of printing. Many were saved from the attempts of the Portuguese and British to confiscate and destroy them because of the radical political content of the text. Abu notes that a large cache of Arabi-Malayalam manuscripts were ruined first by the Portuguese during their attack on costal Muslim settlements in southern Malabar and off late by the British during the Mappila rebellion of 1921.[61] However, most of the manuscripts later on got printed versions, even though only some parts were printed in most of the cases. *Sīratunnbawiyyā,* the work praising the Prophet, written originally in two parts lost the second part while getting printed. So was the case with *Kasfuttārfi A'khbari Malaibār* written by Ibrahim Maulawi- only the first part of it was printed.[62]

2. Works on Medicine and Science

The evolution of prose tradition in Arabi-Malayalam touched its zenith in the 19th century with the publication of a wide spectrum of works dealing with traditional medicinal system. Arabi-Malayalam science literature also reached a maturity by this time with the publication of original contributions of

---

[58] Abu, *Arabic-Malayalam Literary History*, p.129.

[59] Interview with Edathola Gafoor, a keeper of Arabi-Malayalam Quran in manuscript form inherited from his great grandfather held on 12th March, 2012.

[60] Abu Raseeda, "Cālilakath Kudumbakkār", pp.191-193.

[61] Abu, *Arabic-Malayalam Literary History*. pp. 129-30

[62] Ibid., pp.130-131.

home-grown scholars in this field. After having a detailed study of the works published in this category, scholars have come to some assumptions.[63] Firstly, the knowledge of medicine was inherited from Sufis, scholars and traders who came and settled in Malabar mainly from Southern Arabia and Iran. Secondly, the local scholars who had possessed enormous amount of knowledge of theology at the same time had maintained a keen interest in practicing medicine also. Thirdly, Mappila Muslims turned to such scholars seeking remedy for their mental and physical illness. Fourthly, the traditional medicinal system prevailed among Mappilas of Malabar traces its root to the local practices and the knowledge acquired from canonical texts of both Ayurveda and Unani. Apart from this, some of the practitioners depended on *Asmah,* a system of medicine used mainly for the treatment of mental illness believed to have come to Malabar via Persian Sufi scholars.[64]

Arabi-Malayalam literature on medicine witnessed a sudden increase in number since the days when Konkanam Veetil Ahmed Bawa Musliyar wrote his masterpiece *Sarva Rōga Cikitsa Sāram* aka *Valiya Vaidya Sāram.* Published in the year 1890, this work provides essential clues to some Kerala-Muslim specific indigenous medicinal systems, prescriptions for some generic diseases, ingredients of some the then popular medicinal mix.[65] The author has also made an attempt to connect it to the medicinal system prevalent in Arab/Islamic word since the time of the Prophet. Irresistibly drawn to the study of Ayurveda, Arab and Persian medicinal systems, Bawa Musliyar has authored several works in this field. The other works of him- *Upakāram Tarjama* and *Kodumudi-* represent an attempt in juxtaposing the principles of local system of medicine, Ayurveda and Perso-Islamic tradition in a common synthesis. Taking cues from the Persian texts, his work *Farofakāram* deals exclusively with *Asmah* and other mantra-based medicinal practices.[66] Bawa Musliyar seems to depart slightly from the traditional Indian system of medicine based on the theory of *pancabūta* or five spirits-air, fire, space, earth and water and shows a profound inclination towards the Greek system of medicine.[67] What he employed in *Upakāram* is a fusion of Arab and Greek traditions in place of the Sanskritized one substituting sight with fire, smell with water, taste with earth and sound with air.[68]

Following Bawa Musliyar, many scholars cum medical practitioners sought to reach the widest audience possible through the regular publication of their works in Arabi-Malayalam. The emergence of Arabi-Malayalam periodicals and the increased printing facilities had brought about further spurt in publishing such texts. However, Karakkal Mammadu Musliyar's *Vishaviadyam* was the only worthy successor to Bawa Musliyar's works in terms of research and comprehensiveness in coverage. Hakeem P.B. K. Kunhamu Maulawi's work on Ayurveda, *Fawaīdu Mufradātt bi Dalailil Adaviyāt* containing description of 537 *ottamūlikaḷ* also belongs to this category. The list of works on Ayurveda in Arabi-

[63] This was one of the major findings of National Workshop on *Arabic, Arabic-Malayalam, Urdu and Persian Manuscripts in Malabar*, held at the University of Calicut on 7-19 February, 2011. Cited in Yousaf Muhammed Nadwi, "Keralatile Arabi, Arabi-Malayala Vaidyaṣastra Grandaṉal", *Bodhanam*, 29 September, 2014., pp. 94-96.

[64] The word *Asmah* is derived from *Asmahul Husna* or the names of God. This system of medicine, closely resembles to sorcery, is based on the basic belief that reciting and writing the names of God bring cure. See also Nadwi, "Keralatile Arabi, Arabi-Malayala Vaidyaṣastra Grandaṉal", pp.94-96.

[65] Mohamedkunhi, *Musliṉalum Kerala Samskāṟavum*, pp.174-77.

[66] Nadwi, "Keralatile Arabi, Arabi-Malayala Vaidyaṣastra Grandaṉal", pp. 94-96.

[67] P.A. Aboobacker, "śastra Sahityavum Kerala Muslimkalum", *Bodhanam,* Januray-March, 2014, pp. 34-49., p. 45.

[68] Ibid.,p. 46.

Malayalam also includes *Valiya Vaidyasāram* and *Ottamūli* (single medicine therapy-Plate 4.3) and *Bālacikista* (pediatric treatment-Plate 4.4) by C.H. Ibrahim Kutty. Even *Aṣhtangahradaya*- a canonical text in Ayurveda was translated and published in Arabi-Malayalam language by Kunhimayin Kutty Vaidyar.[69]

The science literature in Arabi-Malayalam had been initiated in the late 19th century. The growth of it was substantial in the subsequent decades. The works published in the category of science literature, according to Aboobacker, can be bifurcated broadly into pure and applied science literature.[70] While astronomy and mathematics are considered to be a part of pure science, architecture becomes a part of applied science. However, of the texts of science, astronomy and geography occupied a pivotal position as the daily prayer and major festivals of Muslims are closely connected to the position of Qibla[71], movement of sun and sighting moon. Astronomy is considered to be the most developed branch of science literature in Arabi-Malayalam and the origin of it has been traced back by some of the scholars to a period close to the first work in this language, though there is no material evidence to that.[72]

The most massive contribution to Arabi-Malayalam science literature has, naturally, been by *Ain al-Qibla Vivādam*, a dispute hinging on the actual position of Qibla in the early 20th century. This dispute, in a sense, was a rallying point for a set of theological and scientific discourses to produce a large cache of literature in Arabi-Malayalam. The dispute emerged in early the 1900s, when a group of scholars under the leadership of Mawlana Chalilakath Kunhamed Haji put an argument that the *Salah* or compulsory prayer of a believer would be valid only one performs it facing the exact direction of Qibla.[73] The proponents of *Ain al-Qibla* theory went to the extent of demolishing all the mosques which were not Qibla-facing. The opposite group sticking to the *Jihatul Qibla* theory on the other side argued that it hardly matters whether one performs prayer facing Qibla exactly or not. Even an approximate position would serve the purpose. Quite interestingly, the people who were a part of this dispute were renowned scholars and prolific authors of Islamic jurisprudence, astronomy and mathematics as well.[74]

Scholars lined up in two camps debated openly and such debates often led to the compilation of each group's arguments and publication of it in the book form. The dispute, thus, engendered many interesting works favouring and opposing *Ain al-Qibla* in Arabi-Malayalam. Of which the most prominent was Chalilakath Kunhamed Haji *Ada'wayum Tuhfatul Akhtabum*. This work, analyzing canonical works in this field of Islamic astronomy such as *Ilmul Falakh, Ilmul Hisab* and *Ilmul Meekhat*, substantiated the argument of *Ain al-Qibla*. It also contained *fatwas* by eminent scholars from within and outside India issued in the similar or related contexts. Haji could manage to get fatwa issued in favour of his position from Mecca and Medina.[75] Haji's arguments favouring *Ain al-Qibla* were

---

[69] Ibid., p.44.

[70] Ibid., p. 45.

[71] The direction of Kaaba towards which a Muslim should face while offering *salat.*

[72] Mohamedkunhi, *Musliṅalum Kerala Samskaravum,*pp.174-76.

[73] See M.K. Noushad Kalikavu, "Ain al-Qibla Vivādam: Matavum Ṣastravum Onnica Sandarbam", *Bodhanam*, 29th September, 2014, pp. 57-61, p.58-59.

[74] Ibid.

[75] Kareem, *K.M.Maulawi Jīacaṅtram*, p.32.

augmented further through a series of articles published in an Arabi-Malayalam journal *Maṉiviḷakku* published from Alapuzha.[76] This series included the translation of his own Arabic work *Ada'wa* in Arabi-Malayalam. Apart from these works, arguments and counter arguments of scholars from both sides had been edited and published by P.N.Ahmed Maulawi in the form of an Arabi-Malayalam leaflet entitled *Iṣtihar Adava Viḷambaram.*[77] The opposite group reciprocated it by publishing another work, *Tuhfatul Afbab* by Mangalapuram Denchilpadi Sulyman Musliyar.[78]

Arabi-Malayalam calendar is another major contribution of Mappila Muslims to the field of science literature. It was actually their pressing need to calculate the timing of daily prayer that eventually led to the preparation of this calendar which was otherwise known popularly as *adikkaṉakku bayt*. This calendar which became a part of Arabi-Malayalam literature with its highly poetic nature starts with following lines:[79]

Mēdam va Ciṉ̂am randilum samāniya

fī idavamīnam karkkadatil tāsi'a...

(Seventh in Mēdam and Ciṉ̂am

Ninth in Idavam, Mīnam and Karkkidakam[80])

Although Malayalam names were used for months in the calendar, *rāsis* or zodiac signs have been given Arabic nomenclature. Following are the Arabic names (corresponding Malayalam and English names are also given) for twelve zodiac signs.[81]

Hamal (Médam, Aries)

Sawr (Idavam, Taurus)

Jawsa' (Midunam, Gemini)

Sartan (Karkkadakam, Cancer)

Asad (Ciṉ̂am, Leo)

Sunbula (Kanni, Virgo)

Mīzan (Tulām, Libra)

Akhrāb (Vriscikam, Scorpio)

Khaws (Danu, Sagittarius)

Jadyu (Makaram, Capricon)

Dalvu (Kumbam, Aqaurius)

---

[76] Ibid. p.46.

[77] P.N.Ahmed Maulawi, *Iṣtihar Adava Vilambaram*, (Tirurangadi: Amirul Islma Press, 1910).

[78] Kalikavu, "Ain al-Qibla Vivadam", pp.58-59.

[79] Aboobacker, "Ṣāstra Sāhityavum Kerala Muslimkalum" p. 45.

[80] Mēdam, Ciṉ̂am, Idavam, Mīnam, Karkkidakam are the months in Malayalam calendar.

[81] Aboobacker, "Ṣastra Sahityavum Kerala Muslimkalum", p. 47.

Hūth (Mīnam, Pisces)

However, for *ritus* or seasons, *Adikanakku bayt* depends exclusively on Arabic nomenclature. *Saif, Rabiu, Ṣit'a and Kharīf* are used to mark all the seasons.[82] This calendar continued to be in use until around the middle of the 20th century. The increase in popularity of Gregorian calendar which was of course a corollary of modern education led to its gradual decline. Nevertheless, some of the scholars and mosque authorities in Malabar still use Arabi-Malayalam calendar and the publishers bring out the copies of it almost on regular basis.

3. Documents Legitimizing Doctrinal Claims

As discussed earlier, Hadrami Sayyids and Kondōṭṭy Taṉals with their huge spheres of influence represented two opposite versions of Islam in Malabar for three centuries from the 18th century. The former inculcated the Sunni inclination, transmitting their emphasis on the orthodoxy of the *Shafi* School, the dominant legal school of the Southern Arabia as against the Persian-Sufi orientation of Kondōṭṭy Taṉals. The doctrinal beliefs and practices of the Hadrami Sayyids exemplified a pious orthodoxy, stressing on strict adherence to the Quran, Sunnah and the traditions of the Prophet.[83] The latter have always been under attack by the Hadami Sayyids for their alleged 'Shite orientation'.

Kondōṭṭy Taṉals were an exceptional group forming the only known Perso-Islamic Sufi order in northern Kerala.[84] The Persian speaking Shia Muslim Sheikh Muhammed Shah, who was the founder of this group, therefore, had an alien stature among the Muslim scholars.[85] Some of his practices like the celebration of the Muharram festival and the insistence for the prostration of *murids* or disciples before him often invited popular suspicion of his Shiite lineage.[86] Hadrami Sayyids and *Kondōṭṭy* Taṉals engaged in de-legitimating the claims of each other with fatwas and counter-fatwas. This theological rift which came to be known as *Ponnāni-Kondōṭṭy Kaitarkkam*[87] or factional feud has spawned an extra ordinary amount of interesting documents in Arabi-Malayalam. For the purpose of validating their claims each group managed to get rulings and scholarly opinions on matters of Islamic law from recognized authorities inside and outside India and compiled them in Arabic or Arabi-Malayalam language.

There was an obvious political angle to the dispute between these two groups. While Sayyids of Hadramawt enjoyed a huge sphere of influence among Mappila Muslims, Kondōṭṭy faction gained consistent political support from the colonial rulers. When the British took over the rule of Malabar in 1792, they confirmed the position of Muhmmad Shah as Inamdar,[88] the position which was originally

---

[82] Ibid.

[83] Stephen Dale, *The Māppiḷas of Malabar: 1498-1922, Islamic Society on the South Asian Frontier*, (London: Clarendon Press, 1980).

[84] Miller, Mappila Muslims of Kerala, p. 112.

[85] Ibid.

[86] A.P. Ibrahim Kunju, *Mappila Muslims of Kerala,* (Thiruvananthapuram: Sandhya Publications, 1993), pp. 26-27.

[87] *Kai* refers to faction or order and *tarkam* means dispute in Malayalam Language.

[88] The state dignitary who has been given rent free lands as gifts. See Hussain Randathani, *Mappila Muslims: A Study on Society and Anti-Colonial Struggles*, (Calicut: Other Books, 2007), 51.

granted by Tipu Sultan of Mysore. To reciprocate it, Kondōṭṭy Taṉals were always loyal to the British and were successful in preventing their adherents from participating in the periodic Mappila outbreaks in which Mampuram Taṉals actively participated and taken the leadership role.

As the keepers of Perso-Islamic tradition and with loyalty to the British, Kondōṭṭy faction was able to attract only a miniscule few population in Malabar. Adhered closely to the teachings of Hadrami Sayyids, Mappila *ulema*, anathematized Muhmmad Shah and his disciples as heretics.[89] It was their alleged Shia practices that attracted the wrath of Hadrami Sayyids who succeeded in damaging the legitimacy of Kondōṭṭy Taṉals through a series of *fatwas*. Inclination of Shah towards Shia'sm met stiff opposition from Makhdumis of Ponnāni,[90]another group of diasporic scholars of Arab origin who had maintained strong ties with Hadrami Sayyids. This dispute gained further religious significance with the pronouncement of heresy against Muhmmad Shah by Sheikh Jifri.[91] He criticized Shah and his disciples for their Shia connection, though the latter denied it and claimed to be a Sufi belonging to Sunni sect.[92] His work *Kanz-al Barahin* in Arabic language, calling Muhammad Shah a pseudo-Sufi with an agenda of misleading Muslims of Malabar has been the most prominent work with an overt anti-Shiite nature. [93]

On his part, Muhammad Shah established a *takiya* or commune at Kondōṭṭy with the purpose to propagate his views and to give religious instructions to disciples. Though Muhammad Shah himself rejected a connection with Shiism, Shiite rituals and ceremonies were reported to have followed at Kondōṭṭy. The way, Muharam was observed with a procession bearing close resemblance to *Ashura* along with other practices like the prostration of *murids* before Taṉal, invited a popular suspicion.[94] The most objectionable practices which provoked the Sunni *ulema*, according to Alikutty Musliyar were abstinence from compulsory prayers, women taking pledge by seizing the hands of the Sheikh and using intoxicants like hashish and alcohol by Muhammad Shah and his disciples.[95] Kondōṭṭy faction had given up obligatory prayers during *dikr* or litany and gone to the extent of considering *zakat* and *hajj* not compulsory.[96]

Kondōṭṭy-Ponnani Kaitharkkam has engendered a plethora of literature in Arabic and Arabic-Malayalam defending and opposing the views of each faction. This seminal event also marks an important phase in Arabi-Malayalam literary history. The works came attached to the dispute generally include *fatwas,* counter-*fawatas* and *malas* or devotional compositions that eulogize the life and deed of people from both the factions. The Ponnāni faction with their wider influence, managed to get a set of *fatwas* favouring their position in the dispute form the renowned Arab scholars of that time including the Mufti of Mecca. This can be seen as a part of larger universe of anti-Shia discourse that emerged in the Islamic world. Maulana Khussayi Haji in his Arabi-Malayalam work *Fatwa majuma'*

---

[89] Ibid.

[90] Ponnani, a coastal town in Malabar was the centre of Sunni Orthodoxy led by Makhdums.

[91] A prominent Hadarmi Sayyid scholar reached Malabar Coast in the year 1746.

[92] Randathani, *Mappila Muslims*, p.53.

[93] Sayyid Sheikh Jifri, *Kanz al Barahin,* (MS, 1784).

[94] Kunju, *Mappila Muslims of Kerala*, pp. 26-27.

[95] See Alikutty Musliyar, *Fatwa* (1891), Cholayil Ahammed et. al., *Fatwa al-Radd Kondotty* (MS, 1861).

[96] Randathani, *Mappila Muslims of Kerala,* p. 57.

compiled and interpreted all these fatwas.[97] Mundampra Unni Mammad has composed *Kodikeṭṭa Mala,* a poem with the purpose of exposing the anti-Islamic rituals connected to the annual festival at Kondōṭṭy.

Sheikh Jifris' arguments presented in *Kanz al-Barāhīn* were meticulously countered by another set of Arabi-Malayalam *fatwas* by Kondōṭṭy faction. Muslirakat Aziz Musliyar composed a *mawlīd* entitled *Mohammed Shah Mawlīd* criticizing Jifri and his enthusiasm in indulging into the internal affairs of Kondōṭṭy faction.[98] Quoting Imam Shafi, the renowned Islamic jurist, Musliyar reiterated that "the theologians have nothing to do with the practices of Sufis who are quite immune from the rigidities of *Shariah*."[99] Manuscripts containing these *fatwas* continue to be a great source for theologians in contemporary Malabar on various issues and are, therefore, well preserved in some of the mosque libraries and in private collections for further reference.[100] The alleged Shite practices at Kondōṭṭy takiya, besides provoking many eminent Sunni scholars of Malabar and outside to issue fatwas against them had attracted the notice of scholars and motivated them to participate in the debate by writing leaflets and books.[101]

The most remarkable and comprehensive one in that lot was Ponnani Puthiyakat Musliyar's work answering to the questions and concerns of various sorts on the Kondōṭṭy faction by taking examples and quotations from canonical works in Islamic jurisprudence.[102] Musliyar stressed on the prostration that the *faqirs* at Kondōṭṭy demanded from *murids* or disciples and denounced it as something amounts to polytheism.[103] Pulthodikakattil Ali Musliyar, the then Qazi of Kondōṭṭy takiya responded to it by justifying the prostration before *faqirs* as something sanctified in Isalm. Musliyar writes;

> One should come to know the difference between the prostration before God and respectable persons. The former one, prostration as a part of worship differs from the one that is meant to honour a noble person. Both the prostration as *ibadat* (worship) and *tahiyyat* (honour) are sanctified in Islam.[104]

Another scholar belonging to the court of Kondōṭṭy Taṉals, Koyamutti Musliyar also joined the row and issued a set of fatwas in Arabi-Malayalam giving sanctity to Kondōṭṭy order in general and their allegedly un-Islamic prostration in particular.[105] These fatwas and counter fatwas led further to a series of public debates which ultimately to the publication of a wide range of texts on diverse aspects of Islamic jurisprudence in Arabi-Malayalam language. Musliyarkath Ahmed Kutty Musliyar published a

---

[97] Abu Raseeda, "Cālilakat Kudumbakkār", p. 189

[98] *Mahatāya Mappiḷa Sāhitya Pārambaraym*, p. 318.

[99] Cited in Pudiyakath Bawa Musliyar, *Answer to the Questions of Kunheedu* (MS).

[100] Edathola Bhavanam in Malappuram, mosque libraries of Thanur and Kakkov and are the major keepers of these fatwas in manuscript form.

[101] Randathani, *Mappila Muslims,* p. 58.

[102] Maulawi and Kareem, *Mahatāya Mappiḷa Sāhitya Pārambaraym* Mahataya, p. 318-19.

[103] Puthiyakath Bawa Musliyar, Answer to the Questions of Kunheedu (MS).

[104] Maulawi and Kareem, *Mahatāya Mappiḷa Sāhitya Pārambaraym*, p. 321.

[105] Ibid., p. 321

work, *al-Bustān* presenting the Kondōṭṭy order as a part of broader *Qadiriya* Sufi network.[106] He made trenchant criticism on the attempt of Ponnani faction to portray the faqirs of Kondōṭṭy order-from Mohammed Shah to Ishtiyaq Shah- as Shias. In an act of tit-for-tat reciprocation, Ponnani Puthenveettil Ahmed Musliyar authored an Arabi-Malayalam work entitled *Hayattuddīn Vamamātul Muaniddīn*[107] which was published by Malharatul Muhimmat Press at Talasserry in 1308 Hijra.

4. Literature of Anti-colonial Nature

The anti-colonial Mappila rebellion spanning around two centuries (19th and 20th) also has spawned an extraordinary amount of Arabi-Malayalam literature, especially verses. With massive movements of resistance of Mappilas, Malabar in 19th century was a major theatre of popular revolt against the British in South India. There is ample evidence for direct role of scholars and *ulema* leadership in instigating Mappilas to participate in this revolt. They could convince the need of strong leadership mobilizing local Mappila population at a massive level against the colonizers.[108] Besides the religious positions they maintained, Hadrami Sayyids were also very active in anti-colonial struggles in Malabar. As the charismatic leaders, they gave spiritual benediction to several outbreaks of the Mappilas against the oppressions of colonial powers. Several of their fatwas were instrumental in cultivating a revolutionary spirit among Mappila Muslims of Malabar.

Anti-colonial posture of *ulema* leadership in Malabar, however, traces back to the 16th and 17th centuries when they rose politically first time and became very vocal about the Portuguese oppression against Mappilas. The adoption of themes from Islamic history in the early writings in Arabi-Malayalam like *Mohiyuddīn Māla* was not a natural choice. Publication of a considerably huge body of texts in this language (mainly songs that praise saints and other seminal figures in Islamic history) with themes taken from Arab/ Muslim history during the Portuguese period is seen by many authors as a part of resistance tradition and an attempt in rejuvenating the Mappila Muslim spirit.[109]

Looking at the early anti-colonial literature, one can see that the genesis of which traces back to a poem entitled *Manatparambil Kuññimarakkar Māla*. This work with unknown authorship helped ignite an anti-Portuguese feeling all over the South Malabar.[110] Although the year of publication remains unknown, this work unfolds the legendary life and resistance of Kunhimarikkar of Veliyamkode against the Portuguese.[111] The focal theme of this work revolves around the brave act of the person referred to while attempting to rescue a Muslim girl who was under the captivity of the Portuguese. *Ramantaḷi Māla,* composed in the form of eulogy also has a similar sort of plot to narrate. This work chronicles the adventures of a set of 17 Mappilas from Ramanthali village of north Kerala, who took the mission of taking on the Portuguese militarily when the latter's tyrannous rule exceeded all the limits.[112] This

---

[106] Musliyarakath Ahmed Kutty Musliyar, *Al-Bustan* (MS).

[107] As shown in the text, this work was printed in Muhimatul Press, Thalasery in the year 1891.

[108] M. Gangadaran, "Mampuram Thangalmarude Kalavm Akalavum", in K.K.N.Kurup and P.K.Pokker (eds.) *Mampuram Sayid Fadl Pūkkōya Tangal: Adhiniveṣa Virudha Caritratile Nitya Sānnidyam,* (Thiruvananthapuram: Chintha Publishers, 2006).

[109] Sainuddin Mandalamkunnu, *Mappila Samarangalum Ulema Nethrathwavum*, (Calicut: Nanma Books, 2009), p. 67.

[110] M.P Mujeeb Rahman, "Adinivesavirudda Sāhityam Arabiyilum Malayalatilum", in T. Mansurali (ed.), *Arabi-Malayala Sahityava Padanangal*,pp.26-51, p. 36.

[111] Ibid.

[112] Ibid., p. 38.

māla commemorates the courageous and heroic deed of the people who were killed by the Portuguese before accomplishing their mission.

By the end of the 18th century, Mappila *ulemas* became much more concerned about the injustice committed by the British and launched a tradition of indirect challenges against them.[113] As the pioneer, Sheikh Hassan Jifri set in motion an anti-colonial movement, despite the futile exercise of the British administration to appease him. Inculcating the unity of Mappila Muslims, he stressed on the meaninglessness of petty squabbles among them. Sayyid Alawi who was brought into Malabar from Hadramawt by his maternal uncle Sheikh Hassan Jifri in the year 1768 was the first Hadrami Sayyid scholar who had an open and direct involvement in the Mappila rebellion. His teachings initiated a process of revitalization and regeneration among the Mappilas.[114] As Panikkar notes, "...his (Sayyid Alawi's) emphasis was on self purification – a jihad against *nafs* – which he considered essential for the advance of the community."[115] As the most influential *ulema*, Sayyid Alawi gave spiritual sanctions to several outbreaks of the Mappilas. Sayyid Alawi's booklet in Arabic *al-Saiful Batār*[116] (literally means cutting sword) came out in the context of a series of 'outbreaks' by Mappilas in and around Thirurangadi in 1841 resulting in the martyrdom of eleven Mappilas. Justifying the need of waging a holy war against the British till the end, *al-Saiful Batār* ignited a virulent anti-colonial campaign. Though an unsuccessful effort was made by the authority to search and destroy the copy of it, this book is said to have been circulated widely through mosque networks.[117]

Sayyid Alawi in a set of fatwas staunchly argue that *Jehad* becomes mandatory for the believers in the context of foreign invasion. The questions raised in this work cover a wide range of interesting and unique *fiqh* related issues with deep political undertones. They include: how to deal with the believers of other religions who enter into the land of Islam as invaders; how to treat those (fellow Muslims) who keep a soft and tolerant attitude towards them and mingle with their customs and rituals; is it religiously sanctioned or permissible to live in a place which has been invaded by the Christian colonizers?[118] Quoting verses from the Quran, Sayyid Alawi categorically declares that only aged ones, women and children are exempted; all others have to wage an armed struggle against the enemy (the British) who shattered the livelihood of Mappilas.[119]

In one of the fatwas, he goes to the extent of saying that if one supports the Christian rulers, it amounts to a sin and he should repent for it.[120] Praising the rule of *Kuffar* or the infidel makes one an

---

[113] Mandalamkunnu, *Mappila Samarangalum Ulema Nethrathwavum,* p. 67.

[114] K.N. Panikkar, *Against Lord and State: Religion and Peasant Uprisings in Malabar 1836-1921,* (New Delhi, Oxford University Press, 2001), p. 62

[115] Ibid.

[116] *Sayful Bathar* is a collection of fatwas said to have composed in the context of an uprising in Muttiara of South Malabar in 1841 instigating Muslims to fight against the British regime as their religious duty. To substantiate this argument, quotations from the Quran, Hadith and works of leading scholars of Islamic philosophy have lavishly been used. Sayyid Alawi, *Al- Sayful Bathar* (MS, 1841)

[117] Some of the Mosque libraries in South Malabar have got the copies in possession.

[118] Alawi, *Al-Sayful Bathar,* pp.278-79.

[119] To substantiate his rulings, Sayyid Alawi depends on the rulings of similar nature referred in some of the seminal works in Shafi School of jurisprudence like *Bukhari,Muslims, Tharmudi, Abu-Dawood, Nisaee, Ibn Maja, Mustadarak* etc. See Alawi, *Al-Sayful Bathar*.

[120] Ibid., 26

infidel inviting the wrath of God.[121] To the question about Muslims who approach the court for dispute settlement, he reiterates that those who seek a solution from the court with the belief that the legal code of Christians is better than that of Islam, should be considered as *murtad* or apostate.[122] In a cloaked criticism against the British support of Kondōṭṭy faction, Sayyid Alawi states that accepting the supremacy of Islam parallel to maintaining a belief in the superiority of colonial rulings, according to him, makes one a *fasiq* or unreliable.[123]

After the death of Sayyid Alawi, his son Sayyid Fadl assumed the leadership position and inherited father's spiritual and social status and the legacy of political activism legitimised in religious terms. Sayyid Fadl was quick to use his Hadhrami Sayyid lineage and family clout to politically mobilize Mappila Muslims against the British. By then the British administrators had started exercising more cohesive mode of control and stringent methods in dealing with the Mappila outbreaks. Moved by the deplorable condition of Mappila peasants under the British rule, he focused on the importance of a concerted move and sanctioned it taking cues from the religious texts. It was Sayyid Fadl who translated Mappila grievances into an Islamic idiom which acted as a catalyst to transform widespread discontent into specific acts of social protest. He found the market place a more suitable pulpit than the mosque for indoctrinating Mappilas the spirit of anti-colonialism.[124] Sayyid Fadl justified violent action against the British saying in one of his Friday sermon delivered at Thirurarangadi mosque, "It is not a sin, but a merit to kill a *Jenmi* or upper caste Hindu landlord who evicts the poor tenants from their land."[125]

Through several of his fatwas, Sayyid Fadl stressed more on self-respect of Mappilas and he sanctioned armed attacks on upper caste Hindus and the British administrators who had either insulted Mappila peasants or evicted them from their land. His attitude towards the British rule, however, was not just an extension of his religious beliefs. His anti-colonial doctrine rather had a political dimension also; mobilised Muslim peasants to violent but at the same time religiously sanctified protest. Fadl issued some *fatwas* shedding lights on the anti-Islamic conduct of the British and instituted congregational sermons at different places in south Malabar. In these specially designed Friday sermons, he sought not only to direct Mappilas towards the practice of pious Islam, but also attempted to heighten their awareness of their Islamic identity and how to preserve it in the context of colonial invasion.[126] The sermons were therefore a direct challenge to the authority and position of the powerful upper caste Hindu *Jenmis* and British officials.

Sayyid Fadl's fatwas gained wide popularity among the locals and he was suspected of fomenting many anti-British outbreaks. The officials succeeded in linking the Mappila rebellion of 1843 in particular with his fatwas and teachings. It was in this context, two special commissions were constituted to probe into frequent 'Mappila outbreaks' and Fadl's involvement in each one, in the year 1852. The commission recommended removing Sayyid Fadl to Arabia in order to regulate his

---

[121] Ibdid, p.28, 29, 30, 31

[122] K.K. Mohamed Sathar, *Bā-Alawis of Malabar*, Unpublished Manuscript.

[123] Alawi, *Al-Sayful Bathar,* p.37.

[124] Panikkar, *Against Lord and State,* pp. 61-62.

[125] William Logan, *Malabar,* Vol. 1, (Trivandrum, 1981), p. 691.

[126] K.K. Moahmed Abdul Kareem, *Sayyid Alawi Taṉal* (Venniyur, 1982), pp. 66-67.

teaching.[127] The Malabar District administration also felt the necessity of his eviction on the ground of the reports from below and finally, on the 19th March, 1852 Sayyid Fadl, with a group of fifty seven people set sail for Southern Arabia. Sayyid Fadl has authored almost twenty five works on wide range of topics in Arabic and Arabic-Malayalam. They are mostly fatwas in nature with the special purpose of indoctrinating Mappilas of the ill-effects of colonial rule.

The British administration gradually became aware of the influence of the writings of Mappila ulema and scholars. The overwhelming acceptance of these works invited the wrath of the colonial administration. They banned copies of them and destroyed them physically. Keeping the copies of these works, reading and circulating them became an unlawful activity in Malabar. Some the mosque libraries in South Malabar were raided and copies were confiscated. Nallam Beeran, who composed song on the massacre called Wagon Tragedy[128] and popularised it by singing on stage throughout Malabar was imprisoned by the administration.[129] The battle songs such as *Cērur Padappāṭṭu, Mancēri Padappāṭṭu* and *Mannārkkād Pada* were the major works that attracted the sour notice of the British Administration in Malabar. Each one among these works (detailed discussion on these works has been given in chapter four) based on a particular battle that Mappilas waged against the British was composed with the purpose of cultivating anti-colonial feeling Mappila Muslims.

5. Reform Literature

The Islamic reform movement in Kerala which had a genesis in the 19th century is associated mainly with the names of three scholars-Sayyid Sanaulla Makti Taṉ̂al, Chalilakath Kunhammad Haji, Sheikh Hamadani Taṉ̂al, Vakkom Abdul Kader Maulawi and K.M.Maulawi. But there is an alternative view put forward by Sunni[130] scholars tracing the origin of reform tradition to the early attempts of Hadrami Sayyids who came and settled in different parts of Malabar in the 18th century.[131] As discussed elsewhere, Hadrami Sayyids tried to convert Muslims from semi-pantheist mysticism and bring close to 'pure Islam'.[132] The idea of reform, thus, is deeply dependent on the teachings of scholars and religious leaders who came from the Arab world. Inculcation of *Sharia* and reconfiguration of the rituals and practices of Mappilas within a strict Sunni-Shafiite code by the Arab scholars is considered

---

[127] Letter from H.V.Conolly to T. Pycroft, 30 September 1851, Correspondence of Mappila Outrages, Vol.1, 80-81 & Letter from T.L Strange to T Pyfcroft, 25 September, 1852, CMO, Vol.1, 454.

[128] The Wagon Tragedy refers to the massacre of Mappila prisoners on the 20th November, 2021. The incident happened due to the apparent negligence by the British officers caused the death of 67 prisoners who had been taken into custody and transferred from Tanur to the Central prison in Coimbatore in Tamilnadu.

[129] Mohamedali, *Mappila Pattukal Noottandukalilude*, p.55.

[130] Sunni in the context of Kerala does not refer to the Sunni-Shafi bifurcation in Islam. All Kerala Muslims in that sense are Sunnis belonging to Shafi School of Islamic jurisprudence. Since the rise of reform movement, the term Sunni is used to mean 'orthodox' or traditionalist' Muslims or those who opposed to the tradition of 'reform' introduced in Kerala by a set of liberal scholars. See Filippo Osella and Caroline Osella, "Islamism and Social Reform in Kerala, South India", *Modern Asian Studies* 42, 2/3 (2008) pp. 317-346. , p. 320

[131] The spread of the *Shafii* School in Malabar traces back to Hadrami Sayyids who, in fact, had a particular mission of propagating this school against the encirclement of Hanafism and Shiasm from northern parts of India.

[132] Dale, *The Māppiḷas of Malabar*, pp. 115-16

to be the first concerted attempt along the direction of reform by some scholars.[133] In addition to that we must also take serious account of Islamic revivalism spread across the Indian Ocean region with almost similar sort of movements in Southern Arabia and South East Asia. [134]

Islamic reform in the late 19th and early 20th centuries differed slightly and characterized by some peculiarities and therefore cannot be connected immediately to the corresponding movements in the other communities, mainly Hindu and Christian. The experience varies primarily due to the community formation which was largely a product of oceanic trade and trade-induced cultural linkages between Malabar and the Arab world. So the reform does not appear in the literature not essentially as an engagement with the 'modern' European ideals; rationalism and universalism.[135] In place of it, one can see Islamic world-wide strands for reform, which had often been brought into Kerala by the translated works of West Asian Islamic reformists like Jamal Al-Din Afghani, Mohammed Abdu, Rashid Rida and Qasim Amin.[136] The pioneers of reform movement were directly or indirectly attracted to the teachings or works of these scholars.[137] The branches of Salafism that flourished in Kerala was a syncretic one called *al-Salafiyya al-tanwiriyya* which departed from the literalist theological doctrines and took a position on the importance of independent derivation of legal rulings (*ijtihad*). It was chiefly through *al-Manār,* the mouthpiece of reform movement in Egypt, reformers in Kerala were awakened.[138] Through this journal leaders of reform movement became closely acquainted with the developments in larger Islamic world.[139]

Islamic reform movement in Kerala, in fact, represents an analytically important case as any inquiry leading to comprehend it can be done from different vantage points; of reform and revival; assimilation and puritan. Various ideological streams were coexisting under the common rubric of reform. Being a non-monolithic entity, the movement was equally inspired and guided by the ideas of 'revivalist' scholars like Ibn Taimiyya and his disciples, Sheikh Mohammed bin Abdul Wahab, Shah Waliyullah Dahlavi and Sheikh Ismail Shaheed also.[140] However, all diverse streams converged at a common objective to unite the Muslims of Kerala for a fight against superstitions and un-Islamic practices and beliefs, to cultivate the spirit of Quran and Sunnah among them. Unlike their counter

---

[133] See A.K.Abdul Majeed et al., *Kerala Muslim Navōdhānam: Punaṛanweśaṉatinte Prasakti*, (Kozhicode: Islamic Publishing Beaurau, 2010), O.M. Taruvana, *Wahhābi Navōdhanam Oru Nuṉakkadha,*(Kozhicode: Irsad Book Satll, 2005) P.A. Sadiq Faisy Tanoor, Muslim *Navōdhanam: Vazhiyum Vartamānavum,* (Kozhicode: Sifa BooK Stall,2008).

[134] M.H. Ilias, *Hadrami Sancāṛaṉaḷude Dēsāntara Calanaṉal, Teḷicam* (15th Anniversary Issue), 2013,pp.44-47.

[135] Osella and Osella, "Islamism and Social Reform in Kerala, South India", p. 319. Ilias, *Hadrami Sancāṛaṉaḷude Dēsāntara Calanaṉal*, pp.44-47.

[136] Miller, *Mappila Muslims of Kerala,* p. 270

[137] The roots of the Salafist movement in Kerala go back to the late 19th century, in what came to be known as tanwiriyya or "reformist Salafism," a movement that largely mirrored the reformist Salafist movements that had emerged in Egypt with Sheikh Mohammad Abdu, Sheikh Abd al-Rahman al-Kawakibi, Sheikh Jamal al-Dheen Afghani and Sheikh Muhammed Rasheed Rida.

[138] Maulavi C.K.Shirazi, " Reform Movement in Islam", *K.M.Maulawi Smāraka Grantam,* (Thirurangadi K.M.Maulawi Memorial Trust, 1965), p. 92.

[139] Vakkamom Maulawi and K.M.Maulawi had contributed regularly to *al-Manār* published under the leadership of reform movement in Egypt.K.K. Abdul Kareem, *K.M.Maulawi Jīvacaritram,* (Calicut: Yuvata Book House, 1985).

[140] E.K.Ibrahim Kutty, "The Mujahid Movement and its Role in the Islamic Revival in Kerala" in Asgar Ali Enginner (ed.), *Kerala Muslims: A Historical Perspective,* (New Delhi: Ajanta Publications, 1995), pp. 68-83, p. 72.

parts elsewhere in the world, Salafist movement in Kerala stressed more on promoting 'secular' education among the Mappilas.[141]

The application of reform in individual writings appeared first in the works of Makti Taṉal, a pioneering figure in reform movement. But his teachings exemplified an attempt to undo the effects of European modernity and reform which were prevalent in Kerala society.[142] Problematizing 'modern' for its alleged link with European Christian theology, Taṉal emphasized the need to rejuvenate the tradition of reform absorbing elements from Islam. For him, modernity and reform in their real senses were not essentially European. He rather traced out the roots of them in classical Islamic discourse. The 'secular' essentialism also came under a virulent attack from him. However, his major target was European Christian missionaries, who were engaged in criticizing the fundamentals of Islam and the Prophet in the late 19th century.[143] Upset by traditional Mappila scholars' inability to take on the Christian propaganda, Taṉal resigned from the job of Excise and Customs Inspector under the British rule and devoted himself fully to the task of answering the charges of the Christian missionaries.[144] He established Mummadiyya printing press in the 1891 at Cochin with the purpose of bringing out booklets and pamphlets on regular basis.

Though he regarded the practice of using Arabi-Malayalam as something forcibly imposed by a set of scholars with poor knowledge of Malyalam language, Taṉal made extensive use of it in his attempt to disseminate the ideals of reform. He criticized the scholars who write only in Arabi-Malayalam in harsh and reproachful words and inculcated the need of Malayalam. Taṉal writes in his work *Makti Manakḷēśam*;

> Musliyars (religious scholars) write pretending to have mastered all religious knowledge. But the works they churn out in Arabi-Malayalam are on the basis of what they heard and learnt by heart from the older generation. They write on Islamic jurisprudence and even on intricate slices of Islamic history with a high amount of authoritativeness. These works have misled the ordinary people whose proficiency in Malayalam language is poor. It is so sad to see that people write article in the language sans a basic understanding of syntactical structure, tense and gender. People read it ungrudgingly and religiously only on the ground that they are written by the *ulemas*. This tendency has ruined the common wisdom of the community.[145]

Taṉal had a rare insight and width of vision. Most of the works he authored highlighted the prowess of knowledge and deeper understanding of discourse of 'Islamic modernity.' His concerns have been duly reflected in all his works which were mostly the rebuttals of European modernity a

---

[141] P.M.A. Gafoor, *Kālavum Kālppādum: Kerala Muslim Navōdhanatinte Nāyakaniṟayekkuriccu Vēritoru Anwśaṇam,* (Kozhicode: Yuvatha Book House, 2014).

[142] M.Gangadharan, *"Sanaullah Makti Taṉal: Jṉānam Kondu Porutiya Paṟiśkartavu"*, in in K.K.Moammed Abdul Kareem (compiled), *Makti Taṉaḷude SampŪrṇa Kritikal,* (Calicut, Vachanam Books, 2006), pp. 11-22, p. 13.

[143] Kunju, *Mappila Muslims of Kerlala*, p. 227.

[144] Ibid.

[145] Makti Thangal, "Makti Manaklesam", in K.K.Moammed Abdul Kareem (compiled), *Makti Taṉaḷude SampŪrṇa Kritikal,* (Calicut, Vachanam Books, 2006), pp.687-727, p.700.

corollary of reform in Christianity.[146] Keeping the same objective in mind, Taṉ̂al started an Arabi-Malayalam fortnightly called *Tufat ul-Akhyār wa Hidāyat ul-Aṣrār* which apart from making counter-arguments against the charges of Christian missionaries, severely criticized the inertia of tradition-oriented *ulema* in this issue. *Tufat ul-Akhyār wa Hidāyat ul-Aṣrār* was published using standardized Arabi-Malayalam script. With its sharp and penchant content, this fortnightly became the most popular Arabi-Malayalam periodical.[147]

Though he has written only three books in Arabi-Malayalam (*Ta'lim ul-Ikhwān, Mu'allim ul-Ikhwān* and *Islāmum Marumakkatāyavum*), Taṉ̂al's position in the history of evolution of this language is significant. Towards the objective of making Arabi-Malayalam capable enough to accommodate letters from English and Malayalam languages, Taṉ̂al modified the script system in this language. It was in this modified script, his fortnightly Arabi-Malayalam journal was published.

The first organized attempt along the direction of reform came from *Kerala Muslim Aikya Sangham.*[148] It was from this movement the ideal of reform sprang up in other parts of Kerala. Rather than confining to the realm of religion, the activities of reform movement created a general awakening in all spheres. The movement, of course, aimed primarily at restoring the purity of Islam shearing of beliefs and practices alien to the religion.[149] Simultaneously, the pioneers of it endeavoured in spreading modern education along the religious lines.[150] Besides modernizing the curriculum in *Madrassa*, large number of institutions of 'modern education' was established taking inspiration from the movement. Thanks to the movement of reform, a number of ō*ttupaḷḷis*[151] or traditional institutions for imparting religious education were metamorphosed into Arabic colleges and Arts and Science colleges.[152] Disciplines like geography, astronomy, maths, logic, etc. were introduced to the curriculum, scope which was earlier limited to teaching interpretation of Quran, Hadith, Fiqh or Islamic jurisprudence and Islamic history, etc.[153] Women's education was another priority and special institutions were established in order to accomplish this objective.

The situation remained conducive to the emergence of various genres of expressions in Arabi-Malayalam language. Looking at the reform literature, one can see that there was the revival of Arabi-

---

[146] Gangadharan, "Sanāullah Makti Taṉal", pp. 13-14.

[147] Tuhfatul Akbyār Vahidāyatul Aṣrar is supposed to be the first periodical published using standardized Arabi-Malayalam script.

[148] Founded at Kodungallur, which was then a part of erstwhile princely state of Cochin in 1922 by a group of prominent personalities in the community, *Aikya Sangham* could soon be able to reach out to a wide mass.

[149] Kunju, Mappila Muslims of Kerala, p. 150.

[150] Ibid.

[151] The primary level religious or moral education centres were known as *ōttupaḷḷi* or *ōttupura*. Each *ōttupaḷḷi* tutored by Mollakka or teacher was instrumental in imparting religious education to the Mappila children. The mode of teaching was very simple; the Mollakka recites the lessons from the Quran and other canonical texts and the students repeat it again and again until it was learnt by heart.

[152] E. Moidu Maulawi, *Maulawiyude Atmakadha*, (Kottayam: DC Books, 1985), p. 14.

[153] Though the idea of modernizing religious education came little earlier from Maulana Chalilakath Kunjahamad Haji, the pioneers of reform movement took it forward by introducing a set of new disciplines like Islamic aesthetics. See K.K. Mohamed Abdul Kareem, *K.M.Maulawi Jīvacaritram*, (Calicut: Yuvata Book House, 1985), p.31, Umar Maulawi, p. 95.

Malayalam literature as a part of it.[154] Vakkom Maulawi, with a view to communicate the message with the ordinary people widely and clearly, capitalized the potential of Arabi-Malayalam.[155]Apart from being a pioneer of Islamic reform movement, Maulawi is revered and remembered for taking up the task of translating many canonical works pertaining to Islamic revivalism in Arabi-Malayalam language. This includes Allama Sayyid Sulaiman Nadwi's *Ahlusunnati val Jama't.* Reformist and unorthodox in his ways of and views on Islam, Maulawi wrote *Lawussabāh* introducing the thoughts of pioneers of reform tradition like Ibn Taymiyya and Mohamed Ibn Abdul Wahab.[156] His Arabi-Malayalam journal *al-Islām* came out in five issues functioned as an import tool for the reformists to reiterate the need of a return to the Quran, teaching and practices of the Prophet and the pious ancestors. E.K.Maulawi notes, "...*al-Islām* showed the seed of Islamic reform in Kerala...it (*al-Islām*) created a storm from one end of Kerala to the other."[157] Maulawi's Arabi-Malayalam publications with a reformist tinge also include; the translation of al-Ghazali's *Kīmiyā al-Sa'āda* an abbreviation of *Ihyā UlŪmuddīn* and a monthly journal for the women titled *al-nisa.*

Muslim Aikyasangham the group which spearheaded the reform movement in Kerala launched a tradition of challenges against the religious and social norms for their alleged un-Islamic content. Through a set of publications in Arabic, Malayalam and Arabi-Malayalam, they introduced a new Islamic discourse based on the themes of reason and freedom. In its first annual meeting in 1923, the *Aikyasangham* passed a resolution persuading all its members to engage in promoting the ideals of *Islah* or reform and dispiriting practices that challenge *tawhid* or oneness of God. The presidential speech of Hamadani Taṉal prepared and presented originally in Arabic language was also later on translated and published in Arabi-Malayalam with the title *Kutbātul hamadāniyya.* Followed by it, inculcating the urgent need to fight *bida'* or innovations infiltrated into Islam in Kerala through the local contacts, K.M.Maulawi prepared an Arabi-Malayalam booklet entitled *Alhidāya Ilāmahkhil Bidaivaddwalāla* for wider circulation among the members and sympathizers of the *Aikyasangham.* [158]

The discussions taken place in the first meeting of the organization culminated in the publication of *Aikyasangham's* Arabi-Malayalam mouthpiece, *al-Irṣad* under the editorship of E.K Maulawi another key figure in the Islamic reform movement in Kerala.[159] The exponential growth of reform literature in Arabi-Malayalam made the organization to think of establishing a separate press (Muhiyuddin Press at Eriyad) exclusively for printing and publishing Arabi-Malayalam propaganda literature.[160]

However, the first Arabi-Malayalam periodical with reformist zeal, *Hidāyattul Ikhwān* was published by Sayyid Abdullakkoya Taṉal from Thrirurangadi.[161] Playing a crucial role in the history of reform, *Hidāyattul Ikhwān* engaged in persuading its contemporary Muslim public to shun away from

---

[154] Balakrishnan Vallikuunu, *Mappila Sāhityavum Muslim Navōdhanavum,* (Kozhicode: Yuvata Book House, 2008) & Nediyadi, "SāmŪhika Navōdanatinte Māppilapattukaḷ." pp.231- 32.

[155] M.Muhammed Kannu, *Vakkom Maulawiyum Navōdhana Nāyakanmārum* (Trivandrum: The Author, 1982).

[156] Maulawi, *Ormakaḷude Tīṟatu,* p. 54-55.

[157] E.K. maulawi, "Another New Monthly", October, 1958.

[158] Kareem, *K.M.Maulawi Jīvacaritram,*p. 95.

[159] Mansurali Chemmad, *Islāhi Nayakanmār: Smriti Citraṉal,* (Kozhicode: Yuvatha Book House, 2011)

[160] Kareem, *K.M.Maulawi Jīvacaritram,*p. 95.

[161] Abu Raseeda, "Cālilakath Kudumbakkār", *C.H. Ibrahim Hajji Smaranika-2001,* pp. 192.

the anti-British agitations and to involve deeply in the activities to promote modern education.[162] Sulayman Maulawi established a litho press in Alapuzha called Amirul Islam Press in the year 1894 and published an Arabi-Malayalam magazine called *Maṇiviḷakku* in 1899, perhaps the first initiative in this direction from the southern side of Kerala.[163]

Arabi-Malayalam publications by the leaders of reform movement like *al-Islah,*[164] *al-Ittihād* and *Rafīq-ul-Islām* advanced the ideas of the movement further. Among them, *Al-Islah* was published as both monthly and weekly under the editorship of E. Moidu Maulawi, who was initially a part of religious reform movement but off late became one of the most important figures of the national movement in Kerala. But Maulawi's autobiographical work *Maulawiyude Atmakadha* seems to be a critique of this experience:

> Though they were not at all reluctant to take on tradition-oriented ulemas for their alleged acts of polytheism and innovation, the members and sympathizers of Aikyasangham could not do much on anti-colonial front. Two journals-*al-Islah* and *al-Irṣad* were published by them from Kodungallore, but both could not survive long because of resource crunch and acute infighting within. Nonetheless, through these publications, the Aikysangham has contributed a lot to the process of reform within the community.[165]

Similar sort of issues were also discussed in *al-Murśid,* another landmark in the history of Arabi-Malayalam journalism. This monthly started publishing in the year 1935 by Kerala Jamiyyatul Ulema, an organization of reform-oriented religious scholars took out a twin-edge strategy to fight both un-Islamic beliefs and practices and colonial rule. The contributions to it in each issue maintained enormous amount of diversity. The articles ranged from the translation of *Swahihul Buhāri*, a canonical text in the *hadith* literature and *Attarāwīh*, a work falling under the category of Islamic jurisprudence to the articles analysing the reasons of the community's decline in the construction of knowledge in science and literature during the colonial period.[166] The credit of introducing Sheikh Zainuddin Makdum's legendary work of history in Arabic *Tuhfatul Mujahiddīn* in Arabi-Malayalam also goes to this journal.[167]

It is not surprising that some of the columns like *Quranum Amusliṇalum* (the Quran and non-Muslims) and *Kutuba pariṣkaraṇam* (the revision of Friday sermon) handled monthly by C.N Ahmed Maulawi in *al-Murśid,* indeed had raised many eyebrows within and outside the organization. The translation of Maulana Abdul Kalam Azad's famous interpretation of the Quran, *Tarjumānul Quran* appeared first in this journal published part by part. Al- *Murśid* adopted a firm and consistent position against *kurafāt* or un-Islamic practices on one side and against various sects within Islam like Shia and

---

162 K.M.Naseer, " Arabi-Malayalam Patramāsikakaḷ" in T. Mansurali (ed.), *Arabi-Malayala Sāhitya Padanangal*, (Kozhicode: Lead Books, 2014), pp. 127-132., p. 128.

163 Ibid.

164 See, Maulawi, *Maulawiyude Atmakadha,* p.105. Miller, *Mappila Muslims of Kerala,* p.274.

165 Maulawi, *Maulawiyude Atmakadha,* pp.105-106.

166 *Al-Murshid,* February, 1936.

167 Translation of this work was done by K. Moosan Kutty Maulawi. Al-Murshid published it in parts in 1935., *Al-Murshid,* March, June, July, August, September, October, November, December, 1935.

Ahmadiyya[168] on the other. M.C.C Hassan Maulawi's *Khatimunubiyyin* published in this journal played "a crucial role in creating public awareness against the Ahmadiyya movement which was gaining a rapid acceptance among the Muslims in north Kerala."[169] Publication of this article led to a series of heated public debates and open street-level exchanges of words between the Salafis and Ahmadiyyas which were attended by thousands of Mappilas.

The organization of tradition-oriented religious scholars Samsta Kerala Jamiyyattul Ulema started a new Arabi-Malayalam publication *al-Bayan*[170] in 1929 specifically for taking on the Salafi challenge unleashed through *al-Murśid.* Another periodical *al-Hidāya* started publishing in the same year from Malappuram, spent most of its issues to point out a pressing need of reforming religious education in the context of a rapid spread of modern education in the other communities.[171] The last one in the series of magazines and journals published by the people who were a part of reform movement was *al-Ittihād* published under the editorship of E.K.Maulawi from Thirurangadi in the year 1954 with the intention of augmenting the reformist initiative, which by then had a different trajectory with petty ideological squabbles within.[172] The Sunni groups responded to this move by bringing out another magazine called *al-Burhān* printed at Bayaniya press, Parappanangadi. Published almost around a year under the editorship of eminent scholar, K.P.Moahmmed Musliyar in the 1960s, *al-Bruhan* aimed at remedying the cause lacked by the unavailability of Sunni literature on reform. The tradition of publishing Arabi-Malayalam periodicals, however, ended with *al-Mua'llim* a monthly brought out by Samasta Kerala Islām matavidyabhyāsa Board, an association of Sunni teachers of madrassas in Malabar with the prime purpose to keep apprised its individual members of developments in the field of Islamic jurisprudence. For a considerably long time, *al-Muallim* survived as the lone periodical in Arabi-Malayalam succeeded in negotiating the identity of the language which incurred displeasure from the modernists on one side and the revivalists on the other.

The practices which were regarded as either *Ṣhirk* or polytheism or *bid'a* or innovation came under virulent attack of reformists in the first half of Twentieth century.[173] This period also witnessed the publication of Quran translations with reformist interpretations. Ummar Moulawi's experience of translating Quran[174] in Arabi-Malayalam language in three volumes has been described in his autobiography *Ormakalude Tīratu:*

> There have been many translations of the Quran before. Muslim Literature Society had brought out one in 1940s. But for various reasons, my translation stands apart as what

[168] Ahmadiyya, popularly known as *khadiyanism* is an Islamic religious movement founded in British India in the end of the 19th century based on the life and teachings of Mirza Ghulam Ahmad, who claimed to have raised to the prophet hood towards the end of his life.

[169] Kareem, *K.M.Maulawi Jīvacaritram*, p.112.

[170] This journal edited by Pangil Ahmadukutty Musliyar became the chief medium for disseminating anti-Salafi ideology soon after its inception in the late 1920s. This publication of al-Bayān continued for almost ten years from Maḷharatul Muhimmāt Press at Thirurangadi.

[171] Naseer, "Arabi-Malayalam Patramāsikakaḷ", p.129.

[172] Ibid., 130.

[173] E.K. Ahamedkutty, *Islamum Keralatile Sām Ūhyaparivartana Prastānaṅalum,* (Calicut: Kerala Nadvatul Mujahiddin, 1982).

[174] Ummar Maulawi's translation of Quran in Arabi-Malayalam published by C.H.Mohammed and Sons in six volumes is the most accepted one and is still in wide circulation despite the popularity of Malayalam Quran has recently reduced number of copies being sold out.

the others published in Malayalam and Arabi-Malayalam were mainly reinterpretations, abridgements or retellings. Mine was the first ever complete verse-by-verse translation that followed the same metric patterns and order. I prepared it cutting word by word and giving meaning and interpretations of each word below in Arabi-Malayalam. During those days, Arabi-Malayalam had enjoyed a wider acceptance than Malayalam in the Muslim households. So, my intension was to popularize the reformist interpretation among tradition-oriented Sunni Muslim majority whose education was limited to *dars* attached to the local mosques. The effort yielded desired result. I could understand from the publisher that because of easy to grasp and teach interpretation given in it, this translation has been widely used by the Orthodox ulemas.[175]

With the purpose of getting a wide reach for their message among common people, the leaders of reform movement published most of their early works in Arabi-Malayalam language. Preparation of leaflets containing fatwas in this language was the most valued activity for most of them. K. M. Maulavi, for instance, issued and circulated all his fatwas recalling Muslims to the Quran and the true practices of the Prophet in Arabi-Malayalam in way that would reach the ordinary Muslims.[176] "Since a large number of Muslims were illiterate in Malayalam, the pamphlets meant for massive indoctrination were prepared mainly in Arabi-Malayalam" recalls Ummar Maulawi.[177] Maulawi himself has published at least two dozen pamphlets in this language. His *Irshadul Ikhwan,* a compilation of scholarly debates on Friday prayer published in Arabi-Malayalam, is the most notable one that attracted the wrath of many tradition-oriented scholars. Another major work in Arabi-Malayalam to his credit, *Adkārussalāt* dealt with Salafi interpretation of *namāz* or ritual prayer, the second of the five pillars of Islam.

The leaders of national movement in Malabar also have successfully made use of the fame of Arabic-Malayalam. Some of the works published by them launched scathing attack on the ulemas who were closely adhered to the British administration while others either promoted or disparaged *khilāfat* movement, a pan-Islamic, political protest initiated by Muslims in British Malabar which became a part of the wider Indian independence movement.[178] *Mahakkul khilāfati fi silmil 'kāfa'* authored by a group of ulemas who were a part of national movement criticized both the ulemas who showed strong proclivity towards the British rule and those were the partisans of the Indian National Congress.[179] The publication of it led to the deportation of K.M.Maulawi, who was the lead contributor to this work, from Malabar province which was then under the British rule. The spread of this leaflet also resulted in the rigorous imprisonment and torture of E. Moidu Maulawi as the chief architect of anti-colonial Mappila revolts during the 1920s.[180]

The Muslims leaders of the national movement made it a point to 'mainstream' the language which hitherto was totally sidelined.[181] The popularity of Mappila songs cutting across the religious,

---

[175] Maulawi, *Ormakaḷude Tīṟatu,*pp. 185-86.

[176]Maulawi, *Maulawiyude Atmakadha,* pp. 101-102 & Mohamedkunhi, Musliṉalum Kerala Samskāṟavum, pp. 179.

[177]Maulawi, *Ormakaḷude Tīṟatu,* p. 123.

[178] Kareem *K.M.Maulawi Jīvacaritram*,p.61

[179] Ibid.

[180] Maulawi, *Maulawiyude Atmakadha,* pp.59-63.

[181] Mohamedkunhi, *Musliṉalum Kerala Samskaravum* p. 179.

cultural and class lines made them thinking of composing songs of resistance along those lines. Mappila songs became a major attraction on occasions like meeting to mobilize the public massively. Some of the classic Mappila songs had parodies containing serious political messages.[182] Following was a popular Mappila song composed in the form of an appeal to join the Quit India movement; *"Dēṣiya prastāate vaḷartiya nētakkaḷ/Jayili kidannīunnavaṟe vittidān-/Nammaḷ yojikkuka tammil"* (unite and move together/ for the cause of liberating the leaders/who built the national movement/from the jails).[183]

Majlisul Ulema, the movement came into being under the leadership of leaders of the national movement from the community, published a large number of leaflets and news bulletins with serious anti-colonial political content. *Muslim, Malabar, Islam, Khilafat patrika, Mohammedali* were the prominent ones among them dedicated to disseminate the ideology of the movement.[184] Fearing their intense political content, copies of most of these news bulletins and booklets were either confiscated or set ablaze by the British administration in Malabar. They also took serious note of the theme of each Arabi-Malayalam leaflet published by the pro-Khilāfat ulemas and assigned a wide array of pro-British scholars to respond to them in the same language.

However, the literary works written and published in the context of Islamic reform were mostly satirical songs with an intention to address a specific issue in the society or to target a particular group. Dowry or groom-money system, tomb worshiping and belief in superstitious and supernatural elements became the themes of such songs. Pulikootil Hyder has deftly used his lines for criticizing such issues. Un-Islamic practices borrowed from local customs and other traditions were the major targets of his satirical compositions. Veliyankode Umar Kazi, a prominent scholar from South Malabar composed such a poem to criticize the practice of claiming supremacy on the basis of *taravāditam* or birth to a family of high esteem among Mappilas. Kazi in this work reminds Mappilas of the fact that most of their great grand fathers were converts from lower castes.

Āyā faqirān binnasabi kaifatta fāqiru

va aslukkumu-min qablu tīyyan va nāyaru

va āsari va mūsāri va maṉṉānu pāṉṉanu

va koyappanu ceṯṯiyum va nāyadi parayaru.

(Hey, people who are poor for generations,

think, how did you originate?

Your ancestry traces back to Ezhavas, Nairs,

Carpenters, Blacksmith, Mannan, Pananan,

Koyappan, Ceṯṯi, Nāyāi and Parayas.[185]

---

[182] Ibid.

[183] Ibid.

[184] Kareem, *K.M.Maulawi Jīvacaritram*,p.63.

[185] Castes with lower social stature in the hierarchy.

Some blind beliefs and rituals also have attracted the wrath of social reformists. The protest against *katukut kalyāṇam* or ear-boring and *mārkka kalyāṇam* or male circumcision has culminated in writing almost half a dozen works. Of which Marakkar Musliyar's work is a diatribe to the celebration associated with ear-boring.

Kātukut tanne harāmennu vekkumbō

pinnentu kalyāṇamenna cōdyavum.

Mutupēṭakku pōyavar vane

muẓhuvanum kalavennu pularnne.

Ataram tanne kūṭṭayi veḷḷam,

atināl pularnatum kallam.

Etere janam accatīl peṭṭe,

ende pinne atokkeyum kette.

(When ear-boring is forbidden,

question arises then why should it be celebrated.

Those who visited Muthupetta[186] on divine trip

were later on realized it was a big fraud.

Who went for seeing 'divine' water in Kuttayi[187]

were also cheated.

So does happen with those who follow wrong traditions.)[188]

T. Ubaid, Punnayurkkulam Bappu, Mehar and Marancherry Marakkar Musliyar were the notable Mappila poets who have contributed enormously to the development of this genre. Kottakunnan Moahmed of Kondōṭṭy alias Pulavar Mohammed has written a poem entitled *Peṇkeṭṭu Niścayam* criticizing unnecessary functions conducting in connection with Muslim marriages in Malabar. The target of satirical songs also included priesthood in the community and the exploitative activities that they are engaged in, factional feuds and the slandering campaigns that the Muslim organizations launched against others, gender issues etc.

The nature of reform literature, thus, varies from simple efforts to criticize *taklid* or blind beliefs and superstitious practices to the massive indoctrination supporting the reformist ideology of Salafism which had a lively spread during the first half of twentieth century.[189] Pulikottil Hyder and

---

[186] A place with supposed divinity in Tamil Nadu.

[187] The place belonging to South Malabar was famous for its 'divine' water which people of the locality believe brings cure to serious illness.

[188] Maulawi, *Maulawiyude Atmakadha*.

[189] Salafism, a rendering of the Arabic word salafiyya- is a generic term with a wide variety of connotative meanings. Primarily, it refers to the salaf al-salih or "pious ancestors", a designation for Sahaba or the companions of the Prophet Mohammed and the first three generations of Islamic scholars. Salafism calls for a return to the tradition of the Quran,

Marakkar Musliyar were the two eminent poets intimately associated with this movement. Hyder's poems with a definite aim of reforming the Mappilas included *Durācara Māla* (a song exposing the un-Islamic practices involved in many rituals popular among Mappilas), *Kaliyugam, Kātukuttu Māla* (a song on ear-piercing) and *Strīmardi Māla* (a poem composed against women battering).[190]

Kāt kuttum bida'tum kondu!!a

Cétam peruttundu kékkuvin-koncam

Ōtunnita khabarākkuvan.

Kālacerupatil penkuttikaḷe,

Kōlam kedutātirikkuvin-anta

Vēla īn̄enkilum pōkkuvin.

(Listen a while to the ill-effects of

ear-piercing and other bida't (innovations),

that I am reciting for your appraisal.

It is high time to stop this wrong custom,

which mutilates the beauty of young girls.[191]

Subscribed to the ideology of reform, the poems like *Aikya BhŪṣhaṇam* and *Kurāfat Māla* (N. Kunhikammu) and *Kodikutu Māla* (Kannan Pareekutty) launched virulent attacks on the anti-Islamic rituals associated with *nērcaa* or annual *urs*-like offerings at the shrines of the saints and tomb worship. The reformist literature in Arabi-Malayalam was effectively countered by 'orthodox' poets. In their attempt to defend traditions, they despised the revivalist ideologies (mainly Salafism and its variant Wahhabism[192]) as *bid'a* or innovation. Kadampattu Alavikutty's *Pariṣhkaramāla* published in 1932 disparaged the ideology of Mohammed Ibn Abdul Wahab for spreading *fitna* or rebellion against the rightful way. In an act of reciprocation, the reformist poet Hyder in the same year wrote *Pariṣkara Gaṇdanakāvyam* critiquing the efforts of conservative poets to ridicule Wahhabism.[193]

Hadith and the salutary example of pious epigones (the Salaf) who learned about Islam directly from the Prophet or those who had first-hand experience of the rise of Islam and commanded a pure understanding of the religion.

[190] M.N. Karasserry, "Preface", in C.N.Ahmed Moulavi and K.K.abdul Kareem, *Mahatāya Mappiḷa Sāhitya Pārambaraym,*(Calicut: Authors, 1978),p. XVI.

[191] Lines from Hyder's *Kātukutu Māla* criticizing a popular custom called Katukutu or ear-boring.

[192] Wahhabism a variant of Salafism associated with the eighteenth century Saudi scholar Mohamed ibn Abd-al Wahab adopted a form of formalism on the top of literalism. Wahhab's main concerns were related to the centrality of *tawhid* or monotheism and the dangers posed to Islam by *bid'a*. He firmly held the view that Muslims had become ignorant of their religion and were living in a barbaric stage of *jahiliyya* or ignorance.

[192] For him, the only way to regain and retain the past glory of Islam was the reassertion of *tawhid*--absolute monotheism-as the basis of the Islamic creed and a return to *the Quran* and *Sunnah*.

[193] Maulavi and Kareem, *Mahatāya Mappiḷa Sāhitya Pārambaraym*, pp. 532-35.

A collection of poems titled *wahhabi radd,* countering the arguments of reformists was composed in Malabar during the middle of the 20th century.[194] Even before this work, Samasta Kerala Jamiyyatul Ulema, a collective of tradition-oriented ulema had brought out a huge cache of Arabi-Malayalam literature with a view to establish that the Salafi scholars have been drifted away from the fundamentals of Islam and thereby to delegitimize their claims of reform. Of which the most noteworthy one was *Raddul Wahhabiyya* a treatise composed by Karimpanakkal Cundaṉ̂ayil Moidheenkutty Musliyar in 1928.[195] Provoked by the arguments presented in this work, K.M. Maulawi has written, at least, three Arabi-Malayalam works taking cues from the Quran and teachings of the Prophet. Each of which is still in wider circulation and being used by the Salafi scholars as canonical texts.

Despite the consistent effort from tradition-oriented ulema to forestall its further encirclement, the influence of reform began to spread throughout the Muslim pockets in Kerala. The winds of reform during the 1930s left no field including economy untouched. Deeply felt by the necessity of a process to mobilize the poor Muslims economically, new initiatives were introduced. Consistent debates on this issue finally ended up in establishing a faith-based interest free banking on the basis of Islamic principles.[196] E. Moidu Maulawi notes;

> K. M. Maulawi was asked to issue a *fatwa* by those who took initiative to establish it (the bank). Orthodox factions increasingly took an open stand against banking and criticized it for promoting interest. A rift was developed within the reform movement as some of the people inside openly criticised the idea of banking. The fissure led to war of words within the movement and also on several occasions to open demonstrations against the bank by the people within.

However, the leaders of the movement under the strong back up of K.M. Maulawi who had by then enjoyed an undisputable position in the community because of his deep knowledge of Quran, Hadith and Islamic jurisprudence. Maulawi issued a fatwa favouring it and published an Arabi-Malayalam work *Risālatun filbānk* legitimizing the endeavour to establish the bank taking materials to substantiate it from the canonical texts of *Shāfi* jurisprudence.

---

[194] PP Abdul Razak, *Cololialism and Community Formation in Malabar*, unpublished PhD Thesis, University of Calicut, 2007, p.17.

[195] Kareem, *K.M.Maulawi Jīvacaritram*, p. 94.

[196] Maulawi, *Maulawiyude Atmakadha*, p. 105.

5

Poetical and Peformative Imaginations: Mappiḷappāṭṭu Tradition

1. Mappila Songs

The literary corpus that contains Arabi-Malayalam songs is generally termed as *Māppiḷapāṭṭu* or Mappila Songs.[1] Though indeed closely related to performance, the term Mappila Songs also refers to literary compositions in prose or in poetic form consciously composed for artistic consumption rather than for performance. The aspirations, angers, agonies, struggles, imaginations and other emotional aspects of the Mappila community have been reflected in Mappila songs.[2] Mappila songs are being transmitted, generally, in two ways; oral and written. The textual tradition used Arabic-Malayalam language in preparing the lines and the songs which are preserved in booklets and leaflets and kept in Muslim households, are generally called *sabīna ēdu* or pages of *sabīna*. Women are the main keepers of this tradition and they actively engage in preservation and dissemination of Mappila songs either orally or in writing.

There are several publications of Mappila songs and in each the general tendency is to classify the songs according to their contents. In northern Malabar, there was a tradition of *pāṭṭu kacavadakkār* or song traders who were embarked on the mission of promoting *māppiḷapāṭṭu.*[3] The poet/trader composed poems and sold handwritten and printed copies throughout Malabar. The poet in this case takes the roles of composer, publisher and trader of his/her own poem.

Foreign words are abundantly seen in *māppiḷapāṭṭu*. As Fawcett observes:

> The songs are written in Arabic character and their language is a curious polyglot patois of Malayalam, the local vernacular, Tamil, Telugu, Hindustani, Arabic and many other tongues, a word of which is here and there brought in for some special use.[4]

---

[1] O.Abu, *Arabi-Malayala Sāhitya Caṛitram,* (Kottayam: NBS, 1976) & M.N.Karaserry, "Māppiḷapāṭṭu", in Raghavan Payyanadu, *Kerala Folklore,* (Payyannur: Folklore Fellows of Malabar, 1997).

[2] K.K.N.Kurup, *The Legacy of Islam: A study of the Mappila Muslims of Kerala*, (Kannur, Samayam Publications, 2006), p. 19.

[3] Abdullah Abdul Hameed, *Ndauthoppil Abdullah's Akbar Sadaqa Pakshipattu,* (Kasargod: Central University of Kerala, 2012), p.9.

[4] F. Fawcett, "A Popular Mopla Song", *Indian Antiquary*, March 1899, p.64.

In order to be in tune with the rhythm and rhyme scheme of the composition, poets sometimes choose appropriate words from any language irrespective of the nature of that language. Composers often break the boundaries of languages to make the song more appealing. So, a song in Arabi-Malayalam language in normal case possesses words from at least three or more languages.

Mappila poets compose and sing songs on the occasions of wedding, pulling carts, travelling and harvesting. Songs sometimes create motivating ambience for collective works[5]. Though they are composed by a single person, Mappilas songs are not meant for silent or loud solo reading, but for singing collectively.[6] Poets address people in group and expect a collective listening while composing their works. *Māppiḷapāṭṭu* in that sense sometimes turn out to be performing arts with collective singing, clapping and body movements accompany them.[7] There was a tradition in most parts of Malabar among men and women to sit together in horse shoe shape and sing *sabīna* songs. Knowledgeable among them interpret the inner meanings of each line in lucid and simple language for those who do not able to follow the essence of songs.[8] The centres for imparting courses in *māppiḷapāṭṭu*, called *makhāni* had existed in different parts of Malabar. T. Ubaid has given instances of such *makhāni* in Thalankara of Kasargod district that continued to exist until recently.[9] Singing *māppiḷapāṭṭu* in chorus was a valued pastime among those who were engaged in *beedi* making and fishing. The eldest ones sing songs and explain the meaning to others. This tradition is believed to have come to Kerala from Tamil poets of Coromandel Coast.[10]

The origin of *māppiḷapāṭṭu* tradition stretches back to the advent of *bayth* or Arabic poems which happened almost parallel to the establishment of Arab settlements in Malabar in the 12th century.[11] Arabic poems which were in wider circulation in the Indian Ocean region said to have mingled closely with the ballads of Malabar to give birth to first generation Mappila songs.[12] Later on, they took elements from entire corpus of folk traditions prevailed in Kerala and displayed a great deal of diversity in choosing the rhythms. Appropriated themes and lyrics from the daily life of ordinary people, Mappila songs had always been in conflict with the elitist conception of poetry and music.

At the most obvious level, almost all the folklores including *Kuratipāṭṭu, Puḷḷuvanpāṭṭu* and *Pāṉarpāttu*-musical performances mainly of the lower castes of Malabar found expression in Mappila songs.[13] Presenting the story in the cultural milieu of Kerala Muslims, Mappilas have prepared an alternative version of Ramayana in Arabi Malayalam using their own artistic resources and imaginations. This Ramayana is composed strictly according to the poetic rules in Arabi-Malayalam with lots of funs and satirical references to plots in the original Ramayana. Though there are no clues to the precise origin,[14] this work had made the rounds for many years as a ballad and good humoured

---

[5] Karaserry, "Māppiḷapāṭṭu", p.53.
[6] Ibid.
[7] Ibid.
[8] V. P. Mohamedali, *Mappiḷa Pāṭṭukaḷ Nūṯṯāndukaḷilūde*, (Kottayam: Current Books, 2007), p.23.
[9] See T. Ubaid Smaraka Grandham, p. 182 cited in Mohamedali, *Mappiḷa Pāṭṭukaḷ Nūṯṯāndukaḷilūde*, p.23.
[10] Ibid.
[11] Ibid.
[12] P.K.Mohamedkunhi, *Musliṉalum Kerala Samskaravum*, (Thrissur: Kerala Sahitya Academy, 2008), p. 181.
[13] Interview with Balakrishnan Vallikunnu, a scholar of Mappila Pattu by the authors held on 18th March, 2013.
[14] There are two views regarding the period of Mappila Ramayana. Some scholars hold the view that this work is not very

parody.[15] The compilation of this work in the present form was done some 80 years ago by T.H.Kunhiraman Nambiar.

Pandu tadikkaṟan awliya padivanna pāṭṭu

kēṭṭatalle nāmmaḷī Lāmāyanam[16] Kada pāṭṭu.

Karkidakam katu katu kutiṟikkum pāṭṭu,

kātu ṟandilum viṟal celutitu orikūṭṭum pāṭṭu.

(The song sung by a bearded awliya (saint) during the olden days,

The song Ramayana story song, we used to listen to...

The song, waiting for heavy rain to come,

The song sung keeping fingers in both ears.[17])

"Mappila songs, however, cannot be put under the rubric of folklore, though there are consistent efforts from the scholars for doing so", argues Mohamedali.[18]He tries to substantiate this argument on the ground that Mappila songs are not composed extempore but meant for singing on certain occasions. For the purpose of maintaining aesthetic standards, they follow some strict rules. The factors which make Mappila Songs different from others are; themes are normally related to the historical past and present of the Mappila community; the rhythms follow certain patterns specific to Arab-Mappila tradition; the vocabularies are not loaned from a single language but a set of languages and the lyrics are reflective exclusively of community's imagination.[19] *Māppiḷapāṭṭu* encompasses an eclectic mix of identities - Arab, Kerala and Mappila.

The number of published Mappila songs in Arabi-Malayalam, according to Ubaid is around four thousand, but Pillai contradicts this figure in his work by suggesting a number around five thousand.[20] Many Arabi-Malayalam songs which were popular once did not caught the attention of the public and many authors were disappeared unnoticed because of not getting printed and republished.

Among the first generation of Mappila poets of the 19th and 20th centuries, Moyin Kutty Vaidyar of Kondotty, Ahmed Kutty Molla of Ponnani, Kunjayan Musaliyar (whose works kappāpattu and Nūlmālal have been discussed about in this chapter) Abdul Qadir Mastan (the author of many philosophical songs) Chettuvay Pareekutty (Fathuśām) were the prominent ones who inspired the generations to follow. Of this lot, the most renowned was Vaidyar whose fame came chiefly from Badarul Munīr-Hussanul Jamāl, a kessupāṭṭu that pushed the boundaries of Mappila imagination

old as the language of it appears to be a standardized one while the others argue that the standardization happened while copying it. Mohamedkunhi, *Musliṉalum Kerala Samskaravum* p. 183.

15 Mini Krishnan, "Remembering Mappila Ramakatha in Ramayana Month", *The Hindu,* 31 July, 2016.

16 The letter 'L' has been used in place of 'R' throughout the text. The opening stanza of Ramayana, therefore, becomes "Sreelama! Lama! Lama-Lama, Sreelamachandra Jayaa...". Krishnan, "Remembering Mappila Ramakatha in Ramayana Month"

17 As sung by Bharthan, a perfomer of Mappila Ramayana.

18 Mohamedali, *Mappiḷa Pāṭṭukaḷ Nūṯṯāndukaḷilūde*, p.23.

19 Ibrahim Bevincha, *Varadhyamadhyamam*, 22 April, 2001

20 Erumeli Parameswaran Pillai, *Malayala Sāhityam Kālagaṭṭaṉaḷilūde*, (Kottayam: Current Books, 1998), p.155.

beyond Arabic bayts and devotional compositions like mālas with highly romantic lines. The credit of revitalizing the language which was in a moribund state under the colonial dispensation and shaping it to a language of de-colonization through dozens of war songs goes to none other than Vaidyar.

The second wave of Arabi-Malayalam poets in the early 20th century included Kunhammad Koya (whose fame is associated with the Oppana song taśrif); Mankkantakathu Kunihkkoya Thangal of Kuttayi (the author of Nasīhath māla); Naduthoppil Abdulla (Akbar Sadaqa Pakṣipāṭṭu); Kulangarveettil Moidu Musaliyar (Safalamāla) and Nallalam Beeran. The third phase was represented by an array of women poets like P.K.Haleema Beevi (Candirasundari māla), Naduthoppil V.Ayishakutty (Paẓhaya wafātmāla of Fatima) and Kundil Kunjamina (Sarabi's Kissa) who left remarkable imprints in Arabi-Malayalam literature. The list also includes the major Mappila poets of bygone era like Chakkiri Moidheenkutty (Cākkiri Badṛ) Mundambra Unni Mohammed (Karbala) and Pulikottil Hyder (composer of many popular songs).

The current phase of evolution of Mappila songs traces its origin to the 1970s. This period also witnessed a massive exodus of Mappila Muslims to the countries of Persian Gulf. Oil boom generated economic development in the Gulf and economic slump in the state of Kerala were the major pull and push factors that fostered the process of migration.[21] The *mappila* songs that were sung at homes and on special occasions in the past, began to find their way into stage shows in Kerala and the Gulf where they had massive audiences.[22] Music clubs in Malabar also were instrumental in promoting this tradition of concerts fully equipped with supporting musical instruments. A new generation of singers like V.M.Kutty, Edava Basheer, Peer Mohammed, S.A.Jameel and Ramla Beegum emerged with fame that spilled over even to the Gulf countries. Stage shows and audio-cassettes became the most popular tools for the dissemination of Mappila songs.[23] That tradition continued to flourish with a long army of contemporary Mappila poets like P.T.Abdul Rahiman, Kanesh Punur, O.M.Karuvarakkkundu, Bappu Veliparambu, etc.

Parallel to this, since the 1950s, Malayalam film industry also has played a crucial role in making Mappila songs popular in the Malayali public sphere.[24] Most of the Malayalam films in the 1950s, '60s and '70s had at least one Mappila song and each one of them was well-liked by the public. This is very much evident from the popularity of the song composed by P.Bhaskaran for the film *Nīlakkuyil* came out in the year 1954.

Kāyalarikatu valayeriñappoḷ
vaḷa kilukkiya sundaṛī...
Peṇṇukettinu kuriyedukkumbo-
ḷoru narukkinu cerkkaṇē.

[21]B.A. Prakash, "Impact of Foreign Remittances: A Case Study of Chavakkad Village in Kerala", *Economic and Political Weekly,* 13 (1978), pp.3210-15

[22]Umar Taharamel, "Māppiḷapāttu-Performancite Sādyatakaḷum Prasnavalkaṛanavum", in T.Mansurali, (ed.), *Arabi-Malayala Sāhitya Padanangal*, (Kozhicode: Lead Books, 2014), pp.53-54.

[23] Ibid, p. 54.

[24] Faisal Elettil, in T.Mansurali, (ed.), *Arabi-Malayala Sāhitya Padanangal*, (Kozhicode: Lead Books, 2014), pp.98-102.

(The pretty lady, who shook the bangles,

while throwing net on the lakeshore.

Make me a part,

while you draw the lot on the occasion of wedding.)

This song composed adhering to the style and structure of Mappila songs, was well-received not as a film song, but as a Mappila song in a film. However, it may be naïve to say that this distinctivess of Mappila songs were well-accepted during that period. As what happened to Arabi-Malayalam literature, Mappila songs in Malayalam films were also approached from a distance and gingerly held out at an arm's length by the cultural theorists. Ironically enough, Mappila songs composed by the renowned music director of Malayalam cinema, M.S.Baburaj failed to gain critics' praise while most of his songs belonging to genre of film songs attracted wide acclaim.

But, sociologically speaking, besides serving some artistic functions, Mappila songs in these films provided an avenue for identification for the people of lower strata as the other songs were literarily high-sounding and beyond the reach of their imagination. In a very apparent manner, the language (often highly sanskritized) and imagination in most of the songs of this period made them alien to the ordinary people. Mappila songs, on the other hand, with their widespread cultural elements that were perpetuated through a society's vernacular language, could make deep inroads into the popular imagination. A crucial contribution to the filmy- Mappila song-genre was made by Mehboob, the renowned Malayalam play back singer whose songs finding specific roots in lived cultures of ordinary people had obviously set in motion a new trend in Malayalam film industry in the 1960s.

The tradition is continuing to find its place in the recent films also. *Appaṉaḷellam Cuṭṭammāyi*, a song falling under the category of traditional wedding song recently got a reincarnation in digital form in a Malayalam movie *Ustād Hotel* (2012). [25] Similalry, some of the old compositions in Mappila songs also are staging a comeback through the reality shows on Malayalam televison channels. In theatre also, with language close to the life and not-so-complicated lyrics, the songs which were composed following the styles and meters of Mappila songs outnumbered the songs that adhered to the classical tradition.

It is also interesting to know about the technological sophistications and the means through which these sophistications engendered and developed new genres in Mappila songs. The development in communication technology and new media now play a key mediatory role within an expanding arena of Mappila songs. The trajectory began with radio and gramophone records. [26] Although there was a state monopoly over it, radio had been utilized at its maximum for the dissemination of Mappila songs. Music companies such as HMV and Columbia had a crucial role in electronically popularizing the songs which were once transmitted only through small gatherings of music lovers called *Sīra pāṛāyaṇa sadassu.*[27]

---

[25] Tharamel, "Māppiḷapāttu-Performancite Sādyatakaḷum Prasnavalkaṛanavum", p.53.

[26] Ibid., p. 52.

[27] The singers on such occasions used to sing the songs and interpret them for the general public in simple manner.

In the late 1970s and '80s audio-cassettes emerged as a major electronic tool for ideological indoctrination and a vehicle for the transmission of Mappila songs. This development was closely paralleled everywhere in the Islamic world. Cutting across the denominational lines, compositions of renowned musicians and sermons and speeches of scholars recorded in audio-casttes caught up the popular imagination and listening to such songs and sermons became a common and valued activity for millions of ordinary Muslims around the world.[28] During this period, sermon tapes provided one of the prime means by which Islamic moral/ethical traditions have been recalibrated to a new political order.[29] While cassette sermons in the Arab world became associated with a miniscule few groups of Islamic preachers, audio-cassettes have spawned interesting literary genres in Kerala; *Kattupāṭṭukaḷ* -- letters sending in the form of recorded song to spouses and parents back at home have been the most dynamic one.[30] The popularity of audio-cassettes also served the purpose of giving public prominence to new breed of singers like V.M.Kutty, Ernajoli Musa, Peer Mohammed, etc. with high competency in singing in the company of well equipped orchestra. This development also marked the beginning of a new tradition, Mappila *Gānamēḷa,* on-stage performance of singers with western musical instruments.[31]

In the late 1990s, the Internet quickly became one of the most important tools for both ideological indoctrination and transmission of Mappila songs. The *māppiḷapāṭṭu* singers soon realized the potential of this new space and astonishing amount of songs were put online. As happens elsewhere, new media have now provided many singers with an intermediate virtual space between them and the fans in the GCC countries beyond the physical one. The extensive application of new media as a means of transmitting Mappila songs represents a technologically adept integration of communty's imagination and non-traditional ways of expressing it. This development is more conspicuous with the non-film music albums and Youtube clippings and other related sites of musical expressions on the net. Not only were Mappila songs lending themselves to popular forms of romantic music, but old ballads and narrative poems were beginning to be revived in newer modes of rendition and preserved in the form of digital technology as repositories of social memory. Even *Mohiyuddīn Māla* a long poem composed in the 17th century influenced by Sufi thought has acquired various new styles of recitation on the websites.[32] Thus with the new *Mappila* cultural forms of expression emerged in the wake of new media, there began to be laid the foundations for the institution of a non-film based cultural industry that has survived quite lucratively in a society hitherto dominated by the cultural hegemony of its regional film industry.

---

[28]The reason for rapidly increasing popularity of cassettes partly remained 'political'. Iranian revolution and the circulation of Ayathollah Khomeini's recorded audio-cassette messages played a key role in the mobilization of radicals in the Islamic world.The menacing image of the cassette sermon as a symbol of Islamic fanaticism, according to Charles Hirschkind, "goes back to the 1979 Iranian Revolution, when the circulation of Ayattollah Khomeini's recorded missives played a key role in the mobilizations leading up to the overthrow of the Shah. See Charles Hirschkind, *The Ethical Soundscape: Casette sermons and Islamic Counterpublic* (New York: Columbia University Press, 2006), pp. 2,4.

[29] Ibid., p.2.

[30] Prema Kurien, *Kaleidoscopic Ethnicity: International Migration and the Reconstruction of Community Identities in India,* (Rutgers: Rutgers University Press, 2002).

[31] Tharamel, "Māppiḷapāttu-Performancite Sādyatakaḷum Prasnavalkaṛanavum", p.53.

[32] Ibid., p. 55.

2. *Eśals* or *Rāgās*

The rhythm in *māppiḷapāṭṭu* is called *eśal.*[33] There are hundreds of *eśals* known in various appellations like *tonkal, kombu, oppanacayal, oppanamurukkam, virutam,* etc.[34] The influence of Arabic songs was very much evident in the early *eśals*. The first work in Arabi-Malayalam verse, *Mohiyuiddīn māla* was composed in this tradition. But, the later compositions did not take long time to be free from the orbit of Arabic songs and more close to Dravidian style. Now *māppiḷapāṭṭu* characterizes a dynamic convergence of Arabic and Dravidian *eśals*. Since the rhythm is very important in *māppiḷapāṭṭu*, rhyme schemes carry much of weight. *Kambi, kaẓhutu, valkambi, valummal kambi* are the major rhymes schemes. The rules related to the rhyme schemes are borrowed mainly from Tamil and Arabic traditions.[35] *Kambi* refers to the scheme in which the first word in all the second halves would end with the same sound. In *Kaẓhutu* this rule is applicable to all the second words in the fourth line. *Vālkambi*, which is derived from Arabic song tradition, denotes to the scheme seen with the last words.[36] The scheme in which a new stanza starting from the last word or a group of words used in the previous one is known as *valummalkambi*.

There are almost five hundred *eśals* or ragas said to have existed in Arabi-Malayalam. Each *eśal* is based on a rhythm. So the change of rhythm creates a new *eśal*. The *eśals* are generally flexible and it is this flexibility that makes *māppiḷapāṭṭu* more enjoyable and attractive. The composition of *eśal* also requires high amount of creativity and imagination. Following are some of the *eśals* widely used in composing *māppiḷapāṭṭu: Akabalippu, Tongal, Ceruṭṭonkal, Oppanaṭṭonkal, Birutam, Arabirutaṃ, Adikabirutaṃ, ceruvirutaṃ, Cāyalbirutaṃ, Oṭṭabirutaṃ, Tālarbirutaṃ, Tudarbirutaṃ, Asudbirutaṃ, Tuḷḷalbirutaṃ, Koncalbirutaṃ, Pukarbirutam, Kalakabirutam, Kavibirutam, Bērbirutam, Cāyal, Cāyal Irakkaṃ, Onnāṃccel, Randāṃccel, Mōnaṃccel, Nālamccel, Ancāmccel Cāyal Murukkaṃ, Arāmccel, Pathamccel, Tiruppukal, Caralam, Eamānkavi, Kavi, A'di Antaṃ Onnēkal, Onnāṃtudi, Randāṃtudi, Mōnnaṃtudi, Nālaṃtudi, Elāmtudi, Kombu, Kombu Caaralaṃ, Kombu Cāttaṃ, Tālelaṃ, Talelachāl, Kavitālelaṃ, Padaṃ, Ceruccintu, Nādabāmbu, Ōśanada, Aruḷnada, Cerunada, Cayippu, Cintucayippu, Poncayippu, Iraṭṭakavi, Oppanacayal, Oppanamurukkam, Kammi, Cembaka, Madirakavi andKessu.*

3. *Mālappāṭṭukaḷ*

The most significant form of verse tradition in Arabi-Malayalam is *mālas* or song stories which commemorate the miraculous stories of Muslim saints or heroic events in the history of the community. The genesis of this tradition stretches back to *Mohiyudddīn Māla* which is believed to have composed in AD 1607 by Khazi Mohammed of Calicut. This popular devotional classic depicts the history of the famous Sufi saint Sheikh Mohiyuddīn Abdul Kader of al-Jilani of Baghdad, the founder of *Qādiri* order. It predates five years to Thunchathu Ramanujan Ezhuthachan's *Adhyātma Rāmayanaṃ Kiḷippāṭṭu*, which was supposed to be the first literary work in Malayalam language that conforms to the standard norms. Though the genesis of this tradition stretches back to *Mohiyudddīn Māla,* the

---

[33] The term eśal, according to Mohammedkunhi, is derived from the Tamil word *eyal*. Mohammedkunhi, *Musliṃalum Kerala Samskaravum,* p.185.

[34] Karasserry, "Māppiḷapāṭṭu", p.49.

[35] Ibid., p. 50.

[36] Ibid.

well-developed and advanced composition of this work indicates that there must have been considerably huge amount of literary works in this tradition before this work.

Another famous work belonging to this tradition is *Nafīsat mala* which hinges around the saintly life of Nafeesatul Misriya of Egypt. There is a widely held belief among the Mappilas that frequent recitation of this work brings smooth delivery for pregnant women. *Mālas* are sung on the occasions like delivery, house warming, weddings, male circumcision, harvesting, etc. The practice of singing *mālas* on such special occasions has a long history spanning almost around four centuries. Within the family circle there is a private reading of *mālas,* which commemorate the divine acts and miracles of Muslim saints or heroic events in the history of local community mainly by women.[37] Other works in this genre include: *Rifāyi Māla, Badr Māla and Mañakkulam Māla, Nafīsat Māla, Nasīhat Māla* and *Vafāt Māla.*

Mālas written in the form eulogies are the most popular genre among the *māppiḷappāṭṭu.* They normally refer to the formidable episodes in the life histories of first generation of Muslims and Sufi saints. Apart from these, there are some compositions with resemblance to *mālas* commemorating the eventful lives of notable Sufis or Scholars in Islamic history or local history. Such compositions, being sung by the disciples of Sufis on the occasion of their birth or martyrs day, are called *Nercappāṭṭu. Māla* and *Nērcapāṭṭu* are sometimes used as coterminous forms though there is a slight difference between the two. Both are sung by the devotees in a completely divine ambience bringing the recovery from illness and for turbulence-free life. *Nērcas* are commemoration of the martyrdoms of Muslim saints or local Mappila heroes those who were killed during Mappila rebellion of early twentieth century.[38] During the colonial invasions, there had been a considerably big number of martyrs from the community, whose memories have been perpetuated through *nērcas.*[39] There are songs where one can see the convergence of both *māla* and *nērcapattu*. *Kōṭṭuppaḷḷi Māla*, a ritualistic song which commemorates the martyrdom of Kunhi Marakkar is the major one among them. Marakkar's heroic martyrdom has been well preserved and recollected in the annual festival of Veliyankode Nerca.[40] *Kōṭṭuppaḷḷi Māla* is sung for divine blessing on this occasion.

The tradition of *mālappāṭṭu* had been vehemently opposed by the proponents of Islamic reform and this difference in views with regard to *mālas* had led to somewhat violent factional squabbles between "modernists" and "traditionalists" within the Mappila community in Kerala. Though both the factions agreed to that the life-histories of those who were subjects of *mālas* are worth-praising, the revivalists were of the view that including such saints' names in the prayer as mediators between God and human being amounts to *shirk* or polytheism. Taking cues from the holy text and teaching of prophet, the Sunnis or those who follow the tradition argued that reciting *mālas* are not forbidden in Islam and there is nothing un-Islamic about reciting it. [41] The moderate faction,

---

[37] R.E. Miller, *Mappila Muslims of Kerala: A study in the Islamic Trends*, (Hyderabad: Oriental Longman, 1992), p.241.

[38] Stephen F. Dale and M.Gangadhara Menon, "Nercca: Saint Martyr Worship Among the Muslims of Kerala", in Asgar Ali Engineer (ed.), *Kerala Muslims: A Historical Perspective*,(New Delhi: Ajanta Publications, 1995) pp.174-199.

[39] K.K.N.Kurup, *The Legacy of Islam: A study of the Mappila Muslims of Kerala*, p. 14.

[40] Ibid., p.53.

[41] Mustafa Faisy, *Sampūrna Mohiyuddīn Māla Vyāghyānam*, (Puthanathani: Oasis Books, 2010).

represented mainly by Jama't e-Islami, however, started recognizing the literary and historical values of *mālas*, though they did not endorse the divinity of them.

Mālas makes up the large chunk of song tradition in Arabi-Malayalam. Written in the form of eulogies, *mālas* commemorate miraculous stories of Muslim saints, Sufi sages, martyrs and heroic events in the history of Mappila community. The word mala derives from the Arabic word *mawlīd* which simply means 'something for recitation' in honour of a saintly figure.[42] The scope of *mawlid* also includes a liturgical recital in honour of an *auliya* or a saint. But there is a diverse opinion. Scholars trace out the origin of this term to a Malayalam word *mala* referring to a collection of verses closely interwoven as if in a garland.[43] *Mawlīd* written in Arabic language were the pioneers in the evolution. Publication of *bayt* with similar plots represents the second phase.[44] With the same sort of themes, *bayts* composed in pure Arabic, were later on replaced by Arabi-Malayalam *mālas*.[45]

The spread of *mālas* closely intertwined with the spread of Sufi *tariqahs* or Sufi orders in Malabar. Each *tariqah* resorted to *māla* tradition in popularizing their order. The themes of *mālas* revolved mostly around the life and miraculous deeds of pioneering figures of these *tariqahs*. The purpose varied from instilling the spirit of a particular Sufi order to re-orient people along that order. So, naturally the 18th and 19th centuries with mushrooming *tariqahs*, marked the peak of mala writing. Scholars see this as a variant of Bakti tradition emerged among Mappila Muslims but influenced very little by the corresponding ones happened in other communities.[46]

With lavish praise of the prophet and saintly figures and descriptions of seminal events in Islamic history, reciting *māla* is being considered as a divine ritual. So as to inculcate the element of divinity, miraculous life histories of saintly figures are narrated with greater amount of fantasies.[47] The events carry descriptions in a most embellished and inspiring manner. *Mālas* are sung as *nērca* or offering on occasions of personal loss and illness and for relief from the stress and crisis-ridden periods in life because of its devotional content. Since there is a high regard for *auliyas* with indication of divine powers, Mappilas turn for help to such saints reciting verses from *mālas* for the solutions to certain problems.

The first generation of Mala composers was deeply influenced by the Arabi-Tamil poets. They followed *kōrvēy* or the narrative strategy popular in Arabi-Tamil poems. Stylistic combination of Dravidian and Arabic meters made it more complex. The influence of Tamil language seen in *Mohiyuddīn Māla* is, to a certain extent, because of the author's association with *pulavars* or poets from Tamil Nadu who frequented some parts of Malabar with their works.[48] The publication of works like *Mohiyudhīn Āndavar Mālai* in Arabi-Tamil had heralded the Bhakti movement among Tamil Muslims towards the end of the 16th century.[49]

---

[42] Ramesh.V.K. "Mālapāttukaḷ: Oṟu Caritrānwēṣanam", *Oruma*, 2014, pp.23-25.

[43] *Mala* literally means necklaces in Malayalam.

[44] A.P.Ahmed, scholar of Mappila songs in an interview with the authors held on 14th March, 2013.

[45] Ibid.

[46] Mohamedali, *Mappiḷa Pāṭṭukaḷ Nūṯṯāndukaḷilūde*,p. 33.

[47] Abu, *Arabi-Malayala Sāhitya Caṟitram,* p.67.

[48] Mohamedali, *Mappiḷa Pāṭṭukaḷ Nūṯṯāndukaḷilūde*,p. 34-35.

[49] Ibid., p.34.

As discussed earlier, *Mohiyuddīn Māla* predates five years to Thunchathu Ramanujan Ezhuthachan's *Adhyātma Rāmāyanam Kiḷippāṭṭu*, publication of which marked the beginning of *bhakti* literature in Malayalam. There is a widely held trend placing *mālas* as the contribution of Kerala Muslims to the *bhakti* movement which had a spill-over effect all over India. But the recent studies trace *mālas'* connection to a tradition of Islamic revivalism widely-spread in the Indian Ocean region. Works of similar sort existed among South East Asian Muslims provide testimony to this theory. "The limitation that characterizes our discussion about the political and religious aspects of *mālappāṭṭu* is its tendency to reduce the scope of discussion to the Indian situation", notes Pavithran.[50] Even before the invasion of Brahmins and the advent of Aryans, Semitic religious had maintained close linkages with Kerala. *Mohiyuddīn Mala*, in fact, bears a continuity of this cultural linkage.[51] Pavithran traces its origin to the 'reform' tradition which had lively spread all over the Indian Ocean region.[52]

Mālas, apart from giving clues to the historical past of the community, try to connect it with present in a more emotional way. Through the recreation of history, *mālas* refashioned the memories of Muslims in Malabar. Concept of martyrdom became a recurring theme in most of *mālas*. Badar *māla* the second oldest mala after *Mohiyuddīn Māla* written during the colonial period, for example, praises *śahids* or martyrs who were killed in the battle of Badar by name. It is interesting to note that the choice of martyrdom as the focal theme appears to be intentional. Each attack on the foreign forces was considered as a *jehād*. The virtue of Martyrdom and the ensured entry to heaven it gives motivated many in Malabar to launch a tradition of resistance against the colonial forces; mainly the Portuguese and the British.[53] Fighters from the community who were revered as *śahids* have found place in many *mālas.*

Mālas were traditionally named after the saints or Sufi sages referred in those *mālas*. But this tradition in picking up the themes and nomenclature, later on, undergone some changes. Certain slices of Islamic history and Kerala Muslim history also became theme of *mālas*. *Badr Māla* dealing with the battle of *Badr,* a legendary episode in Islamic history is an example for such a transition. Though content and structure vary, *mālas* show some commonalities. Each one in two sections consists of three hundred to six hundred lines. Beginning with praise of God, *mālas* turn eventually to eulogize *karāmat* or divine powers of persons referred in. Towards the end, there would be a section called *iravu* or *edatāṭṭaṃ* literally means begging. This section consists of a prayer for forgiveness by the mercy of the saint. Some *mālas* have more than one *iravu* (eg. *Nafīsat Māla*).[54] The *iravu* is normally in the form of request to the saintly figure referred into mediate between God and the person who prays.

Aḷḷah tiruperum tutiyum swalavātum,

atinal tudañuvān arul ceyta vedāmbar.

Ālam udayōvan ēkal arulāle,

---

[50] Pavithran, a scholar of Malayalam language and literature in an interview with the authors held on, 25th June, 2013.
[51] Ibid.
[52] Ibid.
[53] K.N. Panikkar, *Against Lord and State: Religion and Peasant Uprisings in Malabar 1836-1921,* (New Delhi, Oxford University Press, 2001).
[54] *Nafīsath mala* has got two *Iravus.*

āye Mohammed avarkiḷa ānōvar.

(The one who commanded to start

with *swalat* and praise of God.

The one who born in the clan of Mohamed,

as per the order of God.)

3.1. *Mohiyuddīn Māla*

This work seems to be the first work in the category of *mālapaṭṭu* as well as in the entire *māppilappāṭṭu* tradition. This popular devotional classic depicts the life history of an eleventh century Sufi saint Sheikh Mohiyuddīn Abdul Kader Jilani of Baghdad, the founder of *Qādiriyya* order. In Kerala this Sufi order had a lively spread thanks to the preaching of Makhdumis, a clan of scholars who came and settled in Malabar from Hadramaut of Southern Arabia. The litanies and devotional songs of *Qādiriyya tariqah* gained wide popularity among Mappila Muslims. The period of this work is evident from the author's words:

Kollam eẕhunūṯṯi eṉpatiraṉdil ñan

Kōrtēn immālēne nūṯṯampatacummal.

Muttum mānikkavum onnāyi kōrtapōl,

Mohiyuddīne mālēne kōrtēn ñan lōkare.

(In the 782nd year of Kollam era[55],

I prepared this mala in 155 lines.

Like a string of pearls and rubies together,

Oh people! I have roved this necklace (this mala).

Mohiyuddīn Māla represents a vast range of linguistic influences including Arabic, Farsi, Tamil and Malayalam. This intermingling of vocabularies from four different languages adds to *Mohiyuddīn Māla*'s charm and makes its recitation more appealing. The poet himself says that he has composed this work mixing various languages as if stringing a necklace with pearl and ruby. Early works of Arabi-Malayalam literature generally inherit this eclecticism from *Manipravāla* tradition, works in which were admixtures of Tamil, Malayalam and Sanskrit.[56] Most of the Mala composers closely followed this pattern and prepared alternative versions of *Manipravāla* mixing Tamil, Malayalam and Arabic in place of Sanskrit. But, with regard to the narrative strategy and style, *Mohiyuddīn Māla* takes inspiration from two major works in Arabic, namely *Bahja* and *Takmīla*.[57] The *eśal* of *Mohiyuddīn Māla* owes

---

[55] Malayalam calendar which was widely used in Kerala.

[56] Manipravalam was a literary style used in medieval liturgical texts in South India, which used an admixture of Tamil, Malayalam and Sanskrit.

[57] Mohamedali, *Mappiḷa Pāṭṭukaḷ Nūṯṯāndukaḷilūde*, p. 34-35.

much to the Arabic meter *Khafīf* and *Madīd.*[58] All *mālas*, except *Nafīsath* Māla and *Mampuraṃ Māla* have followed the same *eśal*.[59]

Simplicity and easy to recite nature of the lyrics are the peculiarities of *Mohiyuddīn Māla*. Most of the words are in Mappila Malayalam.

Pāmbinte koltil jihnnukal vannāre

pasamētum kūdate eduteriñovar.

(Jihn came in the form of snake,

Sheikh threw it away without any trace of fear.[60])

The colloquial term *paśam*, for instance, has been used to denote fear in earlier texts. But with the standardization of language Malayalam term *bhayam* has substituted it. This replacement, according to Rahman, has made a lot of damages to the charm of *Mohiyuddīn Māla*.[61]

Mohiyuddīn Māla comprises 310 lines; of which certain lines are narrated as if Sheikh presents his life in his own words. Towards the end of *Mohiyuddīn Māla* there is an *iravu* or prayer composed in 152 lines. Of the 583 words, almost two hundred are Arabic. But these words were not foreign to Mappilas who showed a tendency to use Arabic words intermingling with Malayalam ones even in casual talks. The narrative strategy of *Mohiyddīn Māla*, according to Ramesh, has been influenced to a great extent by the folk songs of Kerala mainly *Vadakkan Pāṭṭukaḷ* or the ballads of North Malabar of medieval orgin.[62]

Within the family circle there is a private reading of *Mohiyuddīn Māla*. Knowing this *māla* by heart was once considered to be an obligatory asset for Mappila girls before marriage. *Mālas* are memorized and sung at length, especially by Mappila women, on special occasion. They are generally performed with the purpose of getting relief from illness, poverty and other miseries and agonies in the life. *Nafīsat Māla* is sung for smooth delivery, while *Rifa'n M*āla is sung to get protection from the anger of snakes.

Mohiyuddīn Māla was written in the context of increased squabbles among the Mappilas along the line of various Sufi orders.[63]The clashes over the claims of various orders had often gone to the extent of street fights. Kazi Mohammed who took over the leadership of the community in Calicut was very much upset with such petty quarrels. He made an attempt to bring peace among the groups locking horns with each other and to mobilize them under a single *tariqah, Qādiryya.*[64] The

---

[58] Mohamedkunhi, *Musliṅalum Kerala Samskaravum,* p. 186 & Moahamedali, *Mappiḷa Pāṭṭukaḷ Nūṯṯāndukaḷilūde,* p. 37.

[59] Same *eśal* has been used in two recently composed Mālas composed by by Kutty and Karaserry with the life of Malayalam author Vaikkam Mohamed Basheer as the central plot.

[60] Faisy, *Sampūrna Mohiyuddīn Māla Vyāghyānam.*

[61] B.F Abdul Rahman, a composer and performer of Mappila songs in an interview with the authors held on 2nd January, 2014.

[62] Ramesh, "Mālapāttukaḷ: Oṛu Caritrānwēṣanam", p.23.

[63] C.N.Ahmed Moulavi and K.K.abdul Kareem, *Mahatāya Māppila Sāhitya Pāṛambaraym,* (Calicut: Authors, 1978), pp. 152-53.

[64] Ibid.

composition of *Mohiyuddīn Māla* characterizes a peculiar construct-juxtaposing the imagination of a poet and the narratives in the history of a community in a peculiar balance.[65] Historical facts and popular myths are intertwined with each other in an amazing synthesis. It may be true that this is an important theological text, but the poetic beauty and imageries used in it overpowers the former aspect of it.[66] All the later *Mālapāṭṭus* were modelled after *Mohiyuddīn Māla* and hence it remained as the core text from where the later poets derived their modular forms.

3.2. *Badr Māla*

This *māla*, written by Mambattil Kunhirayan is believed to be the second oldest *māla* after *Mohiyuddīn Māla*. *Eśal* and the lyrics of this work, more or less, show some resemblances to *Mohiyuddīn Māla*. Inspired by similar works in Arabic like *Badr Mawlīd* and *Badr Bayt* with heroic stories of *śahids* who fought the war of *Badr*, the poet has taken this battle as the major thematic premise of *Badr Māla* (Plate 5.1).

Cuttiyiruḷu qabaril adaṉum naḷ

mūppar badreenkaḷ kāvalil ēkaḷḷah.

Teṯṯate vistaram ceyyum samayatil

dīrar badreenkaḷ kāvalil ēkaḷḷah.

(Oh God!, Provide me with the protection of Badreengal[67]

when the darkness wrap my burial place.

Save me from giving wrong answers,

when angles question me after death.)

Each śuhada or martyr has been praised individually by name in this mala. Reciting their names in such works, the poet himself writes in the mala, would bring sudden result for the prayer. Most of the lines are dedicated exclusively for the wonders that the recitation of this work would create. Unlike *Mohiyuddīn Māla,* the lyrics of this mala are plain and straightforward and do not carry much of imageries and symbols.

3.3 *Nafīsat Māla*

Another popular work belonging to this genre is *Nafīsat Māla* composed by Nalakath Kunhimoidheen of Tirur.[68] *Nafīsat Māla* (Plate 5.2) deals with the miracles of a Sufi Saint, Nafeesatul Misriya, the granddaughter of the fourth Caliph Ali, who lived in 8th Century AD in Egypt. This work, according to Razak, reminds the people of nothingness of material life and the permanence of life-after death.[69] In

---

[65] Balakrishnan Vallikkunnu, *Mappila Sahityavum, Navodhanavum*, (Kozhicode: Yuvata Books, 2008), p. 30.

[66] Ibid.

[67] Martyrs of the battle of *Badr.* Veneration of them, Mappilas believe would bring solutions to the problems in the daily life.

[68] Nafeesath Mala is his magnum opus, though Kunhimidheen has authored a novel entitled Chahar Darvesh and a poem, called *Akhbarul Ajeeb.*

[69] PP Abdul Razak, *Cololialism and Community Formation in Malabar*, unpublished PhD Thesis, University of Calicut, 2007,

terms of popularity, this *māla* is second only to *Mohiyiddīn Māla*. Women are the major takers of this mala which has been specifically recited by women of Malabar for smooth delivery.[70] "Until recently, families of pregnant women used to book a troop in advance to recite *Nafīsat Māla* along with midwives", recalls Usman.[71] "By the time the troop finish reciting this mala, one can witness to a smooth delivery and the cry of newborn baby"[72] The basis of this belief lies in this mala itself:

Śemitoru sīrikku pēṯṯu nōmbalaṃ piditē

śeṣikeṭṭu randu nāḷ vare bējāril nilate

samayaṃ intē bībi pēril nērcaye kupate

sadiyam moẕhi mudiyum mun avaḷuṃ petē.

(The pain of a pregnant women lasted two days.

Pain made her restless and women lost her patience.

After an offering in the name of Bibi[73],

with her grace, the women gave birth to a babe soon.)

The lyrics of *Nafīsat Māla* are reflective of poet's proficiency in handling Persian, Tamil and Arabic languages. This work composed in the *esal, ādiantam,* has adopted a style more close to Arabic *bayts* taking rhyme schemes directly from them.[74] It also has a long list of nicely-knit Arabic words to denote specific situations.

Munlirun mubaśirun mukaramum kaleemuḷḷah

Muslihun mukaramun mubeenu sīrathuḷḷah

Nafeesatul Misriya belonging to the family of the Prophet had captured the imagination of a long array of Arabi-Malayalam poets. Like other *mālas, Nafīsat Māla* also starts with a hymn in praise of God. In the beginning, there is section fully dedicated to commemorate the Prophet, four Orthodox Khalifs in Islam and people in *Ahlul Bait* or the family of the Prophet.

3.4. *Rifa'in Māla*

Another well-known Mala, *Rifa'in Māla* chronicles the life of Sheikh Rifa'i with a number of disciples in South and North Malabar. This mala is believed to have written in 1623. The author of this mala remains unknown as the name of the author has been mentioned nowhere in the text against the tradition.[75] The miracles of the Sheikh Refai described in this mala include cure from burns of snake

---

pp. 8-9.

70 Ibid., pp. 8-9

71 Shared by Kalaparambath Usman with the authors during the field work.

72 Ibid.

73 A generic term referring to noble women of Sayyid origin belonging to the family of the Prophet. Nafeesatul Misriya in this specific context.

74 Ramesh, "Mālapāttukaḷ: Oṛu Caritrānwēṣanam",p. 24.

75 Razak, *Cololialism and Community Formation in Malabar,* pp.6-7.

bites.[76] A true disciple who chants this mala with the grace of Sheikh, according to the poet, would brave the bite of snake. Other rewards for those who recite Rifa'i mala have also been mentioned in the mala.

> *Ente muride perumbambu tīndukil*
>
> *ētum viṣhamilla ennu paraňovar.*
>
> (...)
>
> *Nannāyi sūkṣiccitine pādunnōrkku,*
>
> *nalavukaḷ ēṯṯam kodukkum atennōvar.*
>
> *Baṇṇam curukki pakarccayil colvōrkku,*
>
> *Valiya halākkiyattaḷḷa kodukkume.*
>
> (My disciples are immune,
>
> even from the bite of python.)
>
> (...)
>
> The amount of property will be high,
>
> for those who recite it in a highly devotional manner
>
> Hell to those,
>
> who handle it in a ridiculous way.

Most of the *Kutrātībs*[77] performed in Malabar use Rifa'i mala for creating a devotional ambience. Believers in crew first taking knife, dagger and a drum in the hands, utter the name of Sheikh and making blood-drenched wounds on the body by knife at the peak of *rātib*. Chanting Rifa'i mala towards the end, according to a popular belief, would heal these marks.[78]

3.5. *Mampuram Māla*

Mampuram Māla portrays the life history of the Arab Scholar Sayyid Alawi Mauladaweela, who lived at Tirurangadi during the first half of 19th century. Sayyid Alawi known popularly as Mampuram Thangal was believed to have come from Hadramawt. The mausoleum of Sayyid Alawi has been the chief centre of pilgrimage in Malabar. At times of need or special undertakings, devotees visit the shrine to make an offering and reciting *Mampuram Māla*. The lyrics of this *māla* deal with with the life and miracle of Sayid Alawi whose life has also been the plot for several other *mālas* composed in

[76] A section among the Mappila community believes that reciting Refai Mala on regular basis would bring rescue from serpent's attack.

[77] With the practice of beating up or making wounds on one's own body, *Kuturātīb* shows some similarities with Tansiya, a performance attached to Asura procession of Shia Muslims.

[78] Interview with Koya Kappad, a performer of *Kuturātīb* held on 4th January, 2014.

Malabar.[79] Most of these *mālas* were of anonymous authorship but published in large number of editions.[80]

Travelled all the way,

crossing seven seas.

Born in the family of the prophet as the 32nd member,

Sayyid Alawi was brought up in Hadhramawt.[81]

3.6. Other *Mālās*

V.Ayisakutty's *Vafāt Māla* gives an account of sorrow of the family of the Prophet on the sad demise of Khadeeja, prophet Mohamed's first wife. This *māla* is narrated in the form of sharing anxieties about her daughter Fatima's future with Khadeeja's friend Asma. Most of them are written along the line of devotional ones but there are some with the prime purpose of entertainment. Such compositions marked a transition in the mala tradition with the notable absence of devotional and metaphysical content. They do not have the portion of *iravu* or prayer which is otherwise considered to be an unavoidable stuff in other compositions. *Kiḷḷati Māla* of Moinkutty vaidyar and *Māta Mōhini Māla* of Edavlan Moidheen belong to this genre.

Kiḷḷati Māla was written with the purpose of singing on the occasion of wedding. Illustrating the heroic life of Hussain, the grandson of Prophet who was killed in the battle of Karbala, this *māla* shows a strong inclination towards Shia literature. *Salīkat Māla* in which Vaidyar wished to pay homage to a lineage of saintly figures from the family of Kondotty Thangals, also add to the category of Shia literature in Arabi-Malayalam language.[82] This work, with its copious praise of Ali, the fourth Khalifa in Islam all along the text tries to validate the Shiite claims vouchsafe him as the real successor of the Prophet.[83] *Karāmat Māla,* another eulogy composed by Vaidyar illustrated the divine powers of Ishtiyah Shah Thangal of Kondotty.

Besides it, there are some locally popular *mālas* with the purpose of commemorating the eventful lives of personalities from those localities. *Mañjakkuḷam Māla* with unknown authorship renders the valiant deeds of Khaja Hussain a brave soldier who fought against 'the conqurers of Mysore' under Tipu Sultan and succumbed to death. This *māla* named after the place Manjakkulam where the battle took place had been recited routinely with a high amount of religiosity by the belivers in order to save themselves from the attack of poisonous beasts.[84]

The plot of *Badar Māla* composed by Kanjirala Kunjirayan of Mampad, recounts the battle of Badr, a major landmark in the history of Islam. The lines of this *māla* rhapzodize the heroic act of Muslims participated and killed in the battle. Recitation of this *māla*, people in certain places of

---

79 Abu, *Arabi-Malayala Sāhitya Caṛitra,* pp.121-122.

80 Razak, *Cololialism and Community Formation in Malabar*, p.7.

81 As sung by a team of students of Darul Huda Islamic university, Chemmad on 4th January, 2013.

82 Vaidyar has used the pen name Twabeeb Payal (the son of medical practitioner) in Salīkat Māla. Ramesh, "Mālapāttukaḷ:Oṛu Caritrānwēṣanam", P. 25.

83 Ibid.

84 Ibid.

Malabar, belived would stop the spread of endemic diseases in the locality.[85] *Safala Māla* of Kulangara Veetil Moidu Musaliyar (known populary as Sujai), deals with Islamic mysticism from the genesis to the death of prophet Mohammed. It is a didactic work in Arabi-Malayalam, which invites people, who are lured by worldly pleasures, to the path of spirituality.[86]

Interestingly enough, there are some works which were instrumental in profanating the themes and contents of *mālas*. They collectively tried to make a mock at the divinity attributed to *mālas* by picking up themes from the daily life.[87] Pulikottil Haider's *Duracāra Māla* is a diatribe throwing light on social evils like dowry system, beliefs and customs that were considered to be against the teaching of Islam. Hyder used usual events in the village life in his compositions. Another *māla* composed by him called *Katukutu Māla* openly criticized a widely held celebration *katukuttu* or ear-boring among Muslims. In the recent past, *mālas* began to cover various issues in the life of ordinary people. From depicting the life histories of sacred figures and events, Malas moved to address various issues that represent Mappila life.[88] Hyder's famous *Veḷḷapokkamāla* depicts a flood that people of Malabar suffered in the last century.

. *Candirasundari Māla* composed by P.K.Haleema, the renowned women poet in Arabi-Malayalam is about the marriage of Prophet Mohamed with Aysha, the daughter of Aboobacker Siddique a close disciple of him. This mala remains to be a favourite ingredient in many of the *Oppana* performed on the occasion of wedding. Ahmed Ismail's *Putiyanikah Māla* is presented in the form of moral advice to newly-wed couple.[89] The composer gives some philosophical advises, in a very appealing colloquial language.

Kadannoḷi maniyara āyalopicce

kautuka paṟikaṯṯil camayippicce.

Piccayil kiḷavarum kuṯṯikaḷ venda

nakṣhamayum kedu keṯṯodukkenda

occa kuraññavarum kayarēnda.

Kaimuttum eśal pāṯṯum padiccum kondu,

karutuḷḷa midukkanmar arakku vendum.

(...)

Vendiyavar putumāranekkondu

nīṉiyatode arakkakam vandu,

vīdaṇayum tirumaṉalam kondu.

---

[85] Ibid., p.24.

[86] Razak, *Colonialism and Community Formation in Malabar,* p.8-9.

[87] Ramesh, "Mālapāttukaḷ:Oṟu Caritrānwēṣanam", p. 25.

[88] Interview with Ummar Tharammel, a scholar of Arabi-Malayalam literature by the authors held on 22nd April, 2013.

[89] Abdulla Thanima in an interview conducted by the authors on 2nd Janurary, 2013.

Konduḷḷil alankarapani pāṯṯālo,

Kōnayannabi mēle madhunālō.

(Step into Maniyara[90] with rhythms,

awe-inspiring and well-decorated cot is kept inside

Aged and kids do not enter it and disturb,

people with low voice also.

The chamber needs who are smart and well-built

knowing *esal* songs and clapping.

(...)

The selected ones take the bridegroom into the chamber.

They participate in the function and accompany the bridegroom with songs describing the decorations in the chamber or with songs praising the Prophet.

Forgive whatever said unpleasant.

And start singing *padam*[91], leaving hesitation and shyness.)[92]

The *māla* tradition continues to be popular with composing new ones in praise of personalities and events of contemporary importance. Two separate *mālas* have been written by the eminent social critique, M N Karassery and the renowned *Māppiḷapāṯṯu* singer, V M Kutty as a tribute to the life of Vaikkom Mohammed Basheer who was a paramount figure in Malayalam literature. *Bashīr Māla* is adhered to devotional mala tradition except for its opening stanza for praising God. Being a parody to *Mohiyuddīn Māla*, Karassery's Basheer mala starts with following lines:

Nēśatil olivay vannu pirannoru

Vaikkom Basheerinnu māla paṇiyunnu.

Vēvum piranthukal kalayakki maṯunna

Vaikkom Baseerinte valarma parayunnu.

(I prepare a mala dedicated to Vaikkam Mohamed Basheer,

who was born in this world as a ray of love.

Narrating his craft,

to convert lunacy to exemplary art works.)[93]

---

[90]Chamber specially designated for newlywed couple.

[91] Songs portraying the life histories of the Prophet and other saintly people.

[92] Thanima Abdulla Mogral and Yousuf Kattathadukka (compilation), *Vadakkinte eṣalukal,* (Mogral: Frontline Publications, 2014), pp. 91-102.

[93] As sung by VM Kutty.

Recitation of *mālas* has long been considered to be an indicator of specialized knowledge among Mappilas cutting across the class lines. People who learnt them by heart had enjoyed a special status in the community. The practice still continues and *mālas* are recited in each house as offering and to create devotional ambience for many rituals. However, the collective recitation of *mālas* suffered a setback on the event of emergence of Islamic revivalist movements. The most popular one Mohiyuddīn *Māla*, for instance, has met a stiff opposition from the revivalist movements for its blasphemous content that openly challenges *tawhid* or monotheism, the fundamental concept in Islam.

It is an irony in history that the pioneers of the revivalist movement had successfully utilized the popularity of *mālas* and prepared parodies for most popular ones to spread their message among Mappila Muslims. Through such parodies, they satirized un-Islamic beliefs and customs that were allegedly borrowed from the local traditions. However, among those who follow tradition, the passion of writing *mālas* on Arab and local saints is on increase. New ones are composed on important scholars, *ulemas* and leaders in the community on their death.

4. *Padappāṭṭukaḷ* or War Songs

Padappāṭṭu (literally means battle songs) generally narrate the conflicts between Muslims and the "infidels" in the early history of Islam. A rough estimate says that the number of battle songs composed in Arabi-Malayalam comes around hundred and fifty.[94] Almost all the battles waged by the first generation of Muslims have become the themes for battle songs. *Badr padappāṭṭu, Uhdu padappāṭṭu* (Plate 5.3)*, Makkām padappāṭṭu, Hunain padappāṭṭu* (Plate 5.4)*, khantak padappāṭṭu, Khyber padappāṭṭu* and *futhuśśam* are some of the battle songs that chronicle the wars that waged in the early period of Islamic history.

Padappāṭṭus are the lengthiest compositions which borrow slices from the real history of wars, though the imagination sometimes tends to push the boundaries of real history. It was *padappāṭṭus* written by Moinkutty Vaidyar that elevated him to the status of the Great Mappila Poet. *Malappuram Padappāṭṭu*, Cērūr *Padappāṭṭu, Salasil Kissappāṭṭu, Elippada* (an imaginary war) and *Salīqath Kissappāṭṭu* were Vaidyar's major works in this genre. Cettuvai Parikutty has composed a famous war song called *Fathuśśām* (Plate 5.5), which deals with Syrian victory of first two Caliphs, Aboobacker and Umar, in 1887. Descriptions of wars by both Vaidyar and Parikutty were powerful enough to sneak into the minds of readers. *Padappāṭṭu* functioned as primer for many in the Mappila community those who were ignorant of history of war in Islam. The dramatic description of the sorrow of Umaiban, the wife of martyr Ibn Saeed, whose married life lasted only for a month, according to Maulavi and Kareem touched the hearts of its readers and this was a favourite song of the *kissappāttukār* or story-tellers all over Malabar for many decades.[95] During the colonial period the scope of *padappāṭṭu* had been widened to include local battles that Mappilas fought against the European forces mainly the Portuguese and the British.

[94] Moulavi and Kareem, *Mahatāya Māppila Sāhitya Pāṛambaraym,* pp.395-398.

[95] Ibid., pp.395-398.

War songs constitute a major category of Mappila ballads. If you analyze them as a special category, *padappāṭṭus* outnumber other genres like *mālappāṭṭu, kessu pāttu* and the like. Arabi-Malayalam war songs are divided broadly into two. The first category includes compositions with plots based on armed rebellions took place in Kerala and the second with plots based on wars happened outside Kerala, mainly in Arabia.[96] *Malappuram Padappāṭṭu , Mannarkkad Padappāṭṭu, Cērur Padappāṭṭu, Mancēṛi padappāṭṭu, Kaprāṭṭu Krishna Panikkar pāṭṭu* etc. belong to the first category while *Badr Padappāṭṭu, Uhud Padappāṭṭu, Karbala Padappāṭṭu* (Plate 5.6)*, Zakhūm Padappāṭṭu* (Plate 5.7), *Fathussām Padappāṭṭu, Makkām Fath, Hunain Padappāṭṭu, Khandak Padappāṭṭu,*and *Khaibar Padappāṭṭu,* etc. to the second one. The works belonging to the first category extolled the heroic exploits of not the Islamic war heroes but of Mappila martyrs of Malabar who died in the battles against the native and European enemies.[97] There are almost fifty war songs with themes revolving around the wars in the early history of Islam which in a way became the alternative narratives of Islamic battles in verses. Most of the songs belonging to first category have been destroyed by the administration because of their potential to instigate rebellions in Malabar.

As mentioned earlier, apart from the wars in early Islamic period, rebellions happened during Portuguese and British period also have become the plots for battle songs. Most of such works inspired by the 1921 Mappila uprising had a fate of attracting the wrath of British administration. The British administration was well-aware of the inflammatory nature of such songs and they either proscribed or destroyed such songs.[98] The British officials, who were in search of a cause for the frequent *Mappila* outbreaks of 19th century, connected it to the contents of *padappāṭṭu*.[99] As Razak notes, "these war songs were identified by the British authorities as the inspiration behind many of the rural revolts of Malabar in 19th century." [100] The then Superintendent of Police in British in Malabar Fawcett in a letter to his superior has sketched out the power of war narratives in following words: [101]

> These poems must be read if the Mappilas is to be understood...How much stronger force on life and the Government and use of life there is in songs which stir the heart of a people to the core... No people of Madras presidency sings songs of this kind as do the Mappilas.... You cannot read the songs I am sending you without feeling the terrible strength of the spirit which animates them.[102]

Cērur Padappāṭṭu, *Mancēri Padappāṭṭu* and *Maṉṉarlkād Padappāṭṭu* were included in the list of works that had been confiscated by the officials. However, even when the copies of *Cērur Padappāṭṭu* were confiscated and burnt by British,[103] the poem was transmitted orally and memory of

---

[96] Mohamedali, *Mappiḷa Pāṭṭukaḷ Nūṟṟāndukaḷilūde*, p. 55.

[97] Razak, *Cololialism and Community Formation in Malabar*, pp.10-11.

[98] Ibid., pp.13-14.

[99] See F.Fawcett, "War Songs of Mappilas of Malabar", *Indian Antiquary*, Vol.30, Nov-Dec. 1901. Also see F.Fawcett, letters, No. 1567, Judicial, 30th Sept. 1896, pp.98-100.

[100] PP Abdul Razak, *Cololialism and Community Formation in Malabar*, unpublished PhD Thesis, University of Calicut, 2007, pp.13-14.

[101] F. Fawcett's letter, No.1567, Judicial, dated 30th September 1896,TNA, Madras, p.97

[102] Ibid.

[103] All the copies of this song were seized and burnt by the British and the only remaining copy of it was collected by Burnell. See, A.C. Burnell, *Specimens of South Indian Dialects*, No.2, 1873 as cited in C.K. Kareem (ed.), *O. Abu Smaraka*

the heroic fight was kept alive in Malabar.[104] The second half of the 19th century marked the peak of *padappāṭṭu* writing; about a hundred were composed during this period. Almost fifty works, which withstood consistent British attempt to destroy them physically, remained highly popular in the decades followed.

Almost all battles fought by prophet and Islamic Caliphs during the formative phase of Islam have been dealt with in these songs.[105] Through the narration of seminal episodes in the early history of Islam, Vaidyar and other poets created a new consciousness among Mappilas and inculcated a spirit of pride and valour among them.[106] Vaidyar in his *Malappuram Padappāṭṭu* says, "Nothing is more pleasing to God than sacrificing one's body and soul in defence of God and none are more honoured than these *Śahīds."* [107] This idea has been echoed in the following lines of Badr *Padappāṭṭu* also: "the prophet swore to army that such happiness would be theirs (in paradise) if they died fighting bravely." In short, all war songs reminded Mappilas about the bliss that awaited martyrs who died in the fight against infidels.[108] Another composition, *Hunain Padapāṭṭu* of Maliyekkal Kunhahamed Sahib written in 1879 deals with Hunain War waged between the last Caliph, Ali and Dabul Himar. *Muhtat pada* by Vallanchira Moideen Haji of Manjeri, *Khandak pada* and *Futuh Tayif* by Kodambiyath Kunhiseethi Koya, *Makkām Fath* by Tanur Munhiyudhin Mulla are the other major works in this genre.[109]

4.1. *Malappuram Padappāṭṭu*

Malappuram Padappāṭṭu or *Mātanidimāla* written by Vaidyar in 1886 occupies a prime position in the battle songs based on the uprisings took place in Malabar. There is an oral tradition behind the composition of this war song which says that the major reason behindcomposing this *padappāṭṭu* was the poet's illness. For getting cured, Vaidyar had a peculiar offering -- to write a song dedicated to the memory of martyrs of Malappuram rebellion.[110] In this work, Vaidyar tries to retell the story of Malappuram uprising against upper caste Hindu Jenmis with a stress on the life-stories of the forty four *Śahids* who died in the revolt between the soldiers of Paranambi and Mappilas in 1728. This work is presented in the form of live recording of the rebellion using special sound effects of the movement of horses and howling of people. The poet tries to reproduce the sound of panicked movements of horses participated in the battle by mimicking them in a most hilarious way.

Since Vaidyar did this work on the basis of his own close interactions with the people of this locality, *Malappuram Padappāṭṭu* is considered to be the first attempt to record oral historical accounts on a particular event. So, besides being considered to be a literary work, this work has got a wide scholarly acclaim as a historical text.

Grantham (Mal.), Tellichery, 1982.

104 Razak, *Cololialism and Community Formation in Malabar,* p.14.

105 Ibid.

106 F. Fawcett, "War Songs of Mappilas of Malabar", *Indian Antiquary*, Vol. XXX, Nov. 1901, p.508.

107 Ibid.

108 Razak, *Cololialism and Community Formation in Malabar* 10-11.

109 Ibid.

110 Malappuram rebellion took place in 1720 was actually a local skirmish between upper caste Hindu landlords and their Mappila tenements which later on flared up to a large scale conflict.

Uratāl madavārkaḷ sankadatāl

oḷkkiday miḷinīrum kēṇavastā.

Irkkunna nagaravum paḷḷiyenkaḷ

(Women complained to the ruler,

soldiers[111] ravaged their life.

Shared their grief-ridden situation,

shedding tears every now and then.

To the king who provided them with a place to say

and built a mosque to worship.)

The most worth-noting feature of this work is its attempt to make a delicate balance between real incidents and poet's imagination. All seminal episodes in Kerala Muslim history from Perumal's embracement of Islam to the Malappuram Rebellion have been scrupulously narrated in this work. The poet's description of the arrival and preaching of Malik bin Dinar with a letter of reference from Perumal who had by then embraced Islam and accepted the name, Thajuddin, goes as follows:[112]

Yeti nadanthavar Malayalatil

Inke Kodunkallore nagar thanatil

Katum Mudi ventar mani Thajuddin

Haji vaziyatum kuriyal munthi

Thettatasarar sammatatal Islam

Deenay Nadathinar sarah noolam

(Alas, they reached the land of Malayalam

the town of Kodungallore

travelled all the way

with a coomunication from Haji Thajuddin

to implement his last wish

to preach Islam adhered to its rules completely.)

This poem, came out in the year 1879, is a classic example for conscious use of poetry for political purpose. It fuelled the Rebellion of 1921 as people participated in the rebellion took inspiration from the lyrics of this work and reciting this along with Vaidyar's other work, *Badr Padappāṭṭu* became the

[111] Nair soldiers of the local ruler, Para Nambi

[112] The Ceraman episode in Kerala Muslim history has been discussed in detail in the first chapter.

most-valued activity among Mappila dissidents.[113] This composition contains sixty eight *eśals*, four *vambus* and a *kutiracāṭṭam* or horse's jump.

4.2. *CērŪr Padappāttu*

This *Padappāttu* dealing with the Cherur riot of 1841 in which seven Mappilas died, was composed jointly by Cherur Mammadkutty and Muhiyudhin. Within a short period after the occurrence of the revolt, this poem became very popular in Malabar and was instrumental in instilling anti-British sentiments in the region.[114] Hence the British government banned it and *Malhar ul Muhimmath* press at Thirurangadi, where this work was printed in 1844 was seized by the Government in the same year.[115] Cherur revolt was instigated by the teachings of Sayyid Alawi, who had given spiritual sanctions to several outbreaks of the Mappilas. Sayyid Alawi's booklet *al-Saiful Batār* (literally means cutting sword) came out in the context of a series of 'outbreaks' by Mappilas in and around Thirurangadi in 1841 resulting in the martyrdom of eleven Mappilas. Justifying the need of waging a holy war against the British till the end, *Saiful Batār* ignited a virulent anti-colonial campaign. *Saiful Batār* was a collection of fatwas composed in the context of an uprising in Muttiara of South Malabar in 1841 instigating Muslims to fight against the British regime as their religious duty. Though an unsuccessful effort was made by the authority to search and destroy the copy of it, this book was circulated widely through mosque networks.

Motivated by *al-Saiful Batār,* the followers of Sayyid Alawi attempted to challenge the colonial hegemony by entering into an open conflict with the British force. Almost twenty five soldiers from the British side were killed and around the same number injured. *CērŪr Padappāttu* illustrates the heroic victory of Mappilas in this revolt. The overwhelming acceptance this work gained invited the wrath of the colonial administration. They banned the copies of it and destroyed them physically. Keeping the copies of this work, reading it and circulating it became an unlawful activity in Malabar. Some of the mosque libraries in South Malabar were raided and copies were confiscated. Putting Cherur Revolt as the central theme, Payyal Khayyath of Parappanangadi also has written a poem called *CērŪr Cintu, which* was also banned by the Government.

4.3. *Badr Padappāttu*

Among the battles in Islamic history, the battle of *Badr* was a perennial source of inspiration to scores of *Mappila* poets and around eighteen poems were written in Malabar about *Badr* war.[116] Eminent poets of the 19th and the 20th century Arabi-Malayalam literature like Moinkutty Vaidyar, Chakkiri Moidheen Kutty and M.A. Moulavi have endeavoured in writing songs based on this battle. Vaidyar's *Gasvatul Badrul Kubra* (Plate 5.8) written in 1876 is the most popular one among them. Vaidyar's work is said to have taken inspiration from another work in Arabic of similar nature entitled *Anwa ul Baswar bi Akbārul Badr* by Kaipatta Mohiuddin Moulawi written in 1813.[117] This song which was sung at social gatherings during the Mappila Rebellion continuously reminded the Mappilas of the sacrifice made by

[113] Panikkar, *Against Lord and State..*

[114] Razak, *Colonialism and Community Formation in Malabar,* 13.

[115] Moulavi and Kareem, *Mahatāya Māppila Sāhitya Pāṟambaraym,* p.391.

[116] F.Fawcett, Letter No.1567. Judicial 30th September, 1896, p.99, Madras, TNA. The first edition of *Badar padappattu* came out only in 1888.

[117] M.N.Karaserry, Mathrubhumi, 31st, March, 1993.

the *Śahids* for the cause of Islam and inculcated the need of *Jehad* against tyrannical rule of the British.[118]

The battle of *Badr* has, of course, got a sentimental attachment and a special sanctity in the minds of *Mappilas* because of its recurring presence in many of the Mappila songs.[119] British officials on many occasions had written to their higher authorities about the 'miracle power' this work had possessed. Mappilas for many generations believed that during the turbulent period in life, calling the martyrs of *Badr* provides a relief and mental strength to them. This must be the reason that by 1896 itself, the *Badr Padapāṭṭu* of Moyinkutty Vaidyar had gone three editions of 1000 copies in each one.[120] There were many other instances for the divinity given to *Badr Padapāṭṭu* in Mappila life. A report in a local news paper, *Kerala Sancāri* about the blood stained copy of *Badr Patapāṭṭu* found on the body of a 'fanatic' in Manjeri temple where the Mappilas found dead in the battle against British troops in 1896, was illustrative of this. [121] One of the most popular lines of this battle song depicting the fight between Hamza, a close disciple of the Prophet and Aswad, a soldier from the rival's side goes as follows:

Ānapota Sadul Ilahari Hamza cadiyadutudan

Arada suja'taruta mi howlilninnu kudippavan?

(Hamza who looked like an elephant

jumped out of his seat and challenged Aswad,

who dared to fetch water from the tank of the prophet?)

5. *Katupāṭṭukaḷ* or Letter Songs

Katupāṭṭu refers to sending letters or messages in the form of songs. They are basically songs composed for the purpose of disseminating a message. The *Katupāṭṭu* in its modern form tells a lot about the social context in Malabar following the mass migration to the Gulf. There are no documents with clues to the origin of *Katupāṭṭu* in Malabar. No evidences are there tracing its origin to *sandeśa kavyās* in Sanskrit literature.

Katupāṭṭukaḷ expose a wide variety of themes ranging from expression of love, separation of loved ones and casual chats to serious reporting of issues and events in a more emotional way. Emotional content of them makes *Katupāṭṭukaḷ* more popular in Mappila community which constitutes of a considerably huge population in diaspora. This genre is having a discernible effect on the imagination of the diasporic Mappila community. *Katupāṭṭukaḷ* in the new context is patronized mainly by the Mappila migrants in the Gulf countries and their spouses back in Kerala.

Simple and Straightforward lyrics meant to capture the imagination of ordinary people is the note-worthy feature of *Katupāṭṭu*. Searching for thoughtfully written lines with unseen meaning,

---

[118] V.P.Moahmedali, *Mappiḷa Pāṭṭukaḷ Nūṯṯāndukaḷilūde,* p. 65 and Razak, *Cololialism and Community Formation in Malabar,*p.7-8.

[119] Razak, *Cololialism and Community Formation in Malabar,* p.99.

[120] Ibid.

[121] *Kerala Sanchari*, Calicut, 10th March 1897, as cited in Razak, *Cololialism and Community Formation in Malabar,* 99.

skillfully worded imageries and philosophical intricacies in *katupaṭṭu*, therefore, becomes a futile exercise. *katupāṭṭukaḷ*, rather, speak of people's love, affections and agonies in a touching and not-so subtle and uncomplicated language. Looking at the history, one can find the roots of *katupāṭṭukaḷ* stretching back to the leading poet of Arabi- Malayalam, Moinkutty Vaidyar. Vaidyar's first work functioned as a medium of expression for his yet untold love affair with Bibikutty whose higher social status prevented the poet from revealing it openly. Only option left for him was to write a *katupāṭṭu*. Following are the lyrics from the letter song that Vaidyar has written at his young age.

MullappŪ Bēvikkarivan kurite katu

Munnēne mai tammil kandiṭṭilla perutu

Mallikamulla Muhabbathoppil Mulachu

Manathasayalul valarma muradu vachu

(Writing to the noble lady who outshines jasmine,

though we have met seldom.

Mallikamulla[122] that sprouted in the garden of love,

grew further in my mind.)

According to Ahmed a scholar of *Māppiḷappāṭṭu*, there are three distinctive phases of evolution for *katupāṭṭu*. The first phase represents *katupāṭṭu* as a medium for expressing love. Personal communications were also done through this medium. People used to hire professional *katupāṭṭu* writers to express their affair. This phase, therefore, marks the emergence of an avalanche of lyrics in this genre by a group of highly professional poets of that time.[123] There were a lot of poets who had taken writing letter songs as a profession in Kondotty before and after Moinkutty Vaidyar. Oral traditions have ample reference to such poets who had been hired for writing letters on behalf of lovers. Getting a letter in the form of a song was considered as something precious. There was also a tradition to pay considerably huge amount for well-written letter songs.[124] Each work, besides describing the features of partners in love, contains lavish praise of nature.[125]

Nallalam Beeran's famous *katupāṭṭu* addressed to his lover also belongs to this genre. However, Mappila girl Amina's *katupāṭṭu* remains to be the most popular composition falling under this category. This *katupāṭṭu* is in the format of reply to the letter she received from Ahmed requesting to marry her. The *katupāṭṭu* tradition, however, flourished with the increasing captivity of leaders from the community in various jails for their involvement in anti-colonial Mappila rebellion under the British rule. The resultant separation from the family incited many to write letter in the form of songs. The popularity of *katupāṭṭu* in that sense was reflective of a particular political situation in Malabar, wherein many people were taken into confinement because of their role in anti-colonial stir.[126] They

---

[122] A plant with flowers having aromatic fragrance.

[123] Mohamedkunhi, *Musliṉalum Kerala Samskaravum*, p.190.

[124] A.P.Ahmed, scholar of Mappilapattu in an interview with the authors held on 18th March, 2013.

[125] Ibid..

[126] Hussain Randathani, a scholar of Mappila history in an interview with the authors held on 14th March, 2013.

were the pioneers of *katupāṭṭu* tradition which was strongly encouraged by the British jail authorities. This tradition later on resulted in producing a long array of political prisoners-turned poets.[127]

The most famous work representing this phase in the evolution of *katupāṭṭu* is Pulikottil Haider's *Mariyakuṭṭy's Katupāṭṭu*. This *katupāṭṭu* is presented in the form of a letter from Mariyakutty addressed to her husband Hassan Kutty who is imprisoned in Bellarry central prison because of his involvement in the Mappila Rebellion. Throughout the letter, Mariyakutty tries to prove her innocence which had been questioned by an anonymous letter already sent to her husband from the village. Due to her alleged extra-marital relationship with someone in the village, her husband Hassan kutty takes a painful decision to separate legally from her. Hassan kutty writes a letter to her mother in this regard. Terribly upset Mariyakutty, responds convincing her husband of the reality.

Tēnāre umaikatil paraňja ā vidamuḷḷa

tēdicitaram kāṭṭi nadannōlla

enai oru temmādi taravāṭṭil pirannōḷalla.

(...)

Vallōru fasadunnatu kēṭṭu muṣhiyēnda

vadivuṯorumai ennē upekṣikkēnda-manassilu-

valutaye verupponnum vicarikkanda.

(My beloved, I have never lived

like a prostitute in your absence.

Not borne to a family of rogues.

(....)

Don't be bothered about people's gossips,

do not give me up hearing that

don't keep any hate in your mind.[128])

Deportation of Mappila youth involved in 1921 Mappila Rebellion also has spawned interesting *katupāṭṭus*. The most illustrious example is Puthur Amina's *katupāṭṭu***.** This song, which is believed to have written during 1921, is in the form of a response to the marriage proposal from a person who had undergone imprisonment in Bellari jail. *Katupāṭṭu* tradition got further boost with Mappila migration to Malaysia. People started writing letters narrating the situation in Malaysia.[129] Letter songs, therefore, became the songs of separation-separation among couples and lovers.

---

[127] Ibid.

[128] Pulikottil Hyder, "Mariyakuṭṭiyude Katu", in M.N.Karaserry (ed.), *Pulikōṭṭil Kritikaḷ*, (Thrissur: Kerala Sahitya Academi, 2007), pp. 104-107.

[129] Interview with Randathani.

In the late 1970s and 80s audio-cassettes emerged as a major tool for the dissemination of *katupāṭṭu*. This development was closely paralleled with a massive outflow of Mappila Muslim youth to the Gulf countries. Cutting across the class lines, recorded letter songs caught up the popular imagination. The reason for rapidly increasing popularity of cassettes partly remained 'religious. Parallel to this, cassette sermons of popular ulemas played a key role in the mobilization of Muslims in Kerala. Sermon tapes provided one of the prime means by which Islamic moral traditions have been discussed. Mappila migration to the Gulf introduced the tradition of cassette and sending recorded letter songs became widespread. The style of writing and frequency also got changed. The cassette-songs with vast variety of compositions opened the floodgate.[130]

Listening to the letters, sent in the form of recorded song to spouses, kids and parents back at home became the most valued entertainment especially for many in diaspora. The popularity of *katupāṭṭu* cassette also served the purpose of giving public prominence to new breed of singers. Jameel was the most prominent one among them. "Jameel's songs were the hotcakes in the market. Maintaining a very delicate balance, his songs contained an amalagam - of romance, separation, agonies and pleasure" notes Randathani.[131] The pangs of separation, which the Gulf migrant family experiences, has been a recurrent theme in these *katupāṭṭus*. Two such songs of Jameel had become super hits in the 1970s. The first one entitled *Dubai Katu* is in the form of a letter by a woman addressing her husband in the Gulf. She shares her unfulfilled sexual and emotional needs in a soul-stirring tone. In a pungent language, she questions the meaning of life in which her youth is wasted waiting for her husband.

Eẓhuti ariyikkankāryaṉ̂al nŪrundu

eẓhutukayallāte verentu vaẓhiyundu.

EnmiẓhikaltŪkum kaṇṇīratukondu

enkaraḷvēdana kāṇuvānārundu.

Eṉ̂ine ñ̂jan parayum-ellām ortu

ennenum ñ̂jan karayum-Īkatinu

udanadi oru marupaditannu sankidam

tīrtidaṇē-idakiide-ennēyum ōrtidaṇē.

(There are many things to let you know,

no other way but to write,

No other option but to cry.

Who is there to see the pain in my heart.

How do I say?

Suppressing all these in mind, I keep crying every day.

---

[130] Ibid.

[131] Ibid.

Bring an end to my agonies with a quick-paced reply to this letter

Remember me once a while.[132])

In reply entitled *Marupadikatu*, the heart-broken husband agrees that their financial stability is no recompense for a wasted youth. He compares the life of migrant to that of a cow which has never been milked. This song ends with promise to return at the first available opportunity.

Abu-dhabiluḷḷōreẓhutupeṭṭi

annu turannappōḷ katu kiṭṭi.

En priye nīninte hrudayam poṭṭi

eẓhutiya kattu ñan kaṇu ñeṭṭi

(...)

Ēre foreign paṇam gulīnnu vannālum,

etrayum sūkṣhiccu vīttil nīninnālum,

pa<u>tt</u>ipōum, te<u>tt</u>u pa<u>tt</u>ipōkum,

pa<u>tt</u>ipōkum, peṇṇu te<u>tt</u>ipōkum.

Ayalatu kadameduttidum gaduvatil

nīyum peṭṭupōkum.

(The letter box in Abu Dhabi,

received a letter, when it opened.

Really shocked,

while seeing your heart-broken letter.

(...)

Though a huge amount of money coming from the Gulf,

taking extreme care, mistake is inevitable...mistake is inevitable

will get into the trap, you will also get into the trap lurking in the neighborhood.[133])

The most painful sacrifice of single expatriates, separated spouses, missing fathers and departed parents also became the favourite themes for the *katupāṭṭu* composers. Chinna Avaran of Edappal has written a *katupāṭṭu* in the form of a letter sending to a husband who is abroad by his wife. Following is a *katupāṭṭu* composed by Hamza Padoor with lyrics addressing to a migrant wife.

Peṇṇukeṭṭi annumutal āsa tīrniṭṭilla,

pembarannōḷ kappalēri pōyivanniṭṭilla.

---

[132] S.A. Jameel, *S A Jameelinte Terañeduta Kritikal,* (Thrissur: Kerala Sahitya Academi, 2010), pp.81-84.

[133] Ibid., pp.84-86.

Katirunnu innuvare kaṇṇadacciṭṭilla,

Kalbu nīri kateẓhutiyorabi vanniṭṭilla.

(Un-fulfilled desire persists for long,

the wife went off in a ship hasn't returned so far.

Waiting patiently, I couldn't close my eyes.

Not yet returned from the Arab land,

even after sharing wounded heart.)

As Muslims of Kerala evolved to current state of technological sophistication, *katupāṭṭu* cassette's inherent limitation paved the way to its rejection. *Katupāṭṭu* in recorded format lost its charm and replaced or abandoned for more advanced and effective mode of music albums. From simple recording of songs in audio-cassettes, the form has now moved over to music albums. Correspondingly, there is a video culture characterizing a non-film music industry of albums revolving around tender themes of love and separation. Almost parallel to it, there is the emergence of a new class of singers with target listeners (mostly youth). Inspite of the fact that the forms changed with developments in communication technology, ordinary migrant labourers' suffering at the work place remains to be the most favorite theme for many letter songs.

No surprise, this genre gets wide popularity among a section of diasporic Mappilas who lead the way with innovative experiments and new-fangled aesthetic sense. With many tender themes of love and sex, *katupāṭṭukaḷ* always push the boundaries of imagination of a community. Addressed to women or by women at home to their spouses in the Gulf, *katupāṭṭu* expresses their grief, sharing good and bad news and recounting familial and religious incidents. The interesting aspect about these letter songs is that the use of Arabic in them is restricted to terms of endearment, exclamations, appeals to God, religious vocabulary and pronouncement of good wishes. Words borrowed from other languages are almost completely done away with in favour of the northern dialects of Malayalam.

Letter songs from the Gulf marked the latest phase of *katupāṭṭu* tradition. But, many like Ahmed think this would not be the last one. This tradition would continue with Mappila Muslims' migration to other places.[134] But chance is very less to have more letter songs based on the situation in West Asia as the life in Gulf is becoming more family oriented and the distance to the region is getting reduced due to the new means of communication.[135]

6. *Kessupāṭṭukaḷ* or Story Songs

Kess simply means story in Arabic. Traditionally, the presentation of stories in Islamic history in the form of songs has been the peculiarity of this tradition. *Kissapāṭṭu,* another genre with similar nature also depends on historical anecdotes. *Kissapāṭṭu* strictly depend on the real episodes from the life histories of prophets and historical figures in Islam, while *Kessupāṭṭukaḷ* sometimes widen their scope to include imaginary tales also. *Yūsaf Kissa, Adam Nabi kissa, Ibrāhim kissa* and *Umar kissa* are the

---

134 Interview with Ahmed.

135 Ibid.

major works represent this tradition. *Kissapāṭṭu* narrates mainly the life histories of prophets, their companions and other notable figures in the history of Islam in the form of song-stories. But *kessupāṭṭu* picks up themes from the history of Islam and present with high amount of imagination.

There is a wide spectrum of views regarding the evolution and nature of *kessupāṭṭu*. Some sees this as basic knot or raga which is used in all the Mappila songs.[136] *Mappilapāṭṭu* and *Kessupāṭṭu*, are therefore, often used as conflating terms or as synonym to each other. When you ask to sing a *kessu*, it naturally means to sing a Mappila song.[137] *Kessu* encapsulates all the *eśals* or *rāgās* in Mappila songs. At the same time it is being considered as a key or basic note in *Mappilapāṭṭu*. *Kessu* songs find lyrics and rhythms mostly from local compositions.[138]

Kessupāṭṭu covers most importantly the stories related to seminal historical events through which the Muslim community had passed. Renditions of the stories of Arab and Persian sages and legends, hymns that eulogize the holy figures, wars waged in Islamic history and moral lessons-all become themes for *kessupāṭṭu*.

Badarul hudā yāsīn annabikharajayanneram

balar kodi mundeṇṇam keṭṭide atilondē-abiyaḷu.

Varṇamatam pinrandum asuvadumame.

Sadakudai kōḷponkum tirukaramālondāma-

Tatine mnabitan tōlar Misa'bleentar-avarat

tanai pidi ceytaṯṯal mumbile nilayake.

(The last prophet (Mohammed) began to move to Badar

with three flying flags.

Of which, one is white in front,

rest are black to follow.

The prophet with his widely revered hands holds the first one himself, while his close aide Misa'b stands in front of him keeping the second one.)[139]

In addition to historical recording of holy events and epistolary verses, *kessupāṭṭu* in modern form also includes romantic tales and love lyrics. New songs undergo a gradual transition from historical plots to romantic ones. *Kessu* songs are actually love songs with romance as the recurring theme. In most of such songs of the 19th century marked a golden period in the history of *kessupāṭṭu*.[140] During this

---

136 Interview with Ahmed.

137 Ibid.

138 The Kessupattu singer V.M.Kutty in an interview held on 20th March, 2013 by the authors.

139 As sung by Vellayil Aboobacker, a perfomer of Padapāṭṭu during authors' field work.

140 Interview with Tharammel.

period, *kessu* songs had outnumbered all other genres in Arabi-Malayalam literature including *mālas.*[141] *Kessupāṭṭu* as a separate genre finds its origin to some early works of Moinkutty Vaidyar.

As discussed elsewhere, during the first three centuries of its evolution starting from 17th century, *Mappilappāṭṭu* was dominated mainly by highly devotional and philosophical compositions like *mālās*. Arabic *bayts* written with the purpose of moral teaching and *Madhupāṭṭus* praising the Prophet, his close aides and saintly figures also added to the richness of it. The composers of most of such compositions were a part of the class of religious scholars and ulemas. However, *kessupāṭṭu* brought an end to this tradition with works portraying tender and unrefined themes like love, separation, demise and lust. This is viewed by many scholars as a deliberate attempt to make *Mappiḷapāṭṭu* more popular and organic.[142] Although the plots were taken mostly from Arabic and Persian folklore, they were well presented fitting into the cultural milieu of Malabar. Following lines of K.C.Mohamed Kutty Molla are reflective of this synthesis.

Vambutta Hamza raḷyaḷḷa cadi-

ṭṭambi asvadil māradā.

Vaḷḷar mahmūdar tante hauḷinnu

veḷḷam kudikkunnōnārada.

Ambar śafiyuḷḷa kāmal veccuḷḷa,

Sambaramil vannu cēradā.

Khairul barā nabiyār kuḷatīnu,

Dairiyamundenkil kōredā.

(The brave Hamsa jumped out of his seat and challenged Aswad

Who is dared to fetch water from the tank of the prophet?

Those who are bold enough,

come and grab water from the storage tank

which is under the possession of the great prophet.)

Badarul Munīr-Hussanul Jamāl of Vaidyar and *Saubāgya Sundari* of Chettuvay Pareekutty, the pioneering works in this genre proved that a narration of romance and desire are not alien to *Mappilappāṭṭu*. Aesthetic beauty of lyrics became a prime concern after that. Vaidyar's master piece *Badarul Munīr-Hussanul Jamāl* written in the year 1872 is the first work that conforms to a standard *kessupāṭṭu*. The way in which the story of *Badarul Munīr- Hussanul Jamāl* has been narrated is worth-mentioning. There are a lot of magical elements, superhuman beings, and supernatural beings like *jihns* and angels and bizarre locations.[143]

---

[141] Ibid.

[142] Ibid.

[143] Ibid.

Kandāraṭṭummal vantaraḷa takhttondatilundane oruti

kahaniludite khamarpol mukham katilenki marintanē.

(...)

Undante kattilil cuṯṯilum nalpatu pendikalum tanē kidnatu

okkēyum takōlamikkeyurakkil kidakkeyetrittānē.

(He (Badrul Muneer) came to see

that pretty woman (the queen of jihn) sleeping on a royal bed.

Her face brightened like a full moon rose in the sky.

(....)

Around forty women were laying around,

and each one had competed with each other even in sleep.)

The poem starts with the poet's appealing accounts of the prettiness of Husanul Jamal.

Pūmakaḷaṇu Hussanul Jamal,

punnāratālam mikanta bīvi.

Hemaṉal mette paṇi cittiram,

ābaraṇa kōrvēy aṇinta bīvi.

(Most affectionate and pretty, Husanul Jamal

with beautiful and rhythmic steps,

putting on well-designed golden ornaments.[144])

Badarul Munīr -Hussanul Jamāl illustrates a love story based on Persian novel with same title by Khaja Moinudheen Shah Shiras.[145] The theme of this work revolves around a love affair. Vaidyar's unrevealed affair with a lady from the elite Sayyid family is said to have inspired his imagination. Protagonists in this folklore-turned song are Hussanul Jamal, the daughter of the King Mahasin of Izmeer and Badarul Muneer, the son of his Minister, Masameer. When the circumstances went against their love, they decided to elope. In a futile attempt to do so Hussanul Jamal went missing. Muneer's search for the missing lover ended up in the palace of Qamarban, the queen of *Jihns*. Enchanted by the beauty of Muneer, Qamarban kept him in her custody. Sufaira, the daughter of Shihab, the Emperor of Parijihns, happened to meet Muneer who was sleeping in the garden of Qamarban. Without disturbing his sleep, Sufiara took him on her wings and flew away.

---

[144] As sung by Ramla Beegum, renowned Mappila song singer,during the field work of the authors.

[145] Vaidyar's work is actually based on the translation of Khaja Moinudheen Shah Shiras's Persian work by Nisamudheen Thangal of Kondotty. Moulavi and Kareem, *Mahatāya Māppila Sāhitya Pāṟambaraym*, p.34.

The element of love in Badarul Muneer –Hussanul Jamal can be seen as an element of liberation.[146] With stress on romance, this work demanded a radical change is the social imagination of Mappila Muslims. *Kessupāṭṭu* tradition consists of an amazingly rich tradition of love songs, that blend tenderness, love, imagination, humour in a fine manner. [147] Pareekutty's *Soubāgya Sundari* composed in the year 1868 is considered to be another landmark in the history of *kessupāṭṭu.* This work gives a detailed narration of hurries and the pleasure-filled state of affairs offered for a believer in heaven. Love and pleasure were the major sentiments expressed in Pareekutty's work. Meher another major poet travelled along a different direction concentrating seldom on desire but on pure and uncontaminated love.

There are *Kessupāṭṭu* revolving around the romantic tales taken from Islamic history; mostly tragic ones ending with the poignant silhouette of women lamenting their beloved who fell in the battle field even before the honeymoon days were over. [148] Although most of the *kessu* songs are with threads taken from Islamic history, there are some with stories placed in the cultural context of Kerala.[149] Life histories of many legendary figures in Kerala Muslim history have found place in these songs. Apart from that, some imaginary stories taken from Persian language have successfully been adapted to Kerala's cultural milieu.

While oriented mainly to the past, *kessupāṭṭu* also reflects some of the stresses in the present life of the community. The composers of *Kessupāṭṭu* find elements from contemporary Malayali life simultaneous to render events in Islamic history. Bullock-race, a popular pastime in southern Malabar has been the theme of a *Kessupāṭṭu* composed by Pulikottil Hyder. This work with its amazingly lucid narration, at some point of time, turns to be a live commentary of this sporting event.[150]

Kāḷap Ūṭṭintatisayam-palarume

para ñña cēti-ente

kalikaḷ kondoru dinam

ññan cennaṇa ñña cēti.

Āḷu eṇṇam anavadiyundu

āke vīti atilorukundu

kīḷe veḷḷam caḷiyatilundu

kāḷakal maṯṯanavadiyundu-kannu

oru jōdi teḷicu kadannu

vadiyuḷḷavarokkeyum vannu-nukam

veccu amaccu keṇiccu taṇiccu.

---

[146] Interview with Tharamel.

[147] Krishna Chaithanya, *A History of Malayalam Literature*, Hyderabad: Orient Longman, 1971,p.197.

[148] Ibid.

[149] Interview with Randathani

[150] Interview with Kutty.

Nēru mūlanṭatuvare vadiveccuraccu keṯṯi kannine

Ninnu maṇdatida kodukkāte janaṉal pāṯṯi.

(Having heard amusement-filled affairs of bullock raise from many,

I rushed to see that one day with my two bullocks.

What I saw was:

massive gathering of enthusiasts;

vast expanse of field-with water and mud down;

long army of bullocks apart from mine.

I entered the field riding the pair,

all in the raise fall in line with sticks in hand. [151])

The flood that affected people of Malabar towards the beginning of the 20th century, for instance, has become the theme of a *Kessupāṭṭu.*

Immalayāḷatilikkuri vannatu pōlotoru maẓhaveḷḷam

nammatumumbe keriyatarum kandilla.

Etira padum pīdika vīdum tōdum mala kunnum,

kutiyidinñolippatinottum maṭṭilla.

(We have never seen such a flood before

like the one affected the land of Malayalam this time.

The unhesitant flood, washed away all the shops, rivulets, hills and hillocks,

as soon as it started.[152])

This *kessupāṭṭu* blends different languages and appropriate different poetic structures so as to create a sublime poetic effect. The most renowned work belonging to the category of modern *kessupāṭṭu* is of P.T. Abdul Rahman. His work *Ōttupaḷḷiyil Annu Nammaḷ* is a very powerful manifestation of a nostalgic past of two who fall in love and maintain a keen wish to marry when grow up.

Ōttupaḷḷīannu nammaḷ poyirunna kālam,

ortukaṇṇīr vārtu nilkayāṇu nīlamēgham.

Kōntalakkalannu nīyenikkay keṭṭiya nellikka,

kanducūral vīsiyille nammude mollākka.

(Memorizing our *madrassa* days,

---

[151] Pulikottil Hyder, "Kāḷapūṭṭu Pāṭṭu", in M.N.Karaserry (ed.), *Pulikōṭṭil Kritikaḷ,* (Thrissur: Kerala Sahitya Academi, 2007), p. 51.

[152] As sung by Nallalam Kabeer, a perfomer of Mappila songs,during the field work of authors.

the blue clouds are in tears.

Seeing the gooseberry kept in the lap-pouch for me,

Mulla[153] whipped up his deterrent-stick angrily.)[154]

Although being a fast number composed for a Malayalam movie, *Ōttupaḷḷiyilannu Nammaḷ* there are three varying styles for singing this song. With its simple and touching lyrics, plain and easy to elaborate compositions, Malayalam films have successfully made use of *kessupāṭṭu*. Though written in Malayalam language, these *kessupāṭṭu* have borrowed considerably huge vocabularies from Arabic and Arabi-Malayalam. Music composers in the Malayalam film industry depend on this genre, especially to visualize fond memories of childhood and past affairs. Malayalam playback singer Mehboob has composed and sung many songs belonging to this genus. The most famous and well accepted one in that list is *Cheruppathil Annu Nammaḷ* which remains to be a text-book example for this tradition.

Cerupatilannu nammaḷ random maṇṇuvari kaḷicappol

annu tammil paraññatum marannupōyō? (2)

Kaliccaṭṭi ciraṭṭayāy muriṉapp Ūpariciṭṭu

Kariveccu kaḷiccatum marannu pōyō?

(Did you forget what we said,

when we played together grabbing soil during our childhood?

Did you forget?

We prepared curries making the coconut shell the utensil,

filling drum-stick flower in it.[155])

Another composition of Mehboob, *Kayalinaṟike* is an instantaneously prepared Kessupattu on the arrival of Cochin port and resultant industrialization of Cochin City.

Kāyalinarike kodikal parati

kuticcu poṉiya companikaḷ.

Kaccavadatinunu kaccamurukki,

kanattu nilkum companikaḷ.

Kayalinarike, Kochi kayalijnarike...

Pears Lessly, Aspin Wall, Vochard,

H& C, Bomaby company Madurai company,

A.V.Thomas company-

---

[153] Instructor in local religious school.

[154] As sung by the renowned Mappila song composer Vatakara Krishnadas.

[155] As sung by Kishore Abu, a perfomer of *Kessu Pāṭṭu*..

aṉine pala pala companikaḷ.

Cochiyileṉum carakku nīkkaṉu, cerakkirakkaṉu,

cerakkukēṯṯaṉu...

Nammude rubberum, corium, teyila kurumuḷakēlam, cemmīn,

tavaḷakal pōlum kayaṯṯiyayakkaṉ.

Namude nadin karaḷu tudikkaṉu, vayaru viśakkaṉu,

"no vacancy"....

(By the side of Kochi lake,

companies coming up,

holding their flags flying high,

prepared well enough to trade.

By the side of lake, by the side of Kochi lake.....

Pears Lessly, Aspin Wall, Vochard

H & C, Bombay Compnay, Madura Compnay

A.V.Thomas Company ...many companies are there.

Loading and off loading goods everywhere in Kochi,

Latex, coir, tea, pepper and prawns, even our frogs are exported.

Beating our lands' heart, but stomachs are still empty-no vacancy.)

Kessupāṭṭu tradition continued to flourish with a long army of contemporary Mappila poets like Kanesh Punur, O.M.Karuvarakkkundu and Bappu Veliparambu and singers like Peer Mohammed, Ramla Beegum, V.M.Kutty, Vilayil Valasa and Eranjoli Moosa. Apart from these, there are some local works with less known or completely unknown authors. Some of them are the finest examples of the aesthetic excellence of *kessupāṭṭu*. Following is such a composition of an anonymous local poet:

Muṯṯatu mātoḷi mūttu paẓhuttappō,

mūtevi peṇṇinte kaṇṇutaṭṭi.

Mūkkatta pūvellām vīṇennu kēṭṭappōḷ,

mūttappa mukkilirunnu ñetti.

Appaḷu, mūkkatte kaṇṇāda vīṇu poṭṭi.

(When the mango turned yellow,

It caught up the notice of the 'naughty girl'.

On hearing- all the flowers fallen down immaturely-

paternal uncle sitting on the corner took it by shock.

Spectacle on his nose then fallen down and got cracked.[156])

7. *Kalyāṇapāṭṭukaḷ* or Wedding Songs

As an important part of community life, Arabi-Malayalam songs have had a special role to play in the Mappila life cycle events. Traditional Mappila weddings, circumcision of boys and ear-piercing of girls were the special occasions where *Māppilapāṭṭu* found to be an inextricable item. The celebration attached to Mappila wedding used to last for three to four days. Nights fully immersed in music were the peculiarity of those occasions. The *mylānci* or applying henna on the hands and legs of the bride one day before the wedding marks the start of celebration. There were compositions specifically meant for *mylānci*. *Maylāncipāṭṭukaḷ* sung mainly by the women is the most prominent one in the category of *kalyāṇapāṭṭukaḷ* or wedding songs. The earliest of this genre, *Ādi mutal purāṇam* by an anonymous poet deals with the life history of the Prophet from his birth to Haleema breast-feeding him.

Ādimutal purāṇam āyetiri mutolivē

Āye padappinellām āridabinnāya telivē

Kātal Muhammadenna kārunapper peṯṯoḷivē

Kālam paśammayil panduḷḷa padacuvacu.

(The shining pearl, existed from the beginning,

revered by all other creatures of God.

A person called Mohamed because of his kindness,

God created his light[157] in the beginning.)

Another popular wedding song *Trikkallyaṇapāttu* depicts the imaginary marriage of Prophet Muhammed in heaven.[158] *Maylāncipāṭṭukaḷ* starts normally around eight in the evening and lasts until dawn. Women in the bride's house split into two or more groups and compete openly with each other in singing.

During the marriage festivities, songs formed an important part of celebrations.[159] *Kalyāṇapāṭṭukaḷ* vary from function to function. There are songs that the music troops sing with the purpose of entertaining the people gathered on the occasion.[160] Sometimes, making fun of the bridegroom turns out to be the major purpose of it. Another variety is accompanied by *Oppana* performed by the bride's friends with claps and body movements. Anyway, the tradition of wedding songs is very rich in composition and imagination.

---

[156] As sung by Kishore Abu.

[157] God, Muslims believe, created the light of the Prophet first even before Adam.

[158] Razak, *Cololialism and Community Formation in Malabar,* p. 16.

[159] Ibid.

[160] Karaserry, "Māppiḷapāṭṭu", p. 53.

Oppana songs like *Ādi mutal purānam* and *Tasrīf* and wedding songs like *Paẓhaya Ammāyipaṭṭu*[161] are the major components of wedding songs. They sometimes include songs describing the specificities and decorations of *pandal* or *shamiana* erected on the occasion of wedding and the ornaments that the bride wear. Here is an example of a wedding song composed in the *eśal, Oppanaccāyal* with the purpose of describing the ornaments that the bride wearing:

Māla bairam ratnamāla

Mikavilārkkum pūtemāla

Mālacakkara minnimāla

Madira cilli enna māla.

(Necklace is of diamond

looks like a bunch of flowers.

The ornament called *madiraccilli*

shines like a star.[162])

Kalyāṇapaṭṭukaḷ, according Razak, provide interesting glimpses of the life world of Mappilas- divergent culinary specialities, the types of ornaments worn by Muslim women, the dress pattern and various ceremonies associated to Mappila marriage.[163]

8. *Vaṭṭappāṭṭu* or Circle Song

Vaṭṭappāṭṭu, 'circle-song', is a house hold performance in Malabar by a group of men with devotional tinge. The name is derived from the word *vaṭṭa* which means circle in Malayalam language. *Vaṭṭappāṭṭu* is performed on the occasion of wedding. There are two varieties of *vaṭṭappāṭṭu*. Male oppana, a dance form performed by the friends of the bride or bridegroom at the wedding is the most popular form of it.[164] As a sophisticated form of *vaṭṭappāṭṭu*, male *oppana* is performed on the stage using a mix of both traditional and modern songs.

Vaṭṭappāṭṭu shows close resemblance to o*ppana*, but with less complex body movements and steps. Facial expressions and hand gestures carry high importance in *oppana* while movements of head and upper portion of the body are important in *vaṭṭappāṭṭu*. Songs used in *oppana* differ in lyrics, composition and rhythm. The style of clapping also varies in male oppana. Two palms are kept close to each other in it, while in female oppana claps are slightly different, keeping palms at some distance from each other.

---

161 Ammayipattus are the preserve of women meant to describe the special treatment given to son-in-laws. Special food items that mother-in-law prepared for the son-in-law would be the theme of Ammayipattu.

162 Lines from *Sakalappōmāla Kalyānappāṭṭukaḷ* as sung by Nallalam Kabeer.

163 Razak, *Cololialism and Community Formation in Malabar,* p.16.

164 Interview with Pareed Gurukkal, a trainer of vattapattu based in Padoor held on 6th July, 2013. See also Iqbal Koppilan, *Vaṭṭapāṭṭu*, (Kondotty: Scarf, 2008) and V.M.Kutty, *Oppana Enna Vaṭṭapāṭṭu,* (Thiruvananthapuram: Kerala Basha Institute, 2011).

The second variety, otherwise known as *kaimuṭṭipāṭṭu,* focuses mainly on songs with clapping while male *oppana* revolves around hand and body gestures along with clapping. The only instrument used in *kaimuṭṭipāṭṭu* is *kiṉṉāram* or copper vessel. The leader uses dried areca palm and beat strongly on the copper vessel in order to make background score. The *vaṭṭappāṭṭu* crew normally consists of eight-ten people called *kaimuṭṭipāṭṭukār* or *ān pāṭṭukar* (male singers) sitting in circle or horse shoe shape. The lead performer or the poet sits in the middle of a circle of singers, who repeat each verse in a chorus, though often they all sing the songs in single voice. Chorus repeats the lines in entirety or *tundam* - a portion of the song. *Vaṭṭappāṭṭu* is performed on the basis of traditional formulaic and thematic patterns.

In male *oppana,* claps are made tilting hands up and down, panning right and left in tune with the changing rhythm of the song. Postures change rapidly moving along a uniform direction, shaking heads in tandem with the tune or kneeling down-all make the performance more attractive. But in traditional *vaṭṭappāṭṭu,* singers sit in a circle with no vigorous body movements. On certain occasions, singers raise their hands giving cues to the others to start singing when they stop. In certain performances, bridegroom sits in the middle. The white knee-length glittering attire gives him a distinctive look from others. A bead over neck and the skull cap also add to this distinctiveness.

Vaṭṭappāṭṭu is performed in ceremonial as well as in ordinary settings. The themes range from anecdotes from Islamic history to contemporary issues like dowry system. The songs that accompany *vaṭṭappāṭṭu* are basically in Arabi-Malayalam and are drawn out of a huge and dynamic corpus of literary expressions in this language. With distinctive performance and linguistic features, *vaṭṭappāṭṭu* songs juxtapose the tradition of classical poems, folk songs and extempore compositions in a single song. Like *oppana, vaṭṭappāṭṭu* is also a rallying point for many song traditions like *madhupāṭṭukaḷ* or praise songs, *ammāyipāṭṭukaḷ* or songs describing mother-in-law's special treatment to son-in-law and *appappāṭṭukaḷ* or songs with the description of food items (mainly bread) prepared for bridegroom. The songs, their contents, their linguistic registers and generic features are designed to fit certain performative concerns according to the occasion. These songs are generally reflective of pragmatic working of language usage and literary genre.

There are no documented evidences to the genesis of *vaṭṭappāṭṭu*. Its spread is also wrapped in mystery. The 17th and the 18th centuries marked the domination of Tamil poets or *pulavars* and their compositions. The teams were brought in to Malabar from Kayal Pattanam area of Tamil Nadu.[165] Ali Pulavar, Gunamkudi Mastan, Usman Nainar Pulavar and Umar Pulavar were the famous poets from Tamil Nadu, whose Arabi-Tamil works have been widely used in *vaṭṭappāṭṭu. Munājat, virutam, mangalam, sīra and padam* which are being considered as the inevitable part of *vaṭṭappāṭṭu* are reflective of Tamil influence. *Vaṭṭappāṭṭu* turned to a different trajectory with the arrival of Moinkutty Vaidya'rs *kiḷḷatamāla, Veṯṯilapāṭṭu, mōlapurānam,* etc..[166] The Tamil tradition remained strong with the Arabi-Malayalam poets including Moinkutty Vaidyar who consistently looked up on their counterparts in Tamil Nadu for new tunes.

---

[165] Koppilan, *Vaṭṭapāṭṭu,*pp.46-51.
[166] Ibid.

By the late 19th and the early 20th century home grown poets like Nallalam Beeran of Calicut emerged and their lyrics gained popularity among Mappila Muslims. By the middle of the 20th century, *Vaṭṭappāṭṭu* departed partly from the Arabi-Tamil orbit with the indigenously written *kalyānapāṭṭukal* or wedding songs. The prominence given to Tamil tradition eventually declined with the emergence of Mappila poets like KT Moidheen. With P.K.Haleema's *Candirasundari Māla, kalyāṉapāṭṭukaḷ* gained wide acceptance in *vaṭṭappāṭṭu* performance. Some works by anonymous or little known authors like *Ādi mutal purānam, Hazatul khuddŪs, Trikkalyānapāṭṭu* and *Tasrīf* gained so much of attention during this period.

Vaṭṭappāṭṭu has got almost four parallel appellations in different parts of Malabar. They are: *Toḷḷappāttu* (songs sing full throated), *kalyānapāṭṭu* (wedding songs), *motaḷapāṭṭu* and *kaimuṭṭipāṭṭu* (clap songs).[167] A normal *vaṭṭappāṭṭu* performance has several segments. Each one differs from other in content, style and speed. Members in the team normally wear white knee length shirts or gowns and a white turban or skull cap. In traditional format, each performance starts with the first segment *vaẓhinīlam.* This segment literally means 'all through the way' refers to the songs or couplets from Arabic literature being used by the people accompanying the bridegroom on their way to bride's house. As per the convention, *Putiyāpḷa* or the bridegroom does not go bride's house directly. A group of close relatives from bride's family has to go in search of the bridegroom.

The second segment called *Mōtaḷa edal* involves a set of songs performed in the context of bridegroom's hair cut and shaving. The *vaṭṭappāṭṭu* crew circles around the bridegroom and the barber with specific songs fitting into the context. The crew continues singing and clapping until the hair cutting or shaving gets finished.[168] *Mōtaḷa* literally means shaving is celebrated in the morning on the day of wedding.[169] The celebration involves troops singing songs describing the beauty of the bride. The metaphors used in these songs sometimes go to the extent of comparing the bride with the *hourries* and angels of the heaven.

BŪvanatileṉum collān ukamilla,

suvantilundu hurānikal,

katiram kattitteḷi mettattirumēnikaḷ.

Avaril hyḷum nifāsum pativilla.

(They are the beauties of heavan,

none is there on the earth to compete with them.

With bodies like flames,

no custom of menses among them.)[170]

---

[167] Interview with Nallalam Kabeer, a vattapattu performer held on 2nd January, 2013.

[168] Ibid.

[169] Ibid.

[170] As sung by Nallalam Kabeer.

On reaching the bride's house, the crew splits in to two and each one sits on a specially designated space for them called *padāpuaram*.[171] A *vaṭṭappāṭṭu* performance, which normally starts around 4 or 5 in the evening, lasts for almost 12 hours. Sometimes stretches up till next day evening. For the convenience of those who were engaged in maritime trade, most of the Muslim weddings were normally held during the night. There may be two teams representing bride's and bridegroom's party. The wedding ceremonies often become a battleground for two parties to compete with each other.

Booking a *vaṭṭappāṭṭu* troupe on the occasion of wedding remained a difficult task earlier. Even the dates of weddings were decided according to the convenience of *vaṭṭappāṭṭu* troupes. The crew comes a little in advance and the leader or poet collects the details of the bride or bridegroom and their parents, siblings and close relatives in order to add it into the lyrics prepared in extempore.

> The poet in the crew prepares lines instantaneously matching with the occasion. Such hurriedly prepared lines sometimes trace out the genealogy of the bride or bridegroom.[172] Even the description of *pandal* or the specially erected *shamiana* at the bride's or bridegroom's place will be covered in these compositions.[173]

Taśrīf[174], the oldest oppana song is the starter. Around that time the team from bride's place in search of the bridegroom reaches and the bridegroom is taken to bride's house by them. The *vaṭṭappāṭṭu* troop from the bridegroom's place also accompanies him throughout the way. After reaching bride's place and identifying the space specially allotted for them, each troop resumes their performances with *salām* and welcome song. The *vaṭṭappāṭṭu* team from bride's place normally sings *bayts* or couplets from Arabic literature called *viḷikkum bayt* or "*bayt* of reception" on this occasion. *vaṭṭappāṭṭu* team accompanying bridegroom find their place usually on the right side of the bride, while the team from bride's side prefers to sit on the left.[175]

From this point onwards, *vaṭṭappāṭṭu* turns out to be a venue for both the teams to compete with each other. Before starting the performance, the team leader seeks the consent and blessings of the eldest person in the family. The first turn always goes to bridegroom's team. To start with, the leaders from each team alone or the full team sing *munjāt*, which refers to a face-off between two teams.

> *Putumāranum sōdararum vannu*
>
> *putupantalakam kadannu,*
>
> *putuvaki keṭṭicamaynte,*
>
> *putuvāki pāṭṭu tudarnnu.*
>
> (There comes the bridegroom and his siblings,
>
> to the newly erected shamiana,

---

[171] Koppilan, *Vaṭṭapāṭṭu,* p.47.
[172] Interview with Ahamed.
[173] Interview with Kabeer.
[174] This work is said to have composed by Kottaparambathu Kunjikakka.
[175] Koppilan, *Vaṭṭapāṭṭu*,p.47.

dressed attractively,

with interesting rhythms that goes on...)[176]

Munajāt is followed by *virutam*, which literally means humming, to be sung by the *vaṭṭappāṭṭu* team from the bride's side. Earlier compositions for virutam were borrowed from Tamil poets' work. Now there are some indigenous ones. Following lines by K.T.Moidheen is the most favourite one among the *vaṭṭappāṭṭu* performers.

Ādirahman taniyanoḷi vilteḷiva,

tākapirantanabiye.

Āśaiymayil veṣamāy nēṣaviṣvāsamā,

yaruḷ peṯṯu vanta nabiye.

Cōti nabiyādam toduttu varunabi mārga

colvaẕhiyil vanta nabiye.

The Prophet of the one who is alone (God) and has been there from the beginning,

invisible but visible everywhere,

Came to the earth with love and trust,

with the words of God.

Inspired by a series of prophets starting from the first one, Adam

he chose the same way, they led.

The team from Bridegroom's side then initiates *kavi* or extempore songs.[177] There are mainly three *kavis*, namely, *salām kavi, mangala kavi* and *saṛasa Kavi.*[178] The other group then reciprocates it with *cāṭṭakavi*. Next segment involves *kalyānpāṭṭu* or wedding songs chronicling generally around the theme of prophet's wedding to Khadeeja or his daughter Fatima's wedding to Ali. The themes also range from the weddings of other historical figures in Islam to marital linkages of the elders in the family of bride or bridegroom. *Sīra* or *madhu* songs praising prophet Mohammed, any other prophets or any saintly figures in Islamic history is the next in line in *vaṭṭappāṭṭu.*

The component *veṯṯilapāṭṭu* deals with specific songs giving signals to the bride's party to bring good-quality betel leaf for the bridegroom's party. With *padam* or recitation of the life history of a holy figure in the form of a song *vaṭṭappāṭṭu* comes to the end. Though coming towards the end, *padam* is an inevitable component of a *vaṭṭappāṭṭu* performance. Bridegroom's party takes the initiative in singing *padam* while the bride's party responds to that. Since it is the last segment, competition enters

---

176 A *munājāt* as sung by Nallam Kabeer, a vattapattu performer.

177 Interview with Kabeer.

178 Koppilan, *Vaṭṭapāṭṭu*, p. 57.

into its peak with *padam*. Both the teams take *padams* from the same book and challenge the other one to complement it. If the latter fails to do so, the former will be declared victorious. [179]

Sometimes, the competition goes on with no one declared victorious until the eldest member of the bridegroom intervenes into with a gentle request to stop it. Weddings in Malabar, thus, become battle ground for professional teams from various parts to take on others.[180]

Until around 1960s, vehicles were not used in transporting bride's and bridegroom's parties in most of the weddings which happened during the night. The guests attending the wedding bear torch and the singers accompany them sing wedding songs all along the way. Adding charm to the procession, *kōlkkaḷi* and *arabanmuṭṭu* were also performed. *Oppana, Mayilāncipāttukal* (songs specially prepared on the occasion of applying Henna) and wedding songs also find place in the celebration. The celebration starts one day before the actual function. The function held in bride's house is called *mylāncirāvu* or henna eve and those at bridegroom's house called *veṯṯilakeṭṭu*. There were separate specialized troops for each. Recently, *vaṭṭappāṭṭu* has made a comeback in the form of male oppana with more modern musical compositions in youth festivals. But, the modified version has attracted the so much of criticism from a section of performers for its alleged tendency to drift away from the traditions.[181]

9. *Pantalpāṭṭukaḷ*

Kalyāṇa pantal or *shamiana* specially erected for weddings were the major attraction of the wedding ceremony. Hence, the descriptions of the *shamiana* became a part of wedding songs. Following are the lines of a wedding song praising shamiana written by K.T.Moidheen:

Maṭṭatil pandal keṭṭicuṯṯum kasēra nirati

moncu parayanentoru kautuka kalliyānamē

Maṭṭil viḷakkukaḷ katum

mlar hāra tōraṇam tūṇum

patara māṯṯoḷi mutu viḷayana

kalyāṇamē- kalyāṇamē.

(Stylish Shamiana erected and chairs put around it,

beauty of it is beyond description-wonderful wedding.

Pretty lamps spread lights around,

garlands of flower hang around,

golden lights generate beads,

Wedding-wedding.

---

[179] Interview with Kabeer.

[180] Interview with Gurukkal.

[181] Ibid.

10. *Oppanappāṭṭukaḷ*

The women perform *oppana* one day before the wedding. Traditionally, elderly women in traditional white dress seat the bride in their midst and sing songs with dance steps and hand clapping faster and faster as the performance proceeds. The two main rhythms of *oppana* songs are *oppana cāyal* (a slow rhythm) and *muṟukkam* (a fast rhythm). Additionally, there is an *oppana* performed by men for the groom. They circle around the groom and sing *oppana* songs accompanied by hand clapping. The songs sung in such events are drawn out of a huge and dynamic corpus that reflects the linguistic and cultural fusion of the regional local Kerala culture with the pan-Muslim culture of Arabia. There are more performative events depicting this fusion, at times leaning more towards the local, and at times leaning more towards the universal Islamic culture.

The origin of this performance traces back to Southern Arabia. *Henne Dance* a performative tradition popular among the Yemeni tribes is believed to be the prototype of *oppana.*[182] This art form is performed mainly by women though not confined to them. Female *oppana* is more colourful and stylish in terms of movements and songs than male *oppana* or *vaṭṭappāṭṭu*. The song with the wedding of the Prophet Mohamed with Khadeeja is the most popular one among the *oppana* songs.

Taruṇimaṇi Beevi Khadeeja māḷika mukaḷil kēriyirunnu

tirutwahā nabiyude varavine kāṇān tuniyunnē.

(Lovely noble lady kadeeja sitting in the balcony,

waiting eagerly for the Prophet's arrival.)[183]

Following is a very famous *oppana* song composed by P.T. Abdul Rahman:

Kaimuṭṭipādai nallōnam-innu

kaḷicirippeṇṇinte kalyāṇam.

Pidayannatikavota peṇṇaṇu-cañju

padaveṭṭum vāḷoḷikaṇṇāṇu.

Tattammakotoru cundāṇu-nalla

mutu niratiya pallāṇu.

kōriruḷotoru mudiyaṇu-teḷi

vāroḷitankakkaviḷānu.

(Clap and sing well-today

wedding of the naughty girl-

with features of female swan-

eyes like fast moving swords in the air,

---

[182] Mohamedali, *Mappiḷa Pāṭṭukaḷ Nūṯṯāndukaḷilūde,* p. 126.
[183] Ibid.

lips reminds that of parrot-nice,

teeth like white beads.

Hair resembling thickly dark night, bright

cheeks shining like moon.)

The wedding songs vary from the ones appreciating the ornaments that the bride wears to the delicious food items that the mother-in-law prepared for the bridegroom. Mother–in-law's concern over the health of the bridegroom manifested through the items prepared for him is a favourite theme of many *appapāṭṭukaḷ*. Looking at the lyrics, one can see a huge list of deliscious Arab dishes popular among the Muslims in Malabar in a*ppapāṭṭu*. Since Mappila communities of certain coastal towns like Calicut, Thalaserry and Ponnani followed matrilineal system, bridegrooms normally live at brides' place after marriage. *Appapāṭṭu* listing down the special items, therefore, in such places occupy a special position in the wedding songs.

Appaṉalembādum cuṭṭammāyi, marumone vīṭṭil viḷiccammāyi.

Appāde appaṉal ōrō taram.

Arikalakki cuṭṭappam,

araśi; varum neyyappam,

maduramuḷḷa kalatappam,

madurамēum idiyappam,

maduramuḷḷa neyyaluva, maiyarayil konduvaccu,

tinnīm mōne-vendammāyi,

iṉal tinnīnnum paraññukondu-marumone

tīṭṭikkunna muttammayi-nalla punnārammayi.

(Preparing all items, mother-in–law feeds son-in-law,

bread made of rice powder, sweet ghee bread, *kaḷatappam*, rice noodles, sweet ghee halwa- all are kept in the *maṉiyara*[184] exclusively for in-law.

Eat my son, please...eat my son, please.

No, mother-in-law...

Mother-in-law compelling and begging him to eat...)

11. *Kissappāṭṭukaḷ* or Story Songs

Kissappāṭṭukaḷ or story songs find themes either from the life histories of the prophets and other eminent personalities or formidable episodes in Islamic history. Majority of the works included in the first category has the Prophet Mohammed's biography as the major plot. Of which *Hijāratunnabi* of

[184] Chamber designated for newlywed couple.

Moinkutty Vaidyar is the most popular one. Being the last work of Vaidyar, this work has gained additional fame. This work portrays the life of the Prophet from the birth to *hijra* or his exile to Medina in the form of a long poetry. Though the work of this peom started in 1887, Vaidyar could finish only a small portion up to Umar's repentance and subsequent embrace of Islam. With unexpected death of the poet, rest of the work was finished jointly by his father Unni Mammad Vaidyar and friend Ambayathnhal Kunhamutty.

> *Etira santośitā ratiru taruḷ*
>
> *Avidame bida nadatudar padi nadu ada*
>
> *Eśi nabiyum atisayatal-munamil*
>
> *Nadatu hamza pintudarnu farookh*
>
> *Ūrippiditu bal iruvarume.*
>
> (He, the noble one,
>
> cheerfully went on the journey.
>
> The Prophet in the middle,
>
> Hamza moved in front with high amount of excitement,
>
> Farook followed him (the Prophet),
>
> both with swords unwrapped.

Other major works in this category are *Yousaf Kissappāṭṭu* (Plate 5.9)*, Ibrahim Nabi Kissappāṭṭu, Suleiman Nabi Kissappāṭṭu* and *Easa Nabi Kissappāṭṭu.* Life histories of the prophet Yousaf and Zuleikh have, actually, been the theme for many story songs, *Yousaf Kissappāṭṭu* by Sardarakat Bawa of Thalaserry being the prominent one.

> *Bīvimey Arasīnal Zuleikha tante*
>
> *Vadan oḷi suhra polnirantu tintu*
>
> (Body of Beebi Zuleikha shined royally,
>
> glow of her face spread around
>
> (....)
>
> One can't stop listening to,
>
> what comes from her lips.)

Mayankutty Ilaya's *Kissat Suleiman ibn Dawūd* popularly known as *Suleiman Nabi Kissappāṭṭu* written in 1847 finds its plot from the eventful life history of the prophet Suleiman. More than narrating his divinity, this work tries to sketch out a profile of the prophet taking cues from his real life. Setting Israel as the locale of the story, the life history of the prophet Daniel has been illustrated in a *Kissappāṭṭu* called *Daniel Nabi Kissappāṭṭu.* Author and period of this work remain unknown. Easa Nabi *Kissappāṭṭu* is based on the biography of the prophet Easa. Though the author and year of publication are remained unknown, a modified version of this work is said to have printed and published from Thalaserry in 1847. [185]

The story songs based on the historical events range from the life and death of holy figures and war heroes to the history of spread of Islam in Kerala and the miracles of Sufi saints. *Mina'tul Bari* composed in 1881 by Chettuvayi Pareekutty, for instance, narrates the story of Islam through the life history of Sayyid Mohammed Moulana, a Sufi sage lived in the 18th century. Besides describing his saintly miracles, this work gives clues to the historical context in which the work was set. The death of the Prophet's beloved daughter Fatima has become the theme of a famous elegy called *Wafath Kissappāṭṭu. Sayyidatunnisah* another story song published from Vengara in the year 1894 by Kodambiyakath Seethi Koya Thangal deals with the life history of Nafeesathul Misriya.

Candam Turaikaḷkkambahsan yennē

arimakkuḷalaḷe vivaram innē

muntum khasayi sul awliyavil

pukaḷi paraymatum kutubukaḷil.

(You are the most knowledgeable among the scholars,

tallest in religious community.

Taking pilgrimage to the graveyard of a person,

who is beloved to Bait ul-Muqaddis.[186])

The life histories of local scholars and anti-colonial champions also have been favourite themes for many *Kissappāṭṭukaḷ*. Vallanchira Kunhammed's *Akhbārul Hind* taking plot from the heroic lives of Sultan Hyderali and his son Tipu of Mysore exemplifies this tradition. The anger towards the British rule and hero worship, two recurring moods throughout the poem echoed the general situation in the then Malabar. Fearing the political consequences of it, the major publishers were not willing to print and publish the copies of this work. [187] So, only manuscripts were spread all across Malabar.

The most important historical narrative came in the form of story song was *Malik ibn Dinar Kissappāṭṭu* written in 1883. The theme of this work revolves around the arrival of Malik Ibn Dinar, the first Muslim scholar who came on the mission of preaching Islam in Kerala. This work along with praising the missionary activity of Dinar, illustrates the social history of the then Kerala through the poetic imagination. The lines describing the place where Dinar stayed are as follows:

Yeriya sugantirētaram avaḷe

yeri minnal oḷihajar teḷunte mādam

yeri niram marmiru aru aru akhḷaru

(A place filled with class apart fragrance,

---

[185] Mohamedali, *Mappiḷa Pāṭṭukaḷ Nūṯṯāndukaḷilūde,* p. 84.

[186] The third holiest shrine in Islam situated in Palestine.

[187] Mohamedali, *Mappiḷa Pāṭṭukaḷ Nūṯṯāndukaḷilūde,* p.86.

the palace is clad with full of stones-

that shine like lightening,

dark green colour burns like *marumir*) [188]

Pulikootil Hyder's *Kerala Caritram Kissappāṭṭu* as the title indicates deals with the history of Kerala. Considerably large portion of this work has been dedicated to how Islam had a lively spread in Malabar. Set in the backdrop of Dinar's arrival, Hyder takes the readers to the social and political situation prevailed in Kerala. Ceraman Perumal's journey to Mecca, his meeting with the Prophet and subsequent conversion to Islam and the arrival of Dinar as his envoy to Kerala-all these episodes in Kerala Muslim history have been narrated with great amount of imagination in this poem. This story song also has candid remarks of warm reception and support to construct mosques in major trade centres extended by the local rulers to Dinar and his team. This poem has a lavish praise for the religious harmony and cosmopolitanism prolonged in Malabar for several centuries.

Annāl toṭṭu Hindu Musalmān tammil

Nannē mairtryil varticcu vanniddey

Anōnyam snēhiccunnum vyāpa-

Ratilum matum tōḷotu pravarticcum

konduḷḷa nimitam

Muslamānkalkkundāyi mahatwam.

(Since then Hindus and Muslims,

lived harmoniously here.

Loved each other,

worked together in trade, which

brought Muslims greatness.

...sectarianism had no place in society,

Muslims then performed well in trade -- gained a lot of profit.

Thanks to that they become prosperous.)

The advent of Portuguese, according to the poet, brought an end to the merry state of affairs and offered woes to the Muslim traders. The work ends with a note on the tradition of resistance launched by Mappilas against the Portuguese under the leadership of Kunhali Marakkar.

Ibrahim Ibn Adham Kissappāṭṭu is supposed to be the one among the oldest composition belonging to the genre of story songs.[189] The first print edition of this work came out from Thalaserry in

[188] The word *marumir* used here has no specific meaning.

[189] Mohamedali, *Mappiḷa Pāṭṭukaḷ Nūṯṯāndukaḷilūde*, p. 87.

1877.[190] The plot hinges on the self imposed exile of the emperor Ibrahim Ibn Adham who ruled Arabia in the 9th century. His wife, who was pregnant at the time of his journey, later on gave birth to a handsome son. Unwilling to say not to his wish to see his father, the mother took him to Mecca where father was reported to be in. Entire work has been written in a very simple, lucid and touching verse.

Mariyum kiṇṇāram, cinnam maniyāram Muśaṉi

Matavu makan makka orumicu nadatam.

Dura kuda puruṣaram oruṉi kāfilayum

(Bells rang to herald their journey,

mother and son made a move together to Mecca.

A long army of people accompanied them,

with camels loads atop.)

Akbar Sadaqa Pakṣhippāṭṭu composed by Naduthoppil Abdulla is another major work belonging to this genre, though there is an alternative opinion that this work with the central plot is narrated by a bird as if it is presenting its version of a particular event belongs to the genre of *kiḷippāṭṭu* or bird song, the movement took its inspiration from *Adhyātma Ramāyanam kiḷippāṭṭu* by Tunchat Ramanujan Ezhuthachan. *Pakṣhippāṭṭu* wth a remarkable touch of imagination and humour presents the story of a female bird who seeks the help of the prophet to convince her mate of her fidelity. This work which recounts the valour of Ali, the son-in-law of the Prophet and a key figure in Shia tradition is considered by many as a part of Shia tradition literature in Arabi-Malayalam language along with the works of Moinkutty Vaidyar.[191] The importance of this poem, as Hameed points out, is interlinked with the importance of *eśal grāmam* or "song village", situated in north Malabar.[192] Mogral known popularly by *eśal grāmam* with its native and visiting poets has contributed a lot to the development of Arabi-Malayalam literature. Though, the village rejected this work and deported the poet for alleged un-Islamic references, this work was eventullay brought back by the next generation poets with great amount of reverence. Now this song is recited by many in the village especially after the evening prayer.[193]

12. *Dāṛsanīka Kāvyaṉaḷ* or Philosophical Poems

Dāṛsanīka Kāvyaṉaḷ are highly devotional and with philosophical undertones. They consist, mainly of lines having hidden, subtle or symbolic meanings. Sufi saints or those who reached the upper heights of devotion are generally the composers of such songs. Most prominent poet of Arabi-Malayalam who enriched this tradition is Abdul Qadir Mastan alias Icha. He was popularly known as Omar Khayam of

---

[190] Ibid.

[191] Paula Richman, "Introduction", in Abdullah abdul Hameed, *Akbar Sadaqa Pakshipattu: Translationa and Study*, (Kasargod: Central Univeristy of Kerala, 2012), p. xxi.

[192] Abdullah abdul Hameed, *Akbar Sadaqa Pakshipattu: Translationa and Study*, (Kasargod Central Univeristy of Kerala, 2012), p.7

[193] Interview with Abdulla Thanima, a scholar of Mappilapattu from Mogral held on 2nd January, 2013.

Malabar. Icha has written almost around twelve thousand mystical poems[194] or *virutaṉaḷ*. They are actually hagiographic poems with a focus of concern over the mystical issues. The poet, who had led a Sufi life and roamed around Malabar, had a habit of writing small haiku-like compositions on the walls and doors of houses. Most of such works were with high-sounding philosophical questions have been compiled later by O. Abu, a scholar of Mappila songs.

Van piẕhai cumanṭ pērkaḷ,

okkeyum halākkilay.

Vambodukkuvor balam

Mautodadukkalāy.

Tanum tanum tauba kaondu,

tan puranil tēdu nī.

Ponnu, veḷḷi ratnavum

falam piditidātta nāḷ.

(Carrying big faults on the shoulder,

everything get spoiled.

Those who think they are mighty enough to face everything,

coming close to death helplessly.

Bow, bow in front of God

with repentance.

The day on which your assets of gold and pearl,

become worthless.)

13. *Madhupāṭṭukaḷ* or Praise Songs and Hagiographic works

Madhu in Arabic means praise and *madhupāṭṭukaḷ* are mainly the songs that are composed with the purpose of praising the Prophet. Mappila hagiographic works which eulogized prophet Mohamed and other historical personalities of Islamic history are generally put in this category. [195] They differ slightly from *mālās* in content. Firstly, the former eulogizes the Prophet only, while the scope of latter extends to Sufi sheikhs, saints and martyrs and other divine figures. Secondly, praise Songs in Arabi-Malayalam are written in the form of poems and the recurring theme in such poems is love.[196] But *mālās* are composed generally to express respect and reverence to the holy figures in Islamic history or Mappila history. Thirdly, while singing *mālā* is considered to be remedy for illness, praise songs are recited with the purpose of showing mere love to the Prophet.

---

[194] Mohamedali, *Mappiḷa Pāṭṭukaḷ Nūṯṯāndukaḷilūde*, p. 157.

[195] Balakrishnan Vallikkunnu and Ummar Tharamel, *Māppiḷapāṭṭu: Pādavum,Padanavum*, (Kottayam: DC Books, 2006), pp.24-25.

[196] Mohamedali, *Mappiḷa Pāṭṭukaḷ Nūṯṯāndukaḷilūde*, p. 147.

13. 1. *Nūlmadhu*

While *mālās* are recited for satiating worldly desires, praise songs represent the selfless urge for union with the prophet.[197] *Madhupāttukaḷ* along with *mālās* and *kissappāṭṭukaḷ* in Arabi-Malayalam have eulogized almost all the seminal figures in Islamic history.[198] However, the most prominent *madhu* is *Nūlmadhu* or *Nūlmāla* of Kunjayan Musaliyar written in 1737 AD. [199] This work extolling the virtue of the prophet Mohammed[200] in 666 verses, comes second in age only to *Mohiyuddīn Māla* in Arabi-Malayalam verse tradition. There is a long gap of hundred and thirty years between the publications of *Mohiyuddīn Māla* and *Nūlmāla*.[201] By the time of the publication of *Nūlmāla,* the Arabi-Malayalam literature had move along orbit of Tamil[202]; so there was an increase in use of Tamil words in the latter than in the former.

Āditan Aruḷinal Perumāl Aṇdayōḷum kadannu

arśit mudi nīnda Mohammed Nabiye

Kānpatuk eni āsakkadal ponkum

atinal immadhu nūlmālai paṇivatuku

Aḷḷāhuve tārum untuṇai kāf.

(Perumal, obeying the instruction of God

moved all the way to meet the Prophet.

I too have a wish to cross the sea to see him (the Prophet)

the noblest person in this universe, Prophet Mohammed.

This *māla*, I prepare for that purpose,

God, please save by supporting me in the endeavor (compsoing this *māla*).

By its content and structure, *Nūlmāla* cannot be put under the rubric of *mālās*. The theme, according to the poet, circles around the "exemplary" and "worth-modeling" life of the Prophet. Kunjayan Musaliyar, who was otherwise the Caliph of *Qadiriya Tariqah* in Malabar, lavishly used metaphors pertaining to sea and sea voyage. This works ends with a keen wish to meet the Prophet in person in the life after death. There existed a tradition of reciting and interpreting *Nūlmāla* which is written with 16 *eśals*, on stage all over Malabar. Because of its particular style of narration, many scholars have

---

[197] Razak,*Cololialism and Community Formation in Malabar*, p. 14.

[198] The most prominent figures among them are prophet Mohamed, prophets like Adam, Yusuf, Ibrahim, Prophet's wives, the pious Caliphs and Caliph Ali's sons - Hassan and Hussain. Razak, *Cololialism and Community Formation in Malabar*, 14-15.

[199] The description given in the text shows that this mala was written in Hijra 1151 by the renowned devotional poet Kunhayan Musaliyar.

[200] *Nūl* in Arabi-Malayalam language refers to the Prophet.

[201] Moahmedali, *Mappiḷa Pāṭṭukaḷ Nūṯṯāndukaḷilūde* p. 147.

[202] Kayalpattanam in Tamil Nadu was once identified as an important centre for the production of Islamic literature in South India. So the early authors in Arabi-Malayalam were largely influenced by the song composers like Umar Pulavar and Kunankuti Mastan Sahib.

equated this work with *Krishnagadha* of Cherusseri, a work said to have written in the same period depicting the life history of Krishna.[203]

This work is an expression of poet's love of him that touches all the zeniths.[204] Throughout this work, portraying the life of the Prophet full of surprises, the poet maintains a longing to meet him in person. Musaliyar in this work has given special attention to pick up and use Malayalam and Tamil words and thereby to avoid using *Sanksritized* Malayalam which was in wider use in other works contemporary to that. Compared to *Mohiyuddīn Māla*, the influence of Tamil is, thus, more apparent in *Nūlmāla* which has made an extensive use of medieval Tamil vocabulary.[205]

This has been seen by many as an act of resistance against the then popular trend of generous use of Sanskrit words.[206] Another worth-mentioning feature of this work is its lavish description of the nature. Forest, beasts and valleys familiar to him in Kerala have been depicted as it is in a very poetic language. *Safala Māla* of Kulangara Veetil Moidu Musaliyar (popularly known as Sujai), is a work with similar nature dealing with Islamic mysticism from the genesis to the death of the prophet Mohammed. It is a didactic work in Arabic-Malayalam, which invites people, who are lured by worldly pleasures, to the path of spirituality.[207]

14. *Kappapāṭṭu* or Ship Song

Kappapāṭṭu or ship song, composed by Kunhayan Musliyar is one among the pioneering works in philosophical poems in Arabi-Malayalam language. The word *safīna* in Arabic means ship and with the publication of ship song, Arabi-Malayalam songs were known as *Safīnappāṭṭukaḷ* or *Safina* songs.[208]Half century ago only, they attained the name *Mappiḷappāṭṭu*.[209] Though second only to *Mohiyuddīn Māla* in popularity, in terms of poetic beauty and profound philosophical undertones this work outshines all other works of similar nature. Using the metaphors of ship and its sail to symbolize the body of a person and his/her life respectively, this work takes the readers to metaphysical aspects of human life. *Kappapāṭṭu* written in the 18th century, as the title itself denotes, equates human life with a ship.

Cāyal oru kappalundu namukku

ccañuḷḷa pāṇdicāṇ onpatu nīlam.

Tālum maṇikkalundettiru pākam

tannil pidice palakayumonnu.

(...)

Kandiṭṭarivānō kaṇṇille poṭṭā

---

[203] Razak, *Cololialism and Community Formation in Malabar*, p. 14.
[204] *Arabi-Malayala Sāhitya Caritram*, p. 78.
[205] Ramesh, "Mālapāttukaḷ: Oṛu Caritrānwēṣanam", p.24.
[206] Mohamedali, *Mappiḷa Pāṭṭukaḷ Nūṯṯāndukaḷilūde*, p. 148.
[207]Similar war songs were popular in Arabi-Tamil called *Padappōr Caritram* during 19th Century AD. See Koppilan, *Vaṭṭapāṭṭu*, pp.37-41.
[208] Abu, *Arabi-Malayala Sāhitya Caritram*, p.84.
[209] Mohamedali, *Mappiḷa Pāṭṭukaḷ Nūṯṯāndukaḷilūde*, p.22.

kāruṇōr conna col kēṭṭillē

Panduḷḷor collilu patirundō poṭṭā

Pai tanna pālil kaypundō poṭṭā

(We have a ship...

By measurement, it is nine *cān*[210] long,

legs with eight *irupākam*[211] size.

The body is like a flat wooden piece fitted into that.

(...)

Hey, are you blind,

not to learn despite seeing repeatedly?

Hey, are you deaf,

haven't you heard the words of elder ones?

Hey deaf, is there anything hollow in what the elders said?

Hey deaf, do the milk of cow taste bitter?)

Burnell writes, "It is an allegory of the fate of the body, which is compared to a ship, the ribs to the framework, and the spine to the keel. It describes the voyage of life and dangers the body meets from rocks and shoals of temptations by *Satan*, its wreck or safe conclusion of voyage."[212] Most interesting feature of this work is the presence of umpteen numbers of anecdotes given as subtexts. Similarly, through some satirical references, this work exposes the fake ones among the religious scholars, mainly those who use Islamic ideology for their own purposes.[213]

15. *Tadiurudi Māla*

Poems which are written in the form of moral lessons are called *Tadiurudis*. The most famous one belonging to this genre is *Tadiurudi Māla* by Aboobacker Kunji Kazi in 1880. This work takes its inspiration from a poem entitled *Elakham Ayyuhal Ikhwan* written in Arabic by Kazi Mohamed, the author of *Mohiyuddīn Māla*. The stanza narrating the doomsday in *Tadiurudi Māla* sounds as follows:

Sūrile ūtetuvōḷam kudiyude vīdakume

sūratellām rūhatiṭṭu purappedum vīdakume

(The body is an abode that surives,

till the *soor* is played on the last day.

The life as an adobe exixts,

---

[210] A measurement for assessing height in Kerala.

[211] Another method for measuring height.

[212] K.K.M Abdul Kareem, *Kappapāṭṭum Nūl Madhum: Oṛu Padanam,* (Tirur, 1983), p.29.

[213] Vallikunnu, *Mappila Sāhityavum, Navōdhanavum,* p. 35.

for reciting the Quran.)

16. *Ambakaḷ*

Ambakal are compositions prepared extempore with the purpose of offering comfort to the workers who are engaged in hard labour. A*mbakal* turn around no fixed rhythms with hilarious lyrics and instantaneously prepared lines. Here is an example for such a work composed for the purpose of easing the difficulty of physical jobs. [214]

First one : "Moosakkakka Sail of a ship"

Chorus : *"Āyimadāme"*

First one : Piece of a coconut in *kalatapatu*

Chorus : *"Āyimadame"*

First one : "When the cat looks"

Chorus : *"Āyimadāme"*

First one : "Head of the village remained in the house"

Chorus : *"Āyimadāme"*

17. Hilarious Songs

There is no dearth for works that hilariously approach social issues in Arabi-Malayalam literature. The songs composed instantaneously with the purpose of crtiticizing some beliefs and customs are the major constituents of this genre.

Cocīum peṇṇilandu, kōyikkōṭṭum peṇṇilandu

kaṭṭutinnaṇṇa pātummānte mōḷe keṭṭi-takida tai.

Peṇṇu kandālaẓhakundu, vīdu kandāl sughamundu,

Ammāyiammade pōru kandā pōrānē tōnnu-takida tai.

(Since there is no girl to marry in Cochin and Calicut,

I married the daughter of Patumma,

who manages her life by stealing things-*takida tai.*[215]

The girl is nice to see, so is the case with the house,

But, none can put up with the quarrelsome nature of mother-in-law.)

Following is a composition with unknown author narrating the predicament of a husband who is being tortured consistently by his wife.

---

[214] Abu, *Arabi-Malayala Sāhitya Caṛitram,* p.118.

[215] A sound with no specific meaning.

Gatikeṭṭa kālam kadiyāne keṭṭi

Kadiyānte koyyōndente kaṇṇu poṭṭi.

Barkat keṭṭuḷḷa kalonnu kuti

varikka pilavinte kombonnu poṭṭi.

(I married Kadeeya in a helpless situation,

my eyes were broken by her hands.

The moment that ill-omen entered into the house,

the twig of jackfruit tree fell down.)

Hilarious songs and parodies were used by the Arabi-Malayalam poets even in their routine conversations with their friends. It is quite interesting to note that though the lyrics were instantaneously prepared, they were strictly adhered to the rules in Arabi-Malayalam poetry.

18. *Kālpantukaḷi Pāttukal* or Soccer Songs

Soccer, a favourite pastime of people of North Kerala, has inspired many Arabi-Malayalam poets to compose works in this genre. Though the number of orally transmitted works in the category of soccer songs in this language is large, the works that put in print are scanty. Following is a song composed by Ahamed Ismail of Mogral on the renowned football club, Mohammedan Sporting of Calcutta:

Mutu Snēhitaṟe prdhanakalkkatayil gōśaviṣēśamē

muntiya pātam pantaluḷḷa kaḷi cintuvānentorunmēśame.

Sattu Muhammed Sportinṉenna, salguṇaṟāya kaḷikkaṟum,

pinne-mecca teamum pala bāgatil ninne.

(Dear friends, (I am) overjoyed to share the news of football,

a great event happening in Calcutta.

Mohammedans Sporting, the masters

along with other heavyweights world over line up on the occassion.)[216]

19. *Sarkīṭ*[217] *Pāṭṭukaḷ* or Travel Songs

The themes of Arabi-Malayalam travel songs range from the traumatic experience of travel and adventures to the minute descriptions of places visited. These songs, which functioned as a window to the world for a place like Malabar where the movement of people was restricted under the colonial rule, were either written in the form of letters or travelogues. People, goods and customs of the places that Arabi-Malayalam poets visited have found place in many travel songs. This genre predates even

---

[216] Ahamed Ismail, "Football Pāttu", in Mogral and Kattathadukka (compilation), *Vadakkinte eṣalukal,* pp.102-103.

[217] The word *sarkeet* in Arabi-Malayalam means travel.

the travel literature in Malayalam literature by many decades.[218] The lyrics in most of the songs were simple and lucid meant to share their experiences with the readers directly.

Shorṉur Yātra of Pulikkottil Hyder, *Hajj Yātra* of P.T.Beerankutty Maulawi *Kolār Yātra* of K. Mammadkutty and *Badravati Sarkīt* of Ottakat Attakoya Tangal are the major works belonging to this genre. The scope of travel songs does not limit to long voyages. It sometimes covers visits to the neighboring villages. The pilgrimages (mainly Hajj) occupy significant position among the themes of travel songs. Beerankutty Maulawi's travel song *Hajj Yātra* is in the form of a letter to his friend and poet Puliokttil Hyder sharing former's experience during the pilgrimage. This song has a detailed descritption of diversity of population people gathered in Mecca during the pilgrimage.

Kōppuḷḷōr ēreyum pārkkunnu makkat

Kūttam akhbareẓhutuvan pōrellō yīkatu.

Pāpam porukkunnu vīd cuttumolanuṅal

paṉoẓhukunne mizril ninne peṉṉuṅal.

Mūppotta vellānakuṭṭikal varum kōlatil

puẓhuṅikkondyrōpyan system hajjin kālatil.

(There are many notables stay in Mecca

This letter doesn't have enough of space to describe each thing.

When the male members take a circumambulation

around the place, which pardons all the sins[219],

women from Egypt move into there swfitly.

The Europeans, who are part of administration, come

like grown up elephants.

Hyder's *Shorṉur Yātra* shares the experiences that the poet had during his trip to the nearby urban space called Shornur, which has centuries old railway station and other amneties.

Turakkamuṭṭayil cenniṭṭoru ticketedutteri-

turuvandikku uḷarntannu śoranūril iraṅi,

cuśennukondoru cāya clubbil kēri.

Parayuvan oru āppum kadi vaṅgi kaẓicannu.

pakal asatm maraṉum bujite pinne

uraṅan patikkoru purayil ṉjan kayaricennē-

cennappōl puratu kutirikkunnundoru māti-

---

[218] Vallikunnu and Tharamel, *Māppiḷapāṭṭu: Pādavum,Padanavum,*p.159.

[219] Ka'ba, the holiest place in Islam where Muslims believe all the sins will be pardoned.

streeyalpoẒhutenne kanint codiccumey
yentinām vannatu atukkuttaram ῆjanoti.
Vannativide parkkuvanaṇṇennu anai uḷḷa
vāstavam paraῆappol urata mulla-
malaren bartav varunnundinnatu padilla-
yennalōatuvenda, puratoru payi
kidakkuvan enikku sammatam tannal mati amayi
anneram anusaricidate vātilum taṭṭi-
adacenne kure cadikkayarccamaṭṭil-kṣaṇmil
akatoru arayil pōy kidannakuṭṭi.
(After taking a passenger ticket from Mukkaṭṭa Station,
boarded on the direct train and got down at Shornur quickly.
Roamed around there and finally stepped into a coffee shop
and had a half glass of tea and snacks for name sake.
After the sunset, having the dinner,
I entered into the nearby house in search of a place to stay.
The middle-aged lady sitting outside asked me politely,
What is the purpose?
When I revealed the fact-seekng a place to stay, she said
since my beloved husband is coming today
you are not allowed to stay inside.
When I asked that aunty for the permission to sleep ouside on a mat,
using harsh and repprochful words, she closed the door mercilessly ,
entered into the inner chamber and slept.)

6

Alternative Construction of Knowledge

While Arabic remained the liturgical language of Malabar Muslims, Arabi-Malayalam represented their literary expression. With a wide array of literary works, this language also set a new paradigm for constructing alternative knowledge and a parallel window to understand reality for the community. Arabi-Malayalam literature provided so many smaller alternative narratives for each and every seminal event in Islamic history and Kerala Muslim history in place of hegemonic and universal ones. Some of the works in this language had gone to the extent of disengaging the traditions and emphasizing on the relativity of facts with diverse versions for understanding each event in Islamic history.

Popularization of this language also marked a change in orientation of Mappila society and their religious consumption. The pattern of religious consumption also underwent a transformation in tune with the changing interpretations of theological texts in this language. Quran, for instance, had almost four different translations and *tafsirs* or interpretations in Arabi-Malayalam. Each one had taken a great deal of freedom to interpret the text matching with the context. The community also moved from the rigid traditions of 'revealed religion' to the 'living practices' of Islam. Re-interpretation of basic texts and reproduction of historical events into the contemporary discourse, Arabi-Malayalam had been instrumental in this transformation. At a most obvious level, the literary works with alternative versions of past and diverse interpretations of the present furthered it.

However, there is a doubt weather this change in orientation of the community has been adequately recorded by the scholars of Kerala history. This issue has been reflected in a widely held trend to consider members of the Mappila community, whose education is confined to Arabi-Malayalam as illiterates. Historically, Muslim women are portrayed marginalized depicting them as uneducated. But, it is not possible to asses them without rejecting the prevalent notions regarding knowledge and literary tradition. They are considered as illiterate because of their abstinence from modern knowledge. Here one has to examine the contribution of Arabi-Malayalam language in developing a parallel way for constructing knowledge and understanding reality.

Arabi-Malayalam is an immensely rich language with a number of scientific, philosophical, and literary works and the entire Mappila community was very proficient in this language. Large number of Mappilas was highly literate in this tradition, despite being considered illiterate by 'modern' standards. They lived in the environments where Arabi-Malayalam texts were read and learnt by-heart and histories were told publically through the genres of songs, ballads and other modes of narration. The public recital of texts or poems meant that its message reached many listeners simultaneously.[1] The realm of literacy in the context of Mappila Muslims contained a vast domain, encompassing many linguistic forms, various genres and literary fusions.

As has been discussed elsewhere, Arabi-Malayalam became the prime medium for routine communication and for letter writing especially among women. Difficulty for getting bridegroom for women who did not know to recite Arabi-Malayalam *mālas* by heart demonstrates the importance that the community had given to this language.[2] The development of this language and its elevation as the medium of instruction in *madrassa* was also instrumental in bringing Mappila women to the centre stage in the literary field. When the mainstream Malayalam literature had not many women writers, women's writing Malayalam literature was well-developed with a wide array of women poets.[3]

Arabic for Mappilas continued to exit as the language of the sacred book, the *Sharia* and prayer. Sanskrit continued to exert its hegemony in Malayalam and the Sanskritisation of Malayalam language furthered Mappilas' alienation with that language. Works in Arabi-Malayalam were written in a style close to ordinary speech, clearly distant from the sankritized verse and prose in Malayalam language. So the texts printed Arabi-Malayalam language received wide acceptance as against the ones that published in other two streams of Malayalam. The first category included texts written in Malayalam close to Sanskrit diction in syntax and semantics circulated among a small section of caste-Hindu population.[4] The second one, influenced greatly by the translation of Bible with words from Hebrew and Syrian languages in abundance and with highly ornamental and flowery vocabulary remained alien to the spoken expression of ordinary people. Because of its poetic beauty, the verse writing in Malayalam had been highly dependent of the latter.[5]

As mentioned earlier, most of the works of prose in Arabi-Malayalam were called as *tarjama* or translation. Despite the fact that translations constituted the largest chunk of prose tradition, all of them were not really translations of works published in other languages.[6] Even some scholar introduced their independent works as *tarjams* using the term, prose as something synonymous to translation.[7] Authenticity of information and authoritativeness of the argument may also be prime factors behind presenting independent works as translations as texts translated from Arabic and Persian had enjoyed special position in Arabi-Malayalam literature. With a view to make it more readable among the ordinary Mappilas, most works in Arabi-Malayalam prose tradition were either written in simple diction or in quasi-verse form.

Works published in this religio-lect were not necessarily with theological content but were adaptations from Persian or Arabic works which the Mappilas considered quite erroneously as being

---

[1] Ronit Ricci, Islam Translated: Literature, Conversion, and the Arabic Cosmopolis of South and Southeast Asia, New Delhi: Permanent Black, 2011, pp. 2-3.

[2] Sameera Haneef, "Arabi-Malayala Sāhityatile Penperuma" (pp.148-153), in T.Mansurali, (ed.), *Arabi-Malayala Sāhitya Padanangal*, (Kozhicode: Lead Books, 2014), p.149.

[3] Ibid.

[4] T.Mansurali, (ed.), *Arabi-Malayala Sāhitya Pādanangal*, (Kozhicode: Lead Books, 2014), p.17.

[5] Ibid.

[6] Ibid., p. 18

[7] Ibid.

connected with Islam.[8] *Badrul Munīr Husanul Jamāl*, the famous poem composed by Moinkutty Vaidyar in 1871 AD is the most illustrious example of this tradition. More than translating Perso-Islamic romantic literature into Arabi-Malayalam, Vaidyar attempted to adapt the whole range of Persian Civilization to the cultural universe of Malabar.[9] This work has also used indigenous metaphors like 'cassia flower', 'plantain tree', 'coral reef', *puliyangam* or fight with Tiger abundantly.[10] It obviously shows that the authors presented Islamic (sometimes even pre-Islamic) imageries and ideas in a form readily familiar to rural Mappilas and they could easily identify the exogenous with indigenous or Arab/Persian with that of Malabar.[11]

Contrary to the general *Sunni-Shāfi* theological orientation of Mappilas, a Shia-Persian influence was also explicit in Arabi-Malayalam literature. This affinity with Persian and *Shi'a* traditions could be detected in the literary works of the late 18th and early 19th centuries such as *Jihnpada, Balqīz kissa, Hassan Kissa, Saqūmpada, Kiḷḷati Māla, Pakṣhippāṭṭu, Kuppippāṭṭu, Salīqat pada, Salāsil pada* etc.[12] Vaidyar's works which exerted a significant influence on later works, address a lot of complex theological and philosophical issues involved in Sunni-Shia divide. His works, at the same time, seem to have been the most important effort to integrate Arabic/Sunni and Persian/ Shia literature.

Arabi-Malayalam literature also has contributed to the *Bakti* tradition in Malayalam. Scholars have suggested that Qazi Muhammad's *Mohiyuddin Māla*, a long story song influenced by Sufi thought, was written five years before Ezhuthachan composed his work, *Adhyātamarāmāyaṇam Kiḷipāṭṭu* and that they shared a common historical context, shared almost similar issues and collectively contributed to enriching Bhakti literature in Kerala.[13]

1. Women's writing

It is to be noted that the women's writing in Arabi-Malayalam predates the same in Malayalam language by decades.[14] Some magazines such as *Nizā-ul-Islam* were published exclusively for women. Although published under the editorship of men, these magazines with fully-dedicated content for women and door-to-door delivery had gained wide acceptance among the Mappila women all over Kerala.[15]Muslim women profusely contributed to them by writing articles, poetry, etc. and actively participated in its publishing them and most of the time by writing critical letters to the editors.[16]

---

8 P.P. Abdul Razak, Colonialism and Community Formation in Malabar, unpublished PhD Thesis, University of Calicut, 2007.

9 Ibid.

10 F.Fawcett, "A Popular Mopla Song", Indian Antiquary, March 1899, p.65.

11 C.K.Kareem, *Muslim Samudāyawum Samskārawum* (Trivandrum: Charithram Publications, 1983)p.67.

12 Razak, *Colonialism and Community Formation in Malabar* p.15.

13 O. Abu, *Arabi-Malayala Sāhitya Caṛitram,* (Kottayam: NBS, 1976), p.75. & P.K.Mohamedkunhi, *Musliṇalum Kerala Samskaravum,* (Thrissur: Kerala Sahitya Academy, 2008), pp.210-11.

14Faisal Elettil, *Mappiḷapāṭṭinṟe Janakiyata,* in T.Mansurali, (ed.), *Arabi-Malayala Sāhitya Padanangal*, (Kozhicode: Lead Books, 2014), pp. 98-102, p. 102.

15 *Nizaul Islam* - a publication for women which was published under leadership of P.N.Haider Mawlawi and the editorship of K.C. Komukutty Mawalawi, adopted the method of direct home delivery to popularize it among the Mappila women.

16Shamshad Hussain, *Nyūnapakshatinum Lingapadavikkum Idayil,* (Thiruvananthapuram:Kerala Basha Institute, 2009)

Similarly, there was an immensely rich Arabi-Malayalam song tradition in which women in large numbers participated as composers and singers. Mappila women disseminated and popularized most of the classics through in-house informal social gatherings. These 'ladies only' gatherings functioned as public spaces where the works major Arabi-Malayalam poets of that time were recited, interpreted, analyzed and criticized. Collective recitation of popular songs followed by the interpretation of it was a major pastime in most of the Muslim dominated areas in Malabar.[17] At some point of time in history, it was difficult for girls who did not know *Mohiyuddīn Māla* to get appropriate groom. This shows the significance that the Mappila community given to their culture and tradition.

Women poets like *P.K.Haleema, Naduthoppil Ayishakutty, C.H.Kunhayisha, T.A. Rabiya and Puthoor Amina* had enjoyed a special position among the Mappila song composers in Arabi-Malayalam and their poems were well-liked by the people from various walks. Apart from being popular, these songs also rejected many traditional patriarchic concepts. The most interesting example of such a tradition was Puthur Amina's *katupāṭṭu* (letter song). This song, which is believed to have written during 1921, is in the form of a response to the marriage proposal from a person who had undergone imprisonment in Bellari jail. The marriage proposal from Ahmed, a prisoner from the Jail who came to know about Amina's talent in composing poems through regular letter songs that she sent to her father who was in the same jail for his involvement in the Malabar Rebellion, also was in the form of *katupāṭṭu*. Amina's expression of unwillingness to marry him through songs provoked him and made him to send threatening letters in song forms. But to all such threats she gave fitting reply in a very sarcastic manner. She writes:

The smugness you brought from Bellari
is not going to work with me.
Why are you wasting time? Do you think?
I will ever marry you? (.....)
I am not exposing your ragged sack.
Don't try to trap me with your proposal-
I replied to your song in befitting style.
This woman has not helped any known criminal.
(......)
Don't be feverish seeing this cot
and don't think that you can devour
everything you desire.
Being well known in this land
proposals are coming to me

[17] Haneef, "Arabi-Malayala Sāhityatile Penperuma", p. 149.

from all four sides.
It is not difficult for me
to, get a man far better than you.
Will be dear and honey
until he (man) accomplished it.
And be dumped in the kitchen
after delivering from him.
And will be thrown to sun
on loosing the sheen.
He will go in search of
yet another green pasture
without any passion.
What nonsense is this?

This poem reveals not only her tenacity to quarrel with an ex-convict but also her views regarding the freedom of woman in choosing her spouse and her attitude about a family structure dominated by men. Apart from this letter song, Amina had composed plenty of *kalyāṇappāṭṭu* (wedding songs) and *kissapāṭṭu* (story songs).

Many of the traditional singers of Mappila songs were women and they had many occasions such as *Mailānci Kallyāṇam* (Mehanty festival on the day before marriage), *Katukuttu Kallyāṇam* (ear piercing ceremony), etc. for performing it. *Nafīsaat Māla* and *Mohiyuddin Māla* were traditionally recited outside the labour room with a belief of bringing easy delivery. There was a long array of women composers and singers of *Mappiḷappāṭṭu* like Haleema who have contributed not just in formulating new tunes for certain old songs by way of improvisation and experimentation but also to compose new popular *eṣals*.

Muslim women had also actively involved in teachings Arabi-Malayalam as the chief medium at *Ōttupaḷḷi* or *madrassa*. There were *madrassas* run exclusively by female teachers who were traditionally called *ustada* or *mollācci*.[18] All these things indicate that Muslim women had their own space which had been utilized by them even in the traditional Muslim societies in Kerala. The Islamic reform movement during the early decades of twentieth century, on its part, contributed in producing many women writers like P.K. Haleema and Aysha Mayan.[19] Both of them braving staunch opposition from the society mobilized Muslim women against the structure of patriarchy. However, it is a sad irony that even though such strong ideas, writings and activities were existed among Muslim women, they had not found a place in 'mainstream' discourse of renaissance. Though the name of Haleema

[18] Mollācci is the feminine gender for the term Mollākka or male teacher of local *madrassa*. See Sadaruddin Vazhakkad, "Ottupaḷḷikaḷile Mollācimār", Prabodhanam Weekly, Vol. 70, No.12, 23 August, 2013.

[19] Hussain, *NyŪnapakshatinum Lingapadavikkum Idayil*, pp.12-14.

occurred in one or two recent studies, she was portrayed only as a product of renaissance movement not as person with notable role in conceptualizing its ideology and implementing them. This, of course, suggests the essentiality of an alternative perspective for identifying the works of Muslim women in Arabi-Malayalam and recognizing them as agency of social reform.

Haleema launched a magazine *Muslim Vanita* in 1938 being herself the printer, publisher and editor of it.[20] She made deep inroads into Mappila literature, by writing in both Malayalam and Arabi-Malayalam, continuously. *Candiṛasundaṛi Māla* composed by her chronicling around the marriage of the Prophet Mohamed with Ayisha is a favourite component in many wedding songs. Her works including *Badarul-Munīr Oppanapāṭṭu, Candiṛasundaṛi Māla, Poṛutam B Āyiśa* and *Rājamangalam* characterize an eclectic mix of languages interwoven in long compositions. Extensive use of word-combinations using old Tamil, Malayalam and Arabic vocabularies made them more attractive. Following lines from *Candiṛasundaṛi Māla* represent such an assortment taking words from four different languages.

Ponnilum punnaṛamil teḷivāya mutu muhammadāṛe

pŪṛaṇōr sakalōrkku munprabhuvaṛaye muzaammilāṛe.

(*Ponnilum, punnaṛamil, teḷivāya, mutu, sakalōrkku*-Malayalam

pŪṛaṇōr -Tamil

munprabhuvaṛaye- Sanskrit and Malayalam

muzaammilāṛe -Arabic-Tamil)

Another interesting work of this period was a fiction *Sultanā's Dream* translated and published in *Muslim Mitram* magazine in 1927. Written originally in Bengali by R.S. Hussain, the story chronicles the dream of a girl maintaining anguish about the plight of Indian Muslim women. This story questions the fundamental notion that the society keeps about man-woman binary. The heroin of the story was laughed at the women on the street she reached in dream. Her friend Sara explains the reason for laughing as her masculine appearance.

Sulthana: Masculinity! What they mean by it?

Sara : They mean you exhibit manly fear and shyness.

The narrator of this story is a purdha-clad girl and living in seclusion from strangers. In the dream world she takes it off jokingly and then becomes very happy thinking that her lifestyle befits man. All the way side sights are strange to her. The most surprising thing is that she never meets a man. She asks surprisingly, "Where are all the men"?

Sara: They are at their places.

Sulthana: What do you mean by 'their places'?

Sara: Oh. I am sorry. Your are here for the first time and you don't know our ways. Our men are kept in houses.

---

[20] Ibid.

> *Sulthana: Like we are protected in our special homes.*
>
> *Sara: Yes, it is so.*

'What a surprise' Sulthana exclaimed. She laughed. Her friend Sara also joined her in laughing.

> *Sara: My dear Sulatana. What an injustice is this? You are locking up innocent women and let loose men.*
>
> *Sulthana. Why? As we are frail by nature, is not living inside house is safe to us?*
>
> *Sara. But we have no safety so long as men are roaming outside. Is it good that a wild animal enters market place?*

In this story Sulthana arrived in a country dominated by women where men are kept inside houses acknowledging their innate limitation. The responsibility of running the state is taken up by women. Men are entrusted with the task of bringing up children and managing domestic affairs. She tells her friend that my friends will be surprised hearing it. The narrator tries to explain the problems faced by women in the society by relocating the traditional positions of man and woman in their spaces.

2. Arabi-Malayalam Printing

Arabi-Malayalam was relatively late to enter the world of press, but it has an impressive history of printing. Contextually, it is to be noted that it was print which saved hundreds of Arabi-Malayalam works, known for literary merit, from literary extinction. Although there is dearth of evidence, the first press for printing Arabi-Malayalam texts was established in Ponnani.[21] Eighteenth and nineteenth centuries witnessed to an exponential growth of literary works –mainly songs- in this language thanks to mushrooming printing press. The earliest works which were put to print in Malabar were the *mālappāṭṭus* (eulogies) and *madhupāṭṭus* (praise songs) which were more popular than even liturgical texts and outnumbered other printed materials during the 19th century.[22]

The first Arabi-Malayalam press in northern Malabar is said to have established at Thalassery in 1867 or 1868 by Theekuthil Kunhamed.[23] He was actually inspired by the Malayalam press established at Thalassery by Basel mission a few years ago. Once the print culture gained popularity among Mappilas, lithographic printing presses were set up at different Muslim centres of Malabar (Plate 6.1). Mappilas leapt at the opportunity provided by lithographic press and everything was published large scale.[24] Almost all works composed before the introduction of press were put to print during the last quarter of 19th century AD.[25]

Towards the end of 19th century there was a spill over effect and a new printing press called *Madhurul Ulūm* Press was started in Thalassery.[26] Those who learnt the printing technology from

---

[21] Interview with Hussain Randathani, a scholar of Kerala Muslim history in an interview with the authors.

[22] Razak, *Colonialism and Community Formation in Malabar*,p.4.

[23] Kunhamed started the press on behalf of his father Melekandi Kunhali Haji by converting Nayyam Veedu an ancestral home which was under his family's possession. Abu, *Arabi- Malayala Sāhitya Caṛitram,* p. 126.

[24] Razak, *Colonialism and Community Formation in Malabar,* pp. 4-5.

[25] Ibid.

[26] Information shared by M.N.Karaserry, a scholar of Arabi-Malayalam literature in interview held on 3rd March, 2013.

Thalassery moved to other places like Valapattanam, Calicut and Thirurangadi and set up printing presses at all these places.[27] The first Arabi-Malayalam Litho press in Thiruragadi called *Āmirul Islām Fi Ma'danil Ulūm* aka *Āmirul Islām* was established by Chalilakath Ahmed in Hijra 1318 (1900 CE). This was supposed to be the first publishing house endeavoured in printing and publishing the Quran in Arabi-Malayalam language commercially.[28] The popularity of printing press in these places also led to the emergence of a plethora of a new generation poets and writers which ultimately ended up in an efflorescence of Arabi-Malayalam literature.[29]

Thirurangadi became a hub of publication in Arabi-Malayalam with the establishment of C.H. Press. *Nūrul Islām* Press in Mogral and *Bayāniya* press in Parappanagadi also functioned as two major centres for Arabi-Malayalam publishing industry. Thanks to *Nūrul Amīn* Press and a long army of Arabi-Malayalam poets from this village, Mogral was later on known to be *eśal grāmam* or song village.[30] The fame of Mogral brought many Arabi-Tamil pulavars or poets and Kannada Muslim poets to this village. There were regular annual gathering of South Indian Muslim poets and music composers in Mogral under the leadership Savukkar Kunnipakki.[31]

However, the printing of Arabai-Malayalam texts of prose doesn't have a long history to trace. It was only in 1901 that Sayyid Sana-Ullah Makthi Thngal, using standardized script that followed some conventions of Urdu orthography published the first prose in Arabi Malayalam -- a short treatise called *Mu'allimu'l-ikhwān* (A Lesson for the Brothers).[32] The first work in the prose tradition, according to Mohammedali is *Veḷḷaṭṭi Masāla* the author of which remains unknown. [33]

Because of the high popularity of printed works, especially songs, the printers and publishers were not concerned much about the quality of production. Though cover pages of works printed in Malayalam language remained impressive and colourful, those of Arabi-Malayalam works did not come up to the level. There was no distinction in quality of papers used for printing cover pages and other pages. Same quality paper was used for printing both inner and cover pages. Sometimes the first page itself turned out to be the cover page. Only font type or style got changed in each work, separate cover pictures were not given (Plate 6.2). A uniform pattern with regard to the design was followed in almost all the works. The cover page, in most of the cases, contained title of the work in different font styles and a brief description of the content. So, without turning over the inside pages, one can have an idea about the content form detailed blurb or jacket information given on the cover page.

As happened in the realm of literature, anti-colonial agitations offered a boost to the printing. Though scholars provide many reasons for that, one can reasonably assume that the denial of justice under the colonial rule, forced the Mappilas to spread the message of anti-colonialism through printed materials.

---

[27] Kunhi, *Musliṇalum Kerala Samskaravum,* p. 176.

[28] Aburaseeda, "Calilakat Kudumbakkār", *C H Imbrahim Haji Smaranika* 2001, p. 197

[29] Razak, *Colonialism and Community Formation in Malabar,* p. 4.

[30] Interview with Abdulla Thanima, a researcher of Mappila songs by the authors.

[31] Interview with Siddiqu Ahamed, great grandson of Savukkar Kunnipakki and a composer of Mappila songs held on 7th January, 2013.

[32] Kunhi, *Musliṇalum Kerala Samskaravum,*p.217 and Uday Kumar, "Shaping a Literary Space", p.32.

[33] V. P. Mohamedali, *Mappiḷa Pāṭṭukaḷ Nūṯṯandukaḷilude,* (Kottayam:Current Books, 2007), p.22.

When the ordinary people were prohibited to come and speak openly, the writers in the community took refuge in printing their works and distributing them through clandestine networks. Because of their inherent militant nature, *Padappāṯṯus* were the most favourite stuffs printed and circulated widely. Most of the Muslim houses in South Malabar kept a copy of them as a sign of solidarity to the fellow-Mappilas fighting with the colonial administration.

Mālās with indications to divinity of saints were another much sought after genre put in print. Mappilas in the late 19th and early 20th century relied much upon descriptions of divine powers lavishly provided in *mālās* for relief. Several such songs were re-published in Malabar during the period 1875-1950, many of which were composed much earlier and several editions of these were printed off late.[34] *Mohiyuddīn Māla which* was composed in 1607 and began to have printed version in 1870s had almost hundreds of editions were brought out from various litho presses within a span of fifty years.[35] The miraculous powers of saintly figures and martyrs referred in *mālās*, Mappilas believed would come for their rescue while passing through the troubled times. Keeping the copy of this māla was considered as act of veneration.

There was a practice of mentioning the name of press in each work.[36] In most of these works, even though the name of author or year of publication had not been given, name of publisher and press were printed with importance.[37] Imprint line of a book published from Malharul Muhimmath Press reads as follows:

> This book is printed at *Malharul Muhimmath* Press owned by Karakkal Abdullah T. Aboobacker of Thalassery on the 20th Jamadul Awal in the year Hijra 1341.

At some point of time in the history of Arabi-Malayalam printing, name of printer and publisher had a prominence than the name of those who composed songs (Plate 6.3). And most of the printers were also publishers who owning up the copy right of publications, gained high reputation and wealth as well. Because of the high monetary value of poems and songs, copy right rules were strictly followed. The following statement given in the first of part of *Sangīta Śirōmaṇi Nērccappāṭṭu* regarding the transfer of copy right of it demonstrates the issue well:

> This song (*Sangīta Śirōmaṇi Nērccappāṭṭu*) is composed by Edathodukayil Kunheedu of Paravannur village of Kalpakancherry province of Ponnani Taluk...the copy right has legally been transferred to me, Kolakkadan Ahamedkutty, a resident of Kakkad...this is to inform that it is a punishable offense to reprint this work without my consent and those who do so will be responsible and liable to all sorts of monetary loss that causes.[38]

The manuscripts of Arabi-Malayalam works were even registered with the local agencies like the Office of Registrar assigned for protecting intellectual property rights under the colonial rule. Following is a

---

[34] Other three popular *malas, Badar Mala, Nafeesath Mala* and *Manjukulam Mala*- in all these, we come across reference to the miraculous power of the respective divinities were also published and circulated in umpteen numbers. See Razak, *Colonialism and Community Formation in Malabar,* p.6.

[35] Ibid., pp.6-7.

[36] Hussain Randathani, a scholar of Kerala Muslim history in an interview with the authors.

[37] Abu, *Arabi-Malayala Sāhitya Caritram,* 126.

[38] Edukathodiyil Kunheedutty, *Sangīta Śirōmaṇi Nērccappāṭṭu* (MS)

legal document given in the opening pages of *Vaidysāram* a work in Ayurveda authored by Konganam Veettil Ahamed alias Bawa Musaliyar.

> This work entitled *Vaidyasāram*, a work of translation done by Konganam Veettil Ahamed alias Bawa Musaliyar had been registered at the Office of Registrar, Madras. The copy right of it, which had originally been transferred to Utuvanganat Maliyekkal Mohamed Musaliyar of Ponnani by the author is now vested up on his nephew and heir apparent, P.M.Abdulla Haji after his death in the year Hijra 1349 (1929). This is to bring into the notice of every one that the reproduction of this work in any form without the prior permission of the bearer of the copy right is a punishable offence under the law.[39]

Now, with the steady increase in education in Malayalam and English in Malabar, the specific need for Arabic-Malayalam literature has been reduced, and book publishers say that it is on the decline.[40] By the 1950-60s, printing Mappila songs and prose switched partly over to Malayalam.[41] There was a massive attempt to rewrite and publish many of the Arabi-Malayalam classics in Malayalam script. Furthermore, a complete sidelining happened because of the wrong notion that Mappila traditions formed the exclusive cultural baggage of Muslims and hence the anti-secular. Overtly religious cultures had no place in the modern secular nationalist consciousness. Nevertheless, Arabi-Malayalam finds it written expression through the text books in almost ten thousand madrassas and certain monthly publications like *Al-Muallim.* Though the publications in this language have considerably been reduced, there are many publishers depending exclusively on the works in Arabi-Malayalam. A rough estimate says that almost thousand books are published every year in this language.[42] A large chunk of them constitute the republication of old works as the new writings are next to nil. The poor remuneration given to the writers and song composers drives them to more lucrative field like the production of Mappila music albums in Malayalam.[43]

---

[39] Cited in Kunhi, *Musliṉ̂alum Kerala Samskaravum*, p.176.

[40] Field work held in CH Press and Ashrafiya Book Stall (Thirurangadi) on 3rd March, 2013.

[41] Mohamedali, *Mappiḷa Pāṭṭukaḷ Nūṯṯandukaḷilude,* p.21.

[42] Field work held in CH Press and Ashrafiya Book Stall (Thirurangadi) on 3rd March, 2013.

[43] Iqbal Koppilan a scholar of Mappila songs in an interview with the authors.

Bibliography

1. Arabic & Arabi-Malayalam Manuscripts

Alawi, Sayyid Al-Sayful Bathar (MS, 1841)

Alikutty Musliyār, Fatwa (MS, 1891)

Cōlayil Ahammed et al., Fatwa al-Radd Kondōṭṭy (MS, 1861).

Jifri, Sayyid Sheikh Kanz al Barahin, (MS, 1784).

Kunheedutty, Edukathodiyil, Sangīta Śirōmaṇi Nērccappāṭṭu (MS)

Musliyar, Pudiyakath Bawa, Answer to the Questions of Kunheedu (MS).

Musliyar, Musliyarakath Ahmed Kutty Al-Bustan (MS).

Musliyar, Putiyakat Kammukutty (MS, 1860).

2. Books/ Articles/ Chapters

2.1. Malayalam

Aboobacker, P.A., "Śastra Sāhityavum Kerala Muslimkaḷum", *Bodhanam,* Januray-March, 2014, pp. 34-49.

Abu, O., *Arabic-Malayala Sāhitya Caritram ,* (Kottayam: NBS, 1976)

Aburaseeda, "Calilakat Kudumbakkār", *C H Imbrahim Haji Smaranika* 2001, p. 197-98.

Ahamed, Jameel, "Arabi-Malayalatil Ninnu Malayāla Islāmilekku" in T. Mansurali (ed.), *Arabi-Malayala Sāhityava Padanaṉaḷ*, (Kozhicode: Lead Books, 2014), pp. 86-98.

Ahamedkutty, E.K.,*Islamum Keralatile SāmŪhyaparivartana Prastānaṉalum*, (Calicut: Kerala Nadvatul Mujahiddin, 1982).

Chemmad, Mansurali, *Islāhi Nayakanmār: Smriti Citraṉal,* (Kozhicode: Yuvatha Book House, 2011).

Elettil, Faisal, in T. Mansurali, (ed.), *Arabi-Malayala Sāhitya Padanaṉal*, (Kozhicode: Lead Books, 2014), pp. 98-102.

Faisy, Mustafa, *SampŪrna Mohiyuddīn Māla Vyāghyānam*, (Puthanathani: Oasis Books,2010).

Gafoor, P.M.A.,*Kālavum Kālppādum: Kerala Muslim Navōdhanatinte Nāyakaniṛayekkuriccu Vēritoru Anwśaṇam,* (Kozhicode: Yuvatha Book House, 2014).

Gangadharan,M., *Māppila Padanaṅal*, (Calicut: Vachanam Books, 2004).

Gangadaran, M., "Mampuram Thaṅalmarude Kalavm Akalavum", in K.K.N.Kurup and P.K. Pokker (eds.) *Mampuram Sayid Fadl PŪkkōya Taṅal: Adhiniveṣa Virudha Caritratile Nitya Sānnidyam,* (Thiruvananthapuram: Chintha Publishers, 2006).

Gangadharan, M., *"Sanaullah Makti Taṅal: Jṅānam Kondu Porutiya Paṙiśkartavu"*, in in K.K.Moammed Abdul Kareem (compiled), *Makti Taṅaḷude SampŪrṇa Kritikal,* (Calicut, Vachanam Books, 2006), pp. 11-22.

Gopalan Nair, C., *Malayalatile Māppiḷamār* (Manglore: Author, 1917)

Gundert, Herman, *Kerlolpathiyum Mattum* (Kottayam, National Book Stall, 1962).

Haneef, Sameera, "Arabi-Malayala Sāhityatile Penperuma" (pp.148-153), in T. Mansurali, (ed.), *Arabi-Malayala Sāhitya Padanaṅal*, (Kozhicode: Lead Books, 2014).

Hussain, Shamshad *NyŪnapakshatinum Lingapadavikkum Idayil*, (Thiruvananthapuram: Kerala Basha Institute, 2009)

Ilias, M.H., *Hadrami Sancāṛaṅaḷude Dēsāntara Calanaṅal, Teḷicam* (15th Anniversary Issue), 2013, pp. 44-47.

Iyer, Ulloor S. Parameswara, *Keraḷa Sāhityacaritram*, vol. 1, (Trivandrum: University of Kerala, 1955).

Kalikavu, Noushad, "Ain al-Qibla Vivādam: Matavum Ṣastravum Onnica Sandarbam", *Bodhanam*, 29th September, 2014, pp. 57-61.

Kannu, M.Muhammed, *Vakkom Maulawiyum Navōdhana Nāyakanmārum* (Trivandrum: The Author, 1982).

Karasserry, M.N., "Preface", in C.N. Ahmed Moulavi and K.K. Abdul Kareem, *Mahatāya Mappiḷa Sāhitya Pārambaraym,*(Calicut: Authors, 1978),pp. XIV-XVI.

Karaserry, M.N., "Māppiḷapāṭṭu", in Raghavan Payyanadu, *Kerala Folklore,* (Payyannur: Folklore Fellows of Malabar, 1997).

Karaserry, M.N., *Kurimānam* (Kozhikkode: Malayalam Publications, 1989).

Kareem, C.K., *Muslim Samudāyawum Samskārawum* (Trivandrum: Charithram Publications, 1983).

Kareem, K.K. Mohammed Abdul, *Hazrat Muhammed Shāh Taṅṅal,* (Kolathur: Islamic Da'wa Centre, 1964).

Kareem, K.K. Moahmed Abdul, *Sayyid Alawi Tanṅal* (Venniyur, Author, 1982).

Kareem, K.K.Mohammed Abdul, *Kappapāṭṭum Nūl Madhum: Oṛu Padanam,* (Tirur, Author, 1983).

Kareem, K.K. Mohammed Abdul, *K.M.Maulawi Jīvacaritram,* (Calicut: Yuvata Book House, 1985).

Koppilan, Iqbal*, Vaṭṭapāṭṭu*, (Kondotty: Scarf, 2008).

Kunhamu, A.P., *"*Malayaḷatile Hajjezhutukaḷ"*, Bodhanam,* January-March, 2013, pp. 5-15.

Kuttaserry, P.Mohamed, "Adunika Arabi Sāhityavum Malayalatile Asparśyatayum"
, *Chandrika Weekly* (Republic Day Special Issue, 1972).

Kutty, V.M., *Oppana Enna Vaṭṭapāṭṭu,* (Thiruvananthapuram: Kerala Basha Institute, 2011).

Latheef, N.K.A., *Mappila śyli* (Kottayam: National Book Stall, 1994)

Leelavathi,M., *Malayāḷa Kavitasāhityacaritram*, (Thrissur: Kerala Sahitya Academy, 2011).

Majeed, A.K.Abdul et al., *Kerala Muslim Navōdhānam: Punaṛanweśaṇatinte Prasakti*, (Kozhicode: Islamic Publishing Beaurau, 2010).

Mandalamkunnu, Sainuddin, *Māppila Samaraṅṅaḷum Ulema Netrathwavum*, (Calicut: Nanma Books, 2009).

Mansurali, T. (ed.), *Arabi-Malayala Sāhityava Padanaṅṅal* , (Kozhicode: Lead Books, 2014)

Maulawi, C.N. Ahmed and Kareem, K.K.abdul, *Mahatāya Māppila Sāhitya Pāṛambaraym,* (Calicut: Authors, 1978).

Maulawi, E. Moidu, *Maulawiyude Ātmakadha*, (Kottayam: DC Books, 1985).

Maulawi, P.N.Ahmed, *Iṣtihar Adava Viḷambaram*, (Tirurangadi: Amirul Islma Press, 1910).

Maulawi, Umar, *Ormakalude Thīrath,* (Cochin: Da'wa Books, 2009).

Meeran, Thoppil Muhammed, "Arabitamiẕh", in T.Mansoorali (ed.), *Arabi-Malāyaḷa Sahitya Pādaṅṅal*, (Kozhicode: Lead Books, 2014), pp.58-71.

Mogral, Tanima Abdulla and Kattathadukka, Yousuf, (compilation), *Vadakkinte eṣalukaḷ,* (Mogral: Frontline Publications, 2014).

Mohammed, T., *Māppiḷa Samudāyam: Cariṯram Samskāram*, (Kozhicode: Islamic Publishing House, 2013).

Mohamedali, V. P., *Māppiḷa Pattukaḷ Nūttandukaḷiḷude*, (Kottayam: Current Books, 2007).

Mohamedkunhi, P.K., *Musliṅṅalum Keraḷa Samskāravum,* (Thrissur: Kerala Sahitya Academy, 2008).

Mujeeburahman, M.P, "Adinivesavirudda Sāhityam Arabiyilum Malayalatilum", in T. Mansurali (ed.), *Arabi-Malayala Sāhityava Padanaṉaḷ*,pp.26-51.

Munafar, Sayyid Abdulla, *Ahlu Baith: Carithra Sangraham*, (Calicut: Vachanam Books, 2002).

Nadwi, Yousaf Muhammed, "Keralatile Arabi, Arabi-Malāyala Vaidyaṣastra Grandaṉaḷ", *Bodhanam*, 29 September, 2014., pp. 94-96.

Naseer, K.M., " Arabi-Malayalam Patramāsikakaḷ" in T. Mansurali (ed.), *Arabi-Malayāla Sāhitya Pādanaṉal*, (Kozhicode: Lead Books, 2014), pp. 127-132.

Nediyadi, Hassan, "SāmŪhika Navōdanatinte Māppilapattukaḷ", in *Mujāhid Samstāna Sammēḷanam Souvenir 2008,* pp.231-32.

Nediyadi, Hassan, *Arabi-Malāyaḷa Padakōsam*, (Thrissur, Kerala Sahitya Academy, 2009).

Parappil, P.P.Mohammed Koya, *Koẓhikoṭṭe Musḷiṉaḷude Caritram,* (Calicut: Focus Publications, 1994).

Pari, Sabna, "Māppila Vamoẓhiyum, Arabi-Malayālavum", in T.Mansoorali (ed.), *Arabi-Malayāla Sāhitya Pādaṉal*, (Kozhicode: Lead Books, 2014)p.117.

Pillai, Elankulam Kunjan, *Keralacharitrathile Iruḷadanja Edukaḷ,* (Kottayam: NBS, 1933).

Pillai, Erumeli Parameswaran, *Malayala Sāhityam Kālagaṭṭaṉaḷilūde*, (Kottayam: Current Books, 1998).

Ramesh.V.K., "Arabi-Malayāḷatile Novelukaḷ", T. Mansurali (ed.), *Arabi-Malayāla Sāhitya Pādaṉal*, (Kozhicode: Lead Books, 2014), pp.143-48.

Ramesh.V.K. "Mālapāttukaḷ:Oṟu Caritrānwēṣanam", *Oruma*, 2014, pp.23-25.

Randathani, Hussain, *Makhdūmum Ponnāniyum,* (Ponnani: Ponnani Juma Masjid Committee, 1998).

Salahuddin.C.T., "Arabi-Malayāḷatile Vaidya Kritikaḷ", in T. Mansurali (ed.), *Arabi-Malayāla Sāhitya Pādaṉal*, (Kozhicode: Lead Books, 2014), pp. 133-146.

Shamsuddin, K.O., *Mappila Malayālam,* (Trivandrum: Author, 1978).

Shirazi, Maulavi C.K., "Navōdana Prastānam Islāmil", *K.M.Maulawi Smāraka Grantam,* (Thirurangadi: K.M.Maulawi Memorial Trust, 1965)pp. 91-94.

Tharamel,Umar,Māppiḷapāttu-Performancite Sādyatakaḷum Prasnavalkaṟanavum", in T.Mansurali, (ed.), *Arabi-Malayāla Sāhitya Pādaṉal*, (Kozhicode: Lead Books, 2014).

Tanoor, P.A. Sadiq Faisy, *Muslim Navōdhanam: Vaẓhiyum Vartamānavum,* (Kozhicode: Shifa Book Stall,2008).

Taruvana, O.M., *Wahhābi Navōdhānam Oru Nuṉakkadha,*(Kozhicode: Irsad Book Satll, 2005).

Thangal, Makti, "Makti Manaklesam", in K.K. Moammed Abdul Kareem (compiled), *Makti Taṉaḷude*

SampŪrṇa Kritikal, (Calicut, Vachanam Books, 2006), pp.687-727.

Vallikkunnu, Balakrishnan and Tharamel, Ummar, *Māppiḷapāṭṭu: Pādavum, Padanavum,* (Kottayam: DC Books, 2006).

Vallikkunnu, Balakrishnan, *Māppila Sāhityavum Navōdhanavum,* (Calicut: Yuvatha Book House, 2008)

Varrier, Raghava, *Keraḷolpatti Chronicles* (Calicut: University of Calicut 1984).

2.2. English

Ahamed, Basheer, *Arabu-Tamil,* (Unpublished Manuscript).

Arasaratnam, Sinnappa, *Maritime Indian in the Seventeenth Century* (New Delhi:Oxford Univeristy Press, 2004).

Abu-Lughod, Janet, *Before European Hegemony: The World System Ad.1250 –1350,* (New York:Oxford University Press, 1989).

Barbosa, Duarta, *The Land of Malabar,* M.Gangadharan (ed.) (Kottayam: Mahatma Gandhi University, 2000).

Buchanen, Francis, *A Journey from Madras: Through the Countries of Mysore, Canara and Malabar* (originally published in 1807 in three volumes), (New Delhi: Asian Educational Society, 1999).

Chaithanya, Krishna, *A History of Malayalam Literature,* (Hyderabad: Orient Longman, 1971).

Clark, Hugh R., "Maritime Diasporas in Asia Before Da Gama: An Introductory Commentary ",*The Journal of the Economic and Social History of the Orient* ,Vol.49,No.4, 2006,pp.391-98.

Cherian, P.J., *Pattanam: South India's Mohanjedaro* (Trivandrum: KCHR, 2006)

Dale, Stephen, *The Mappilas of Malabar 1498 –1922: Islamic Society on the South Asian frontier* (Oxford: Clarendon, 1980).

Dale, Stephen F. and Menon, M.Gangadhara, "Nercca: Saint Martyr Worship Among the Muslims of Kerala", in Asgar Ali Engineer (ed.), *Kerala Muslims: A Historical Perspective,*(New Delhi: Ajanta Publications, 1995) pp.174-199.

D'Souza, V.D., "Status Group Among the Mappila Muslims on the South-West Coast of India",in Imtias Ahmed (ed.),*Social Stratication among Muslims in India* New Delhi: Oxford University Press, 1995), p.45.

Engineer, Asghar Ali (ed.), *Kerala Muslims: A Historical Perspective,*(New Delhi: Ajanta Publishers, 1995).

Fawcett, F., "A Popular Mopla Song", *Indian Antiquary,* March 1899, p.64-72.

Fawcett, F., "War Songs of Mappilas of Malabar", *Indian Antiquary*, Vol.30, Nov-Dec. 1901, pp.12-22.

Gardner, Katy and Osealla, Filippo, "Migration, Modernity and Social Transformation in South Asia: An Introduction", in Filippo Osealla and Katy Gardner (eds.), *Migration, Modernity and Social Transformation in South Asia,* (New Delhi: Sage, 2004).

George, K.M., *A Survey of Malayalam Literature*, (Bombay: Asia Publishing House, 1968).

Gibb, H.A.R., *Ibn Battuta : Travels in Asia and Africa*, (London: Robert M. Mc. Bride and Co., 1929)

Hameed, Abdullah Abdul, *Ndauthoppil Abdullah's Akbar Sadaqa Pakshipāṭṭu,* (Kasargod: Central University of Kerala, 2012).

Harris, V.C., "From Structure to Communitas and Back: Notes on the Arts and festivals of the Muslims of Kerala ",in Asghar Ali Engineer (ed.), *Kerala Muslims: A Historical Perspective*,(New Delhi: Ajanta Publishers, 1995), p. 201-221.

Hirschkind, Charles, *The Ethical Soundscape: Casette sermons and Islamic Counterpublics* (New York: Columbia University Press, 2006).

Hobson, John M., *The Eastern Origins of Western Civilization* (Cambridge: Cambridge University Press, 2004)

Hourani, George F., *Arab Seafaring in the Indian Ocean in Ancient and Early Medieval Times* (Beirut: Khayats, 1963), p. 53.

Hudawi, G.P.Muneer, *Spiritual Leadership in Anti-Colonial Struggle: A Study of Life and Works of Qazi Muhammad Al-Kalikuti* (New Delhi: Writers Choice, 2014).

Ilias, M.H., "Mappila Muslims and the Cultural Content of Arab Trading Diaspora on the Malabar Coast", *Asian Journal of Social Sciences*, 35 (2007), p. 450.

Ilias, M.H., "Ulema and the Internet: A Case Study of Muslim Scholars' Engagement with New Media in Kerala" paper presented at the International Seminar on "Time for Medialization: Integrating Media and Transcultural Communication Research Within Islamic and Areas Studies" held on April (8-10), at Humboldt University, Berlin.

Karaserry, M.N., "Arabic-Malayalam", in Asghar Ali Engineer (ed.), *Kerala Muslims: A Historical Perspectives*, (New Delhi: Ajanta Publications, 1995), pp. 168-172.

Karasserry, M.N., "Arabic-Malayalam: Interactions among Arabs and Mappila Muslims of Kerala", in M.H.Ilias and P. J. Vincent (ed.), *India-West Asia Relations: Understanding Cultural Interplays,* (New Delhi: New Century Publications, 2007), pp.107-112.

Khalid, Omar, "Sayyids of Hadramawt in Medieval and Modern India", *Journal of the Gulf and Arabian Peninsula Studies*, no.127, pp.11-15.

Kumar, Udaya, "Shaping a Literary Space: Early Literary Histories in Malayalam and Normative Uses of the Past", in Hans Harder (ed.) *Literature and nationalist Ideology,* (New Delhi: Social Science Press, 2010).

Kunju, A.P. Ibrahim, *Mappila Muslims of Kerala,* (Thiruvananthapuram: Sandhya Publications, 1993).

Kurien, Prema, *Kaleidoscopic Ethnicity: International Migration and the Reconstruction of Community Identities in India,* (Rutgers: Rutgers University Press, 2002).

Kurup, K.K.N., *The Legacy of Islam: A study of the Mappila Muslims of Kerala,* (Kannur, Samayam Publications, 2006).

Kutty, E.K.Ibrahim, "The Mujahid Movement and its Role in the Islamic Revival in Kerala" in Asgar Ali Enginner (ed.), *Kerala Muslims: A Historical Perspective,* (New Delhi: Ajanta Publications, 1995), pp. 68-83.

Lakshmi, L.R.S., *The Malabar Muslims: A Different Perspectives*, (New Delhi: Cambridge University Press India Ltd, 2012).

Logan, William, *Malabar Manual I*, Pt.1&2, P.J. Cherian et al. (eds.), (Thiruvananthapuram: KCHR, 2008).

Makhdum, Shaykh Zainuddin, *Tuhfat al-Mujāhidīn*, translated by S.M.H.Nainar, (Kuala Lumbur: Islamic Book Trust, 2006).

Mayankutty, O.P., "The Portuguese Advent and the Decline of Arab Trade in Malabar " in M.H.Ilias, *India West Asia Relations: Understanding Cultural Interplays*, (New Delhi: New Centaury Publications, 2007), pp. 90-95.

Menon, Dilip, "Houses by the Sea: State-Formation Experiments in Malabar, 1760-1800", *Economic and Political Weekly*, vol. 34, no. 29 (1999), pp. 1995-2003

Miles, S.B., *The Countries and Tribes of the Gulf,* (London: Harrison & Sons, 1919).

Miller, R.E., *Mappila Muslims of Kerala: A study in the Islamic Trends*, (Hyderabad: Oriental Longman, 1992).

More, JBP, *Origin and Early History of the Muslims of Keralam 700 AD-1600 AD*, (Calicut: Other Books, 2011).

Nainar, S.M.H., *Arab Geographers Knowledge of South India*, (Madras: Madras University Press, 1962).

Narayanan, M.G.S., *Cultural Symbiosis* (Trivandrum: Kerala Historical Society 1972).

Osella, Filippo, and Osella, Caroline, "Islamism and Social Reform in Kerala, South India", *Modern Asian Studies* 42, 2/3 (2008) pp. 317-346.

Osella, Caroline and Osella, Filippo, "Muslim Style in South India," *Fashion Theory*, vol. 11, no. 2-3, pp. 1-4.

Panikkar, K.M., *Malabar and the Portuguese* , (New Delhi: Voice of India, 1997).

Panikkar, K.N., *Against Lord and State: Religion and Peasant Uprisings in Malabr 1836-1921,* (New Delhi, Oxford University Press, 2001).

Prakash, B.A., "Impact of Foreign Remittances: A Case Study of Chavakkad Village in Kerala", *Economic and Political Weekly* 13 (1978), pp.3210-15

Razak, P.P Abdul, *Arabic-Malayalam and the Cultural Lansdcape of Muslims of Malabar* (Unpublished MS).

Razak, PP Abdul, *Cololialism and Community Formation in Malabar* (unpublished PhD Thesis submitted to the University of Calicut, 2007).

Richman, Paula, "Introduction", in Abdullah Abdul Hameed, *Akbar Sadaqa Pakshipattu: Translation and Study,* (Kasargod: Central Univeristy of Kerala, 2012), p. xxi-xxii.

Ricci, Ronit, *Islam Translated: Literature, Conversion, and the Arabic Cosmopolis of South and Southeast Asia*, (New Delhi: Permanent Black, 2011).

Sathar, K.K. Mohamed Abdul, *Bā-Alawis of Malabar*, (Unpublished Manuscript).

Sasthri, S.M. (ed.) "Mc. Crindle's Ancient India as Described by Ptolemy, (Calcutta, 1927).

Serjeant, R.B., *The Saiyids of Hadramawt*, (London: School of Oriental and African Studies, 1957).

Shah, Syed Mohideen, *Islam in Kerala,* (Thrissur: Muslim Educational Association, 1972).

Siddiqui, M.K.H. (ed.), *Marginal Muslim Communities in India*, (New Delhi: Institute of Objective Studies, 2004).

Wink, Andrei, *Al-Hind: The Making of the Indo-Islamic World* ,Vol.1, (New Delhi:Oxford University Press., 1995).

Glossary

abaya	loose over garment worn by women in parts of the Arab world
ahlul Bait	the family of the Prophet
Ain al-Qibla Vivādam	a dispute hinging on the actual position of Qibla in the early 20th century in Malabar
ān pāṭṭukar	male singers
asmah	a system of medicine used mainly for the treatment of mental illness believed to have come to Malabar via Persian Sufi scholars
auliya	saint
azān	call for prayer
Bālacikista	pediatric treatment
bid'a	innovation
Centamil	the classic variety of Tamil language
da'wa	religious preaching
dars	religious schools attached to mosques
dārśanika kāvyangaḷ	philosophical poems
dikr	litany
du'as	prayers
eśal	Scheme of rhythms in *māppiḷapāṭṭu*
fatwas	religious legal ruling
fiqh	Islamic jurisprudence
gānamēḷa	on-stage performance of singers with western musical instruments.
hadith	words of the Prophet Mohammed compiled after his death.
harakats	signs developed to mark new sounds
harām	forbidden
hijra	the Prophet's exile from Mecca to Medina
ijtihad	independent derivation of legal rulings
iravu	request in prayers
jenmi	upper caste land lord

kabilah	clan
kacimundu	waist-cloth used mainly by Mappila women
Kafir	infidel
kaimuṭṭukaḷi	hand-clapping play
kaitharkam	factional feud
kālpantukaḷi Pāttukal	Soccer Songs
kalyānappaṭṭukaḷ	wedding songs
kandūra	the cover-whole gowns of Arab men.
karāmat	possession of divine powers
kattupāṭṭukaḷ	letter songs
katukut kalyāṇam	ear-boring ceremony.
kavi	poet, extempore songs
kessupāṭṭukaḷ	story songs
khahva,	*a* drink made of cinnamon, ginger and coffee beans
kiṇṇāram	copper vessel
kissa	story
kissappāṭṭukaḷ	story songs
kōrvēy	the narrative strategy popular in Arabi-Tamil poems
kufic	the script system in Arabic originated from the Kufa region of Arabian Peninsula
madhupāṭṭukaḷ	praise songs
mafta	head scarf
mālas	song stories
Manipravāḷam	a literary style which had been of wide use in mediaeval South India. This was an admixture of Tamil and Sanskrit.
mārkka kalyāṇam	male circumcision
mawlid	liturgical recital in honour of an *auliya* or a saint
Moulawi	religious teacher
mullaka	religious scholar
mundu	waist-cloth
murtad	apostate
muṟukkam	fast rhythm in Mappila songs
mylānci	applying henna on the hands and legs of the bride on the day before the wedding.
nabātaean	group of languages of the Nabataeans of the Palestine, Jordan and Egypt
nērcas	commemoration of the martyrdoms of Muslim saints or local Mappila heroes those who were killed during the Mappila Rebellions of early Twentieth Century.
oppana cāyal	slow rhythm in Mappila songs
ottamŪli	single medicine therapy
padappāṭṭu	war songs
pancabŪta	five spirits-air, fire, space, earth and water
pantal	shamiana specially erected for weddings

Paradesi	foreigner
paricamuṭṭukaḷi	shield game
Pen pāṭṭukar	female singers
penkuppāyam	waist-length top
pulavars	poets from Tamil Nadu
puliyangam	fight with tiger
Putiyapennu	the bride
Putiyāpḷa	the bridegroom
rāsi	zodiac sign
safīna	ship
śahids	martyrs who were killed for the cause of Islam
sarkīṭ Pāṭṭukaḷ	travel Songs
ṣhāfī	a school of jurisprudence among Sunnī Muslims
Ṣhirk	polytheism
sunna	the teachings of the Prophet
suppara	big plate for collective dining
sīrapārāyana sadassu	Special gathering for the recitation of songs and stories with detailed interpretations
tafsirs	interpretations of the Quran
tariqahs	Sufi orders
tarjama	translation
tawhid	monotheism
tundam	a portion of the song
ulema	Scholar
ustada/ mollācci	female teachers of Islamic studies
v'alu	midnight preaching
vaṭṭazhetu and *kōlezhutu*	Two writing systems originated from the ancient Tamil used to write the Proto-Dravidian languages including Tamil and Malayalam.
yātra	travel

Index